Hospitality Business Development

Hospitality Business Development

Ahmed Hassanien
Crispin Dale
Alan Clarke

ELSEVIER

AMSTERDAM • BOSTON • HEIDELBERG • LONDON • NEW YORK • OXFORD
PARIS • SAN DIEGO • SAN FRANCISCO • SINGAPORE • SYDNEY • TOKYO
Butterworth-Heinemann is an imprint of Elsevier

Butterworth-Heinemann is an Imprint of Elsevier
The Boulevard, Langford Lane, Kidlington, Oxford, OX5 1GB, UK
30 Corporate Drive, Suite 400, Burlington, MA 01803, USA

First edition 2010

British Library Cataloguing in Publication Data
A catalogue record for this book is available from the British Library

Library of Congress Cataloging-in-Publication Data
A catalog record for this book is available from the Library of Congress

ISBN: 978-1-85617-609-5

For information on all Butterworth-Heinemann publications
visit our web site at books.elsevier.com

Printed and bound in Great Britain
10 11 12 10 9 8 7 6 5 4 3 2 1

Working together to grow
libraries in developing countries

www.elsevier.com | www.bookaid.org | www.sabre.org

ELSEVIER   BOOK AID International   Sabre Foundation

Contents

Dedication

We dedicate this book to our respective spouses and children:

EMAN, MARIAM and NOOR (AHMED HASSANIEN)

SUZANNE, SAFFRON and IMOGEN (CRISPIN DALE)

ÁGI, RUTH, JAMIE, DAN and ALEX (ALAN CLARKE)

Preface

The changing business environment has forced hospitality enterprises to reconsider the development of their goods and services. Indeed, consumer tastes, wants and needs are changing all the time and new competitive patterns are emerging. Therefore, it has become essential for organisations to adapt, develop and innovate to achieve a competitive advantage and become successful. Business development is therefore crucial if hospitality firms are to succeed in today's – and tomorrow's – competitive environment.

Business development is an essential activity for firms that desire to face competition on the basis of quality and suitability of purpose. Indeed, there is a strong relationship between business development and success in the hospitality industry. Effective business development can result in the growth and profitability of hospitality firms. Furthermore, business development can promote opportunities for opening up new markets and gaining greater market share. Therefore, business development is fundamental to the sustainable achievement of hospitality organisations.

This book thus addresses issues in business development within the context of the hospitality industry. It draws together, in an accessible form, the principles of business development, as they need to be understood by hospitality professionals. This book investigates and applies theoretical business development concepts and models to hospitality practice. Consequently, examples from the international hospitality industry are used throughout the text in order to link theory to practice. Hospitality managers who value the development of their offerings will gain a new understanding of their business and will be more competent in managing their products efficiently and effectively.

This book examines the nature, and unique characteristics, of the concepts, products and services currently offered within the international hospitality industry. It considers the essential features of business development with which all hospitality organisations operate, and relates key strategic development considerations and frameworks to business development. In advocating a customer-centred approach, it examines the shifting nature of demand, evaluating consumers' dynamics and behaviour, their changing needs, wants and expectations, and hence the nature of, and ongoing variations in, consumer/product relationships. The text also evaluates current and projected business environments, and supply patterns, with particular emphasis upon those research and feasibility issues that are fundamental to the successful and sustainable formulation and development of any hospitality product, namely market research and segmentation, target marketing, positioning, repositioning and location analysis.

In addition, this book considers the significance of effective and appropriate resources and competences in facilitating the planning, delivery and evaluation of the offer as well as enhancing the differentiation and value, of concepts, products and services. It examines key approaches towards addressing competition, and achieving and sustaining competitive advantage. The role of effective marketing planning is analysed, in particular branding, and the increasing adoption of retailing and merchandising techniques within hospitality operations. The critical success factors and challenges of developing new hospitality products are evaluated.

ORGANISATION

The material in this book is presented in five parts that reflect different perspectives and issues regarding hospitality business development. Part I (Chapters 1–3) provides an overview of the hospitality business development and its environment. Chapter 1 explains the nature of hospitality business and the significance of its development. Also, it describes the unique characteristics and challenges of hospitality business development, and the related challenges and implications which these present for hospitality operators. Chapter 2 is concerned with providing an understanding of the concept and scope of hospitality. It examines the different sectors of the hospitality industry. Chapter 3 describes the various layers of the hospitality environment. It relates the nature and significance of common frameworks and methodologies employed when analysing business environments (e.g. PESTEL, SWOT and Porter's Five Forces Model). Finally, it identifies examples of macro- and micro-environmental influences on hospitality organisations.

Part 2 explores the fundamental role of hospitality consumers in business development. Chapter 4 describes the rationale behind the key issues in and the process of positioning and differentiation. Also, the chapter identifies the key steps and issues involved in the hospitality business positioning process. These different issues include topics such as segmentation, targeting, branding, competition, repositioning, market and internal analysis. Chapter 5 explains the principles of customer centricity within the context of the hospitality industry. It relates the fundamental relationship between the consumer and the business development function. In addition, the chapter explores the role of customer attraction, satisfaction and retention in hospitality business development.

Part 3 (Chapters 6–10) focuses on essential management and planning aspects of hospitality businesses. Chapter 6 identifies potential direct and indirect sources of business funding. It also describes the significance of a well researched and written business plan in seeking funding for hospitality business development. Finally, it outlines the structure, and key content, of a well-framed business plan.

Chapter 7 looks at hospitality business growth routes and development processes. It describes generic strategies for the achievement of competitive advantage. It relates specific alternative strategy routes for the achievement of competitive advantage, essentially based upon: (a) 'The strategy clock' and (b) 'The product–market matrix'. Chapter 8 identifies emerging issues and trends in the growth of hospitality businesses. It describes the increasing significance of strategic alliances and their typology. Chapter 9 deals with the major dimensions and characteristics of the new product development (NPD) concept in the marketing of hotel operations. The discussion in this section covers the definition, importance and tools of NPD. This is followed by an investigation of the available NPD strategies or models that can be applied to operations in the hospitality industry. It focuses on different measures of product success and failure. Also, it looks at fundamental considerations relating to effective performance measurement and control within the hospitality industry. Chapter 10 investigates the marketing role played by property renovation in hospitality business development and how the objectives of a renovation programme can be achieved. The presentation includes discussion of terminology, types and significance of renovation. Moreover, the literature on renovation extends into comparing new construction with property renovation in the hospitality industry. Then, the available literature on renovation in the hospitality industry is synthesised in order to develop an understanding of what might make up an approach to the renovation process in the hospitality industry.

The aim of Part 5 (Chapter 11) of this book is to look at the vital requirements for business development through summarising the key messages of the previous chapters. Accordingly, Chapter 10 focuses on different essential requirements for successful and efficient business development in the hospitality industry.

This book is useful for both practitioners and educators. From a teaching perspective, the material covered within this book is of direct importance to students of hospitality on undergraduate and postgraduate programmes as well as to those involved in any industry with links to hospitality and tourism. It is also believed that this book is of value to hospitality marketers, planners and managers who wish to explore the sustainable development of the sophisticated hospitality business.

FEATURES

This book contains several educational features in every chapter to help students grasp the concepts, frameworks, models and techniques presented:

- **Introductions** introduce the key topics that will be presented in the chapter.

- Chapter **learning objectives** list the specific skills, procedures and techniques that students are expected to master after reading the material.

- *Real life and hypothetical* **industry-related examples** *are* included in each chapter to link theory to practice.

- The *chapter* **summary** concisely pulls together the many different points covered in the chapter to help activate students' memories.

- **Discussion questions and activities** *that* ask students to critically analyse and evaluate important concepts, procedures and issues.

- A **case study** at the end of each chapter is to ensure understanding of hospitality business applications and developing conceptual understanding and analysis techniques using realistic business examples. The case study is tied together with the content of its chapter and builds on the concepts learned in it.

- A **glossary** has been designed to summarise the key terms presented in each chapter of this book.

Acknowledgements

The authors would like to thank a number of colleagues who have given support, suggestions and advice, which assisted in the development of this book. We thank them for taking the time and effort to share their thoughts with us or to support us:

- Mr Michael Heriott who was involved in the proposal development stage of this book.

- The three referees who reviewed the proposal and provided us with positive and constructive feedbacks and comments.

- The editors at Elsevier, especially Sarah Long, Francesca Ford, Stephani Allison and Eleanor Blow, have been helpful in bringing the book to publication.

- Professor Clarke would like to thank Petra Gyurácz-Németh for co-authoring Chapters 5 and 6.

- Dr Hassanien would like to thank Mrs Ros Sutherland for her constant support and encouragement.

- Crispin Dale would like to thank Mr Neil Robinson for his academic and personal support.

- Crispin Dale would like to thank his mum, Mrs Isobel Dale, and the immediate family for their support.

- Finally, colleagues at our respective Universities, Edinburgh Napier, Wolverhampton and Pannonia and our colleagues in the hospitality industry.

About the Authors

Ahmed Hassanien is course Leader, Hospitality Management, School of Marketing, Tourism and Languages, Napier Business School, Edinburgh Napier University. He has a PhD in Hospitality Management from Strathclyde University and an MA in Teaching and Learning in Higher Education from the University of Wolverhampton. Ahmed's professional experience includes both practical and academic roles in the hospitality industry. He has more than 15 years of teaching experience in a number of international universities. He is a fellow member of many professional bodies such as the Academy of Higher Education. Before joining the University of Napier, he had been working for five years as a Senior Lecturer in International Hospitality Management at the University of Wolverhampton. He has reviewed many academic articles for international academic periodicals, and is currently an associate editor of the *International Journal of Customer Relationship Marketing & Management*. He has many articles published in international refereed conferences and periodicals. Most of his research work is done in collaboration with international colleagues and postgraduate students. Academic journals that have published his work include *Facilities, Tourism and Hospitality Research: The Surrey Quarterly Review, International Journal of Hospitality & Tourism Administration (IJHTA), Journal of Structural Survey, Journal of Hospitality, Leisure, Sport & Tourism Education (JoHLSTE), Journal of Teaching in Travel and Tourism, Journal of Place Management, Journal of Property Management, Journal of Hospitality and Leisure Marketing* and, *The International Journal of Management Education and Higher Education in Europe*.

Crispin Dale has experience of working in the hospitality industry at both an operational and management level. He has taught hospitality management at undergraduate and postgraduate levels for a number of years. He obtained his Masters degree from Lancaster University and is currently in the final stages of completing his PhD with the University of Wolverhampton. Crispin has published widely on strategic management and business development in books and peer-reviewed journals. His research has focused upon issues including competitive networks and structures, and change management in the hospitality and tourism industries. He has also researched the impact of contemporary strategic management issues on small hospitality and tourism enterprises in the expanding European Union. He has published in journals including the *International Journal of Tourism Research, International Journal of Management Cases, International Journal of Contemporary Hospitality Management, Journal of Hospitality, Leisure, Sport & Tourism Education (JoHLSTE), Journal of Teaching in Travel and Tourism* and the *Journal of Place Branding*. Crispin has also written a resource guide on strategic management for the Hospitality, Leisure, Sport and Tourism subject network of the Higher Education Academy.

Alan Clarke teaches and researches at the University of Pannonia, Hungary. He has a PhD from the Open University and an MA from the University of Sheffield. He has been responsible for developing leisure, tourism and hospitality programmes at the Universities of North London, Sheffield and Derby, where he was made a Professor in 1996. He also regularly collaborates with the Christel DeHaan Tourism and Travel Research Institute at the University of Nottingham, teaching in their master's programme and developing research. His book (with Wei Chen) *International Hospitality Management* (Butterworth Heinemann, 2007) continues to prove popular and he regularly reviews for the *Annals of Tourism Research* and the *Journal of Tourism Management*. He formed his own consultancy company ATTRACTION, which is now working as Vonzero in Hungary, undertaking customer perception research and strategic planning for both public and private sector organisations. His current research interests focus on stakeholder dynamics and partnership building, where he is working with the Assembly of European Regions on a study covering 270 regions to benchmark the best practices in partnership development in the fields of cultural and heritage tourism. He has direct experience in hospitality having run tourist accommodation in Derbyshire, and a bar and a restaurant in Greece. This is coupled by many years of participant observation in pubs, clubs, bars, cafés and restaurants around the world.

List of Figures

List of Tables

List of Case Studies

CHAPTER 1

Introduction to Hospitality Business Development

Learning Objectives

Having completed this chapter, readers should be able to:

- Understand the concept of business development within the context of the hospitality industry.
- Explore the growing importance of hospitality business development with particular emphasis on the motives behind it.
- Investigate the scope of hospitality business development.

CONTENTS

INTRODUCTION

There is no doubt that business development represents the most important single activity of any hospitality organisation in terms of satisfying its target markets. At any one time almost every hospitality business has recently been developed, is under development or needs to be developed. That is because business development is the prime reason for the organisation's survival in the market. Consequently, business development can be regarded as the criteria upon which rest the effective and efficient performance of any hospitality organisation.

In theory, hospitality business development might be seen as a quite obvious, clear and straightforward process. Certainly the process depends on identifying smart goals and objectives, allocating the required resources for its implementation and then getting it done. In reality, nevertheless, business development is not always an easy task for hospitality organisations, because it involves several interacting controllable and uncontrollable factors such as the organisation, its stakeholders and the dynamic changing nature of its micro and macro environments. Until recently, little detailed consideration has been given to appraising the nature of the hospitality business and the significance of its development. As a result, the main goal of this chapter is to look at the concept, significance and scope of hospitality business development.

DEFINING BUSINESS DEVELOPMENT

It is important for the purposes of this book to discuss the term business development to clarify the concept prior to an examination of its scope. However, a review of the literature fails to provide a consistent definition of the concept and its strategies. That is why we can say that despite the wealth of literature, hospitality business development is still an area that needs further research and clarification.

In this book, business development is defined as the process by which a company can improve its performance through: (a) modifying or enhancing the features and attributes of its current products or services, (b) developing new products or services, (c) entering new markets and (d) partnerships or strategic alliances. In other words, hospitality business development refers to the process by which an organisation uses internal, external or joint resources in order to launch, improve, modify or extend its offerings in an existing or in a new market. Despite being a very broad definition, it is essential from a management point of view because it looks at development from different angles that fully reflect the content and context of hospitality business development.

WHY HOSPITALITY BUSINESS DEVELOPMENT?

The success of any hospitality business depends mainly on its development plans. Business development includes a wide range of activities that create new or changed offerings, markets, organisations and processes. It enhances sales, improves customer satisfaction, augments quality, diminishes costs and achieves numerous benefits for organisations. In order for hospitality organisations to be successful, business development needs to be incorporated into the company's business goals and targets. Accordingly, business development should be a strategic part of hospitality organisation's annual business plan. When a hospitality organisation decides to develop its business, it is usually affected by various motives. These motives can be classified as reactive/proactive or internal/external. The following discussion will explain the impact of these motives on hospitality firms in terms of their business development decisions.

■ Profitability

A hospitality business ultimately needs to make some kind of return on investment in the form of profitability. In attempting to achieve profitability decisions about the products cost, production and marketing have to be considered. For instance, if the hospitality business decides to pursue a no-frills strategy of offering a basic product with a minimum level of service so as to minimise its costs and maximise its yield, it has potential to increase its profitability. This strategy is characteristic of the budget hotel sector as explained in the budget hotels example below.

■ To improve market share

Market share is based on the percentage of sales that a product has within a given market or market segment relative to its competitors. The measures of market share are derived from sales revenue or volume of products sold in the market. In the hospitality industry it is not uncommon for organisations to gain market share through the acquisition of other hospitality businesses. This enables the organisations to grow quickly and enter into market areas where they currently may have minimal or no presence.

■ Business growth goals

The objective of the hospitality organisation may be to grow its business rapidly so as to position its business as market leaders. This may initially be at the expense of immediate profitability and return on investment but it will enable the hospitality business to develop brand leadership and gain cost advantages over time. Many of the popular fast food outlets have based their business development decisions on rapid business growth in pursuit of these goals.

■ Managerial urge

Business development can be determined by the instinctive desires of the managers in the hospitality organisation. Decision-making is not always a rational and predetermined process and in many respects can be intuitive and spontaneous in nature. Opportunities may arise in the marketplace that hospitality managers perceive need a reactive response. If these are capitalised upon then the hospitality business can gain an advantage relative to its competitors.

Example: Budget Hotels

Budget hotel operations have become increasingly popular. They offer accommodation that is linked to food operation such as a motorway café or a branded licensed premises where customers can obtain food and beverages. The price for the accommodation is relatively low and costs are kept to a minimum via basic services and limited numbers of personnel to manage and facilitate the premises. In 2004, Whitbread, the owner of budget hotel operator Travel Inn, purchased a rival competitor in the marketplace, Premier Lodge from The Spirit Group for £505 million. Whitbread subsequently rebranded the combined businesses as Premier Travel Inn. The acquisition enabled Whitbread to pursue business growth whilst also claiming the largest share of the budget hotel market, which in 2007 stood at 38%.

Source: www.whitbread.co.uk

■ Unique product or niche

There may be opportunities in the market to develop a product that is currently not being sold by competitors or that which meets the needs and wants of a specialist market segment. Themed hotels that focus on a particular theme are an example of a hospitality product that fulfils the needs of a specialist market segment.

■ New Market Opportunities

New market opportunities may arise as a consequence of trends that may occur in the marketplace. The growth of the Gastropub concept, which is based upon the sale of upmarket food within a public house environment, has emerged as a consequence of changing consumer tastes towards more upmarket dining in an informal environment.

Example: YO! Sushi

In 1997, entrepreneur Simon Woodroffe opened the first YO! Sushi restaurant in London. Based upon the concept of Japanese cuisine that is served via a conveyor belt mechanism, YO! Sushi was an enterprise that exploited an untapped market by offering a product that was unique within its geographical location. After a period of expansion YO! Sushi was purchased by Quilvest SA, the Luxembourg private equity firm, for £51 million.

Source: www.yosushi.com

■ Economies of scale

Economies of scale are when the hospitality organisation purchases products from its suppliers, such as food and drink, in bulk. This enables a lower cost base to be achieved for the hospitality business. The business may then decide to pass these cost savings on to the customer in the form of a reduced price.

Example: JD Wetherspoon

Tim Martin opened the first JD Wetherspoon's pub in London in 1979 and this has since expanded to over 650 outlets. JD Wetherspoon is based upon selling food and alcohol at a low cost. To achieve this strategy it gains economies of scale by buying its food and drink product in bulk and thereby achieving economies of scale. It can negotiate discounts due to the large volume of purchases it makes from its suppliers. This is then passed on to customers in the form of lower prices.

Source: www.jdwetherspoon.co.uk

■ Customer attraction, satisfaction and retention

To ensure that the hospitality business is able to attract, satisfy and retain its customers it has to ensure that it is satisfying their needs and wants. As substitute and complementary products enter the marketplace, it may be necessary for the business to make adaptations to its product offering so as to generate perceived added value for the customer. The same occurs when lifestyle trends emerge that can put the hospitality product at risk. The emergence of healthier lifestyles and eating habits meant that many of the major fast food outlets developed products that met the needs of these changing consumer tastes.

Example: McDonalds Healthy Meals

Accusations that fast food outlets were to blame for the rise in obesity, coupled with changing consumer tastes led McDonalds to introduce alternative meal options in its restaurants. This included salads, fruit juices and carrot sticks. McDonalds also removed its 'Supersize' option where customers could increase the portion size of their meal on request.

Source: www.mcdonalds.com

■ **Legal factors**

Legal factors in the form of new health and safety measures can mean that hospitality businesses have to develop products that meet strict legislative standards of hygiene and production. The introduction of macro-legislative factors such as the smoking ban across all enclosed public places across many countries in Europe meant that hospitality businesses had to develop their products so as to meet the requirements of the legislation.

Example: Mitchells & Butlers and the Smoking Ban

In March 2006 a smoking ban across all enclosed public places was introduced in Scotland. This was followed by England, Wales and Northern Ireland in 2007. Premises that failed to observe the ban would face a £2500 fine. Many thought that the ban would have a major impact upon the wider hospitality industry with a downturn in sales and customer dissatisfaction. However, the smoking ban resulted in an opportunity for many pub restaurant operators. Mitchells & Butlers is the owner of outlets such as All Bar One and Harvester. In these establishments the organisation operates a food-driven business model where food sales become the primary focus of the business. The customer purchase of beverages acts as a means of generating ancillary revenue for the business. Mitchells & Butlers has found that customer in these establishments has increased as a consequence of attracting new markets who previously may not have dined in restaurants due to a smoke-filled atmosphere.

Source: www.mbplc.com

■ **Competition**

In a fiercely competitive marketplace, the hospitality business will be under constant pressure to innovate its product offerings so as to gain a competitive advantage. As new competitors enter the market with similar products the hospitality business will need to be ahead of the game in ensuring its products are perceived by consumers as being better or offering something that is different.

■ **Small and saturated existing market**

The hospitality business may be operating in a sector that is too small in size, and therefore fails to make a sufficient return on investment, or has become overwhelmed with competitors selling a similar product to your own. This can then make it very difficult to compete, with only the brand leader able to sustain itself in the marketplace. The hospitality business may therefore decide to either withdraw the product from the market or make perceived modifications so as to generate further sales.

■ Brand and image improvement

Over time, the products that a hospitality business offers can become stale in the minds of consumers, thus leading to a downturn in overall sales volume. The hospitality business may need to improve or reimage its product brand so as to reinvigorate further sales.

■ Partnership or alliances

If the hospitality business wishes to enter into a new product or geographical area, it may not have the resources to be able to do this alone. Therefore, the business may decide to enter into an alliance or joint venture with another firm that has the resources and capabilities and will enable the business to generate synergies from the partnership.

■ Globalisation or internationalisation

The hospitality business may decide to enter into other geographical market areas in pursuit of a globalisation strategy. However, there are a number of factors that the business has to consider when embarking on this strategy, not least the fact that the product may not be received as favourably in a different country or market area due to cultural differences. The hospitality business may therefore have to make adaptations to the product so as to meet the needs and wants of the local market.

Example: McDonalds in India

McDonalds entered the Indian marketplace in 1996. It is a joint venture between Amit Jatia's company, Hardcastle Restaurants Private Limited and Vikram Bakshi's Connaught Plaza Restaurants Private Limited who operate McDonalds Restaurants in west and north India, respectively. The predominant religion in India is Hinduism where the cow is viewed as being sacred. No beef products are therefore sold in any of the McDonalds restaurants in India. Due to the diversity of other religions in India including Sikhism and Islam, the dietary habits of the majority of India are often vegetarian. To ensure cultural sensitivity and to meet eating tastes in India, McDonalds provide vegetarian burgers in the form of the McVeggie™ and the McAloo Tikki™ and meat options which are chicken based such as Chicken Maharaja Mac™.

Source: www.mcdonalds.com

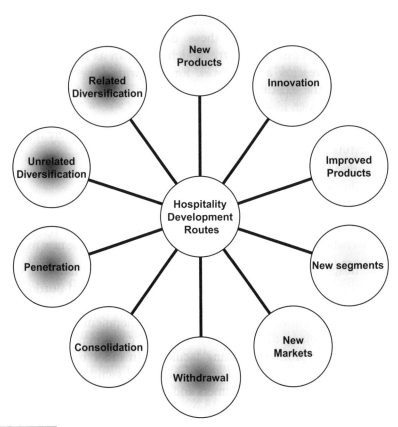

FIGURE 1.1   *Hospitality Development Routes.*
Source: Adapted from Johnson et al. (2008).

Innovation

It will be necessary for hospitality businesses to continually innovate if they are to maintain an advantage over competitors. A culture of creativity needs to be imbued within the organisation so as to encourage the innovation of new products or services. Hospitality organisations sometimes operate a system of idea generation where employees will be given a reward for coming up with a new idea. This could be anything from a completely new product offering to a new method of service delivery. What this develops is an enterprising culture where employees feel that their thoughts are valued, as well as see them get operationalised in practice.

Improved products

If a hospitality product has been in the marketplace for some time it can become stale in the minds of consumers thus leading to a downturn in sales. This can be further compounded by competitors offering new products and services that are perceived as giving greater value to the target market.

The hospitality organisation has to consider strategies to rejuvenate its product. This may be in the form of additional features to the product or offering a more efficient service.

New segments

Opportunities may arise where the hospitality product can be repositioned towards a new market segment. This could be based upon demographic changes and evolving lifestyles in society that have generated new market segments to target. The ageing population has encouraged hospitality organisations to develop products that meet the needs of this expanding market segment. For example, specialised hospitality products such as spa hotels have capitalised upon an ageing demographic and the consumer trend towards health and well-being related experiences.

New markets

The process of globalisation has opened a range of new market opportunities for hospitality organisations to exploit. Growing economic prosperity in countries such as China and India has acted as a catalyst for many large hotel operators such as Holiday Inn and the Accor group to enter the market. This enables them to secure brand recognition early on in the growth of the market as well as exploiting key locational resources over competitors.

New uses

Over the course of their life cycle, new uses may need to be found for hospitality products. As mentioned previously this may be due to declining sales, changing market trends, new market opportunities and so on. A number of traditional licensed premises in the UK have had to develop their product portfolio so as to cater for a more discerning customer who wants more than just an alcoholic beverage. Many public houses now include in-house entertainment and the televising of sports such as football and cricket matches. Not only does this generate an additional use for the premises but can also target new market segments that are attracted to the new use of the product.

Withdrawal

If sales are declining to the extent where it has become unfeasible both in terms of time and resources to attempt to rejuvenate the brand, it may be necessary for the hospitality business to ultimately withdraw the product from the market. This could be due to a range of factors including increased competition, market trends, demographic shifts and so on that have impacted upon the sales of the product in the market.

Consolidation

Consolidation occurs when hospitality businesses decide to merge or acquire one another. Consolidation often occurs when sales growth in the market has peaked and has become saturated with too many competitors selling similar products. It therefore becomes increasingly difficult for all organisations to compete for a share of the same market.

Penetration

The hospitality business may decide to generate further sales from its current market. It may do this by improving the service or quality of the product which it is selling. There has to be scope for the hospitality business to believe that it can sell more of the same products and this will transpire if there is further growth potential in the target market.

Related diversification

Related diversification occurs when the hospitality business decides to enter into product areas that are related to its core business activity. It will do this to exploit further growth potential in the marketplace and to increase market presence. A luxury hotel company, for example, may decide to enter into the budget hotel market. The business will be familiar with the core accommodation product and be able to utilise its existing resource base to develop the related product area.

Unrelated diversification

Hospitality business decides to enter into a product area that is unrelated to its core business activity. For example, a fast food restaurant may decide to enter into the manufacturing of clothing to advertise its brand. The business would either have to acquire a firm that operates in this field or it would have to generate the resources internally to be able to do this on its own. In this example the activity would be very different from the core purpose of the business and therefore the potential risk of pursuing this strategy has to be carefully assessed by the firm.

It should be noted that the above types of development are mainly classified according to the market coverage and the newness of products offered by

Table 1.1	Business Development Classification Criteria
Classification Criteria	**Types Of Development**
Geographic Expansion	Domestic Development National Development Regional Development International Development
Competition	Imitative Development: Developing products similar to existing successful ones in the market. Distinctive Development: a firm protects itself against competitors' attacks by introducing new products or services which are not offered by its competitors. This approach is effective when a firm has a distinctive advantage over its competitors
Customers' Needs	Anticipatory Or Proactive Development: Developing products in anticipation of the evolution of a customers' needs. Adaptive Or Reactive Development: Developing products in order to cope with customers' needs.
Organizational Resources	Internal Or Organic Development: Developing business through the organization's own resources base and competence External Or Inorganic Development: Developing business through mergers and acquisitions Joint Development: Developing business through alliances and partnerships

hospitality organisations. However, customers, competition, market expansion and the methods of development can be considered when we discuss any of the above development routes. These various Business Development Classification Criteria are divided into four groups and discussed in Table 1.1. The first group, classified according to market expansion, business development can be seen as domestic, regional, national or international development. The second group, classified according to competition, includes (1) imitative development and (2) distinctive development. The third group, classified according to customers' needs, includes (1) anticipatory or proactive development and (2) adaptive or reactive development. The fourth group, classified according to organisational resources, includes (1) internal or organic development, (2) external or inorganic development and (3) joint development.

SUMMARY

This chapter deals with various aspects of business and product development in the hospitality industry. It includes discussion of the concept, types, motives and importance of hospitality business development. Finally, this chapter has concluded with an overview of the structure of this book in terms of its content and context. The next chapter will look at the concept and scope of the hospitality industry and its different sectors.

REVIEW QUESTIONS

1. Define the concept of business development and investigate its importance within the context of the hospitality industry.
2. At any one time almost every hospitality business has recently been developed, is under development or needs to be developed. Explore.
3. 'When a hospitality organisation decides to develop its business, it is usually affected by various motives.'
   A. Identify these motives and explain which of them are more reactive than proactive in nature and are driven by internal rather than external factors. Justify the rationale for your answer.
   B. Identify other examples of hospitality business development that have been based upon these motives.
4. 'The scope of business development involves a wide range of routes as shown in Figure 1.1.'
   A. Identify examples from hospitality organisations where each of the Hospitality Development Routes has occurred.
   B. What have been the motives for the hospitality organisation to pursue this particular route?
   C. What has been the outcome of this decision? Consider issues including profitability, market share, brand image and reputation and customer satisfaction and retention when answering this question.

Case Study: Burj Al Arab Hotel, Dubai

Overview

Burj Al Arab Hotel in Dubai was opened in 1999 and recognises itself as a seven star deluxe hotel. It proclaims to be the most luxurious hotel in the World. Dubai is part of the United Arab Emirates (UAE) based in the Middle East. Dubai itself has seen phenomenal growth over the last decade with mass construction and urbanisation of the landscape. The Burj Al Arab, which when translated from Arabic stands for 'Tower of the Arabs', is seen as an iconic symbol that reflects the growing International status of Dubai as a premium hospitality and tourism destination. This is in keeping with Dubai's crown prince, Sheikh Mohammed bin Rashid Al Maktoum, whose vision has been to diversify the country's economy from oil to service-related industries such as hospitality.

Corporate Owner

The hotel is part of Jumeirah, an international hotel group that has representation in destinations across the globe including London, New York, Bermuda, Spain, Thailand and China. Founded in 1997, the focus of Jumeirah was to become a leader in the hospitality industry by developing a portfolio of world class hotels and resorts. Jumeirah distinguishes itself by describing its core philosophy as to STAY Different™. This includes providing guests with unique, innovative and personalised experiences. The Jumeirah Group portfolio of businesses is not exclusively hotels but also includes a water park, an academic institution, a restaurant division, luxury serviced residences and retail stores.

Design and Construction

The Burj Al Arab was designed by a British architect, Tom Wright. The design of the hotel is in the shape of a sail and took five years to build at a cost of $650 million. Standing 321 metres high it was one of the World's tallest hotels. The hotel is built on an artificial island that is located a short distance from the beach off the Persian Gulf and is accessible via a private land bridge. The construction of the hotel was extensive and had to be built within a giant fabric wall. This was to protect the outside of hotel from the high temperatures and heat in Dubai during construction. The hotel was also designed with the World's tallest atrium, which is a large open space that is built up over a number of floors.

Facilities and Services

The hotel's clientele are extremely wealthy and require a superior standard of service. This is reflected in the services and facilities that are offered in the hotel. The hotel has 202 suites across 27 floors. Each floor has its own private reception desk and in suite check-in facilities. The rooms are equipped with in-room office, dining, kitchen and bar facilities, jacuzzi and spa bath facilities, electronic curtains and air conditioning, widescreen plasma TVs and pillow and quilt menus. The rooms use state-of-the-art furnishings and in-room facilities that are associated with recognised brands including Versace bedding and Hermes amenities. The executive and presidential suites have private cinemas and full size bars. The service that is provided in suites is highly personalised with the use of private butlers.

The hotel has nine different restaurants. This includes the Al Muntaha, a 'floating' restaurant that literally hangs in the air and the Al Mahara which is accessed via a simulated submarine voyage and contains an extensive aquarium. In terms of transportation to and from the hotel, all guests have access to chauffeur-driven cars including Rolls Royces and BMWs. The hotel has its own helipad and provides its own private beach which is for the exclusive use of Burj Al Arab guests only. At night the hotel is lit up by an alternating light show that conveys its grandiose exterior to onlookers.

Awards

The Burj Al Arab has received a number of awards including twice winning the Best Hotel in the Middle East at the Ultimate Luxury Travel Related Awards (ULTRAs) and the Best Resort in the Middle East and Africa at the Conde Nast Traveller Reader's Choice Awards 2007 staged in the United States.

Sources

http://www.jumeirah.com/en/Hotels-and-Resorts/Destinations/Dubai/Burj-Al-Arab/

http://en.wikipedia.org/wiki/Burj_Al_Arab http://www.forbestraveler.com/hotel-review/Dubai/Burj-Al-Arab.html

Questions

1. Discuss what the business development motives have been for the Jumeirah Group developing the Burj Al Arab.

2. What business development routes have the Jumeirah Group pursued in the expansion of their business? Why have they used these routes?

3. Evaluate the distinctive features of the Burj Al Arab. How distinctive are they when compared to competitor offerings?

GLOSSARY

Business development   The process by which a company can improve its performance through: (a) modifying or enhancing the features and attributes of its current products or services, (b) developing new products or services, (c) entering new markets and (d) partnerships or strategic alliances.

Consolidation   Consolidation occurs when hospitality businesses decide to merge or acquire one another.

Economies of scale   Economies of scale are when the hospitality organisation purchases products from its suppliers, such as food and drink, in bulk. This enables a lower cost base to be achieved for the hospitality business.

Market development   Finding new markets for the existing products.

Market penetration   Increasing the market share of the existing product in the existing market.

Product development   Developing new products for the existing markets.

Related diversification   Related diversification occurs when the hospitality business decides to enter into product areas that are related to its core business activity.

Unrelated diversification   Hospitality business decides to enter into a product area that is unrelated to its core business activity.

Withdrawal   If sales are declining to the extent where it has become unfeasible both in terms of time and resources to attempt to rejuvenate the brand, it may be necessary for the hospitality business to ultimately withdraw the product from the market.

CHAPTER 2

Scope of the Hospitality Industry

Learning Objectives

- Introduce the concept and scope of the hospitality industry.
- Evaluate the characteristics of services and their impact on hospitality businesses.
- Understand the scope of the hospitality industry and its individual sub-sectors.
- Explore the different levels of the hospitality product.

CONTENTS

INTRODUCTION

This chapter will initially outline what is meant by the hospitality product and its significance to the global economy. This chapter will then progress on to a discussion of the characteristics of services and their influence over product development decision-making by the hospitality manager. A review of the scope of hospitality will then be provided. This chapter will then move on to discuss the hospitality product.

HOSPITALITY AS A SERVICE INDUSTRY

The hospitality industry operates in a service context which makes it different from other industries such as manufacturing and agriculture, and therefore it is presented with a number of unique challenges. Lashley (2000) notes how the focus of service delivery and how it is received are based on first impressions by the customer. These are often described as 'moments of truth' where there is the emotional management of labour to ensure that the customer obtains a quality product and the highest level of service delivery.

These differences manifest themselves in a number of characteristics that are unique to service industries such as hospitality. The hospitality manager has to be familiar with these characteristics as they will influence the operations of the business and decisions made about the product. The characteristics are made up of the following.

Intangibility

The hospitality product is intangible in that it cannot be seen, touched, smelled or tasted prior to purchase. Unlike products such as clothes which can often be tested before being purchased, a couple going out to dinner in a restaurant will be unable to sample the product prior to purchase. This can make the purchase of the product quite risky and, depending on the customers' perception of value, will involve a high degree of involvement in decision-making about what product to purchase. The customer will therefore seek out ways of minimising the risks involved in product purchase. This may include gathering information about the product's quality and reputation. Many hospitality businesses provide customers with Internet-based information about their services. In addition to description, this may include photos or videos that enable the customer to visualise what they will experience if they were to purchase the product. If the customer has been to the restaurant previously then they will have some degree of what to expect both in terms of the service provided and the product being offered. As many hospitality businesses rely on repeat custom it is essential that they ensure quality of service so as to minimise customer anxiety prior to purchase.

Example: Social Networking and Product Decision-Making
The rapid growth and influence of social networking Websites such as You Tube and Facebook have enabled customers to openly express their views and opinions on a variety of subjects. This includes their experiences of hotels, restaurants and so on. Social networking sites have become a means for previous customers to comment on their experiences of products and what they have to offer. These may be both good and bad experiences and have the potential to influence the decisions of others in their search for information about intended hospitality product purchases. This creates both threats and opportunities for hospitality businesses. Negative feedback from customers on these sites has the potential to detract customers whereas positive feedback may have a beneficial effect.

Inseparability

Hospitality goods and services are inseparable. Customers can only consume the good or service in the place or location where it is being produced. For example, the process of having a meal at a restaurant is based on the ordering of the meal, the production of the meal on the premises and the delivery of the meal to the table by the serving staff. This is different from other industries like manufacturing where the product will be produced in a location and then go through a supply chain process from producer to retailer. Staff are therefore part of the production of the experience that the customer receives. This means that the quality of service has to be optimised and the delivery of the product to the customer has to conform to the brand standards of the company so as to maximise customer satisfaction. As all customers will be part of the production process it is in the interest of the hospitality enterprise to ensure that the atmosphere and ambience of the business is maximised.

Example: Park Plaza Hotels Ltd

In 2008, Park Plaza Hotels introduced 'YOU: brand identity, Connect! training pro-gramme'. The programme was introduced to further develop the company's employees to consistently exceed guest expectations and improve performance. The philosophy of the programme is based on a 'reverse thinking' model. This encourages employees to anticipate guest needs so as to surpass their expectations.

Source: http://www.hotelsmag.com/article/CA6554286.html?q=employees+quality

Perishability

The hospitality product is perishable and cannot be stored or stockpiled for later use and sale. The service is time limited and the offer will therefore perish if it has not been sold on any given day. The hoteliers, for example, have to ensure that their accommodation is sold otherwise it will be lost revenue which they will be unable to retrieve due to the perishability of the product. It is not unusual for hotels to implement an over-booking policy where they sell more rooms than they physically have on the premises. The policy is based on revenue management information which determines demand patterns throughout the course of the year. This enables hotels to maximise their yield and the number of rooms that they can sell at any one time. If customers cancel or fail to arrive, the hotel has a fallback position where it can ensure that all the rooms are sold. The drawback to an over-booking policy is when the hotelier finds that all the customers arrive and they have to find alternative accommodation of the same or better value for those whom they do not have rooms for. This has the potential to lead to customer dissatisfaction with the hotel for the possible inconvenience that this may cause.

Lack of ownership

The customers do not own the hospitality product or service and they will be unlikely to be able to take away any physical item from the hospitality premises. This is different from other industries where the purchase of a product such as a car, for example, results in the customer being able to take away what he or she has purchased. The customer will only own the service experience and the memories that this generates. Hospitality businesses therefore have to ensure that the customer is provided with the best possible service and experiences many positive 'moments of truth'.

Heterogeneity

Hospitality services are heterogeneous in that the experience of the service will be different each time it is delivered. This is unlike manufacturing industries where there is the ability to ensure standardisation of the product so that it meets a certain specification. This guarantees that each product will be exactly the same as another of the same kind. The delivery of hospitality services presents many challenges to the hospitality manager in ensuring that each customer obtains an experience which meets with his or her expectations. However, different customers will have different expectations and this compounds the management and delivery of the service for the hospitality business. The standardisation of the service is a method that is used by hospitality businesses to ensure that similar service experiences are achieved. Branded fast food outlets are characteristic of this method of delivery. However, standardising services is not always desirable and can sanitise the overall experience for the customer by removing a sense of personalisation and uniqueness.

Example: Service Scripts

Employees in branded hospitality outlets can be required to adhere to a service script which states specifically how they should interact with customers. However, in a study entitled, 'Service Scripting: A Customer's Perspective of Quality and Performance' the Cornell Centre for Hospitality Research found that employees should not always be required to stick to their service scripts. The research suggests that scripts should be used as a guideline and as part of a customised service experience.

Source: http://www.hotelsmag.com/article/CA6618945.html?q=service+quality, http://www.hotelschool.cornell.edu/research/chr/pubs/reports/2008.html

Example: Standard Operating Procedures

Standard operating procedures (SOPs) enable hospitality businesses to conform to a set of strict principles. The objective of SOPs is to ensure that a desired level of service standards is met. This can include a number of audits including back of house and service and facilities audits, manager walk-throughs, pre-shift meetings, customer survey processes and technology implementation.

Source: http://www.expresshospitality.com/20070315/aahar200706.shtml

Activity

1. Select a hospitality business and think through what the impact of each of the service characteristics on that business will be?
2. How can the hospitality business manage each of the service characteristics?

Table 2.1 identifies the hospitality business management challenges associated with each service characteristic and their possible solutions.

SCOPE OF THE HOSPITALITY PRODUCT

The hospitality industry is broad and complex in scope and is made up of a number of different sectors. It is necessary to outline the scope of the industry so as to understand the different business sectors and how they operate. It should be noted that these sectors are interrelated and therefore should not be viewed in isolation from one another. The sectors will also be made up of sub-categories that further distinguish between hospitality businesses. This impacts on the various decisions that are made about the hospitality products on offer. For the purposes of this discussion the hospitality industry is divided into two broad categories: accommodation and food and beverage operations. Within the context of this discussion different criteria will be presented to classify the scope of these categories.

ACCOMMODATION SECTOR

Accommodation can be commercial, non-commercial and can comprise a wide range of different sub-sectors such as hotels, motels, camps, hostels

Accommodation Type	Examples
Hotels	Transient hotel, Residential hotel, Resort hotel, All-suite hotel, extended stay hotels, casino hotel.
Motels	Motorway and roadside accommodation outlets
Unusual accommodation	Igloo hotel, tree house
Camping & Caravanning	The most common types of camping are: (1) wilderness camping, (2) tent camping and (3) recreational vehicle (RV) or trailer camping.
Event venues	Conference centres
Private homes and timeshares	A private home not dedicated for full time occupation of guests, but is a private house or apartment which is temporarily available for rental, often during peak tourism seasons. (e.g. cottages).
Mobile lodging	Cruises, train sleepers, Recreational Vehicles and Caravans, houseboat and yachts
School accommodation	Boarding Schools, residence halls or dormitory
Clubs	Club ranges from working men clubs, to political party clubs, social club, sports club.
Non-commercial accommodation	Example: Armed forces, prisons, hospitals
Youth Hosels	Hostels and Backpacker accommodation
Guest accommodation	Guest houses, Bed & breakfast, Lodges, Farm stays and pension ■ B&B ■ Guest House ■ Farmhouse ■ Inn ■ Restaurant with rooms
Care accommodation	Nursing home, hospital
Self-catering accommodation	A self-catering establishment may be primarily one of the other accommodation types, but also offers dedicated self-catering facilities.

Table 2.1	Service Characteristics Solutions and Challenges	
Characteristic	**Challenges**	**Solutions**
Intangibility	■ Hospitality service cannot be seen, touched, smelt, or tasted ■ Not easily displayed or sampled prior to purchase ■ Pricing is difficult	■ Make use of tangible clues and physical evidence ■ Ensure quality of service ■ Utilise personal sources of information ■ Utilise social networking technologies ■ Create a strong organisational image
Inseparability	■ Service provider is involved in the production process ■ Customer is involved in the production process ■ Other customers are involved in the production process (shared experience)	■ Effective selection and training of personnel ■ Implementing and ensuring brand standards are maintained across multi-site operations
Heterogenity	■ Standardisation of the hospitality service experience ■ Quality control is difficult to achieve ■ Different customer expectations	■ Standardisation of the hospitality service ■ Customising the service experience so that it meets the customers' needs
Perishability	■ Service is time limited ■ Matching supply and demand challenges	■ Creative pricing and effective reservation systems ■ Effective yield management ■ Development of complementary services ■ Development of non-peak demand strategies
Lack of Ownership	■ Customer does not own the hospitality service ■ Customer only owns memories of the hospitality service experience	■ Ensure quality of the hospitality service experience ■ Ensure the customer experiences 'moments of truth'

Adapted from Hoffman and Bateson (2006).

and villas and apartments for rent. Figure 2.1 illustrates that the accommodation sector consists of a number of different sub-sectors.

Sub-sectors will have their own characteristics that distinguish them from each other. However, there are some common themes that emerge broadly from the accommodation sector as a whole. Medlik and Ingram

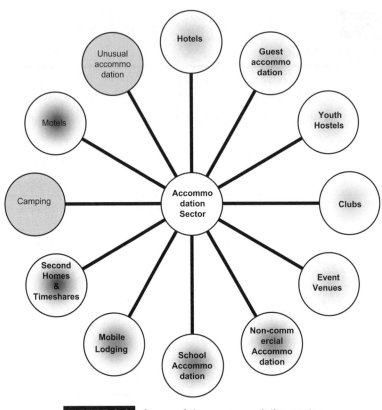

FIGURE 2.1 *Scope of the accommodation sector.*

(2000) have presented a number of criteria that can be used to classify the hotel sector, but these can be broadly used to understand the accommodation sector as a whole. These criteria include the following:

- Location of the accommodation. Is the accommodation based in towns, cities, coastal resorts or in the countryside? What is the position of the accommodation within its location? Is it in city or town centre, along the beach or on a road network?
- Purpose of the visit. Is the accommodation required for leisure, business, health, study or a combination of these different purposes?
- Duration of the stay. Is the stay permanent, semi-permanent or temporary?
- Facilities and services provided. For example, full-service or self-catering.

- Licensed and unlicensed. Does the accommodation provide for the consumption of alcoholic beverages?
- Size of the accommodation. Is it large, medium sized or small?
- Class or grade of the accommodation. Does the accommodation have to conform to a classification standard which denotes its quality and provision of facilities?
- Ownership and management. For example, is it independent, franchised, multi-national or public sector owned?

The largest of the accommodation sectors is hotels. Hotels are where food and beverages are served alongside accommodation. The hotel sector itself is very broad, ranging from small bed and breakfasts to large luxury hotels. Internationally hotel accommodations can be described differently. For example, an Italian guesthouse is called a Pensione and a traditional inn in Japan is called a Ryokan. There are also many unusual types of hotel establishments which include ice hotels, underwater hotels, themed hotels and so on. Each has its own unique characteristics.

Activity: Unique and Unusual Hotels

1. Search the following Website: www.uhotw.com.

2. Using the accommodation criteria above classify the different types of hotels.

3. What is unique about the hotels which make them different from each other?

4. Think of some further unique and unusual hotels which are not listed on the Website and could be developed into a hotel business.

Hotel establishments are usually distinguishable by the classification that denotes the hotels' level of facilities and the quality of service. This includes the number of restaurants and bars, conference facilities, in-house leisure and spa facilities, room and concierge service and so on. Classification systems enable the customer to identify the different hospitality products on offer ensuring ease when making purchase decisions. Most countries operate a star-based categorisation system that ranges from one to five stars. It should be noted that these systems are not unified globally and therefore it is not unusual for customers to receive a standard of service that compares differently from one country to another, irrespective of whether the establishments have the same classification or star grading. This is further compounded when different types of accommodation have alternative methods of classi-fying the product and when there are additional classification schemes for hotels that, for example, demonstrate accessibility and green credentials as they now do in the Caribbean.

The hotel sector has evolved quite significantly over the years and now incorporates a broad range of establishments with the growth in budget, boutique and eco hotel products becoming increasingly popular. These can provide challenges to the traditional classification systems. For example many boutique hotels are too small to meet all the criteria for five star hotels, but they argue that their quality of service and experience is equal to or better than their standardised competitors. They have therefore refused to be classified, but then this causes problems if customers are using Internet search engines, which routinely ask for what sort of accommodation they require by reference to the star ratings.

FOOD AND BEVERAGE SECTOR

Figure 2.2 outlines the broad scope of the product sectors that make up the food and beverage sector.

The offers may be differentiated by matching them to the following factors:

- Variations of foodservice operation among establishments
- Type of restaurants (e.g., fast food, ethnic, speciality, fine dining, themed and family restaurants)
- Location
- Type of Menu (a la carte, fixed, speciality or cyclical menu)
- Food quality
- Menu prices
- Service (pre-plated, French, Russian or English service)
- Ambience
- Range of facilities and services (e.g., full-service, limited, self-catering restaurants)
- Licensed and unlicensed
- Size (e.g., large, medium-sized or small restaurants)
- Class or grade (e.g., five star or four star restaurants)
- Ownership and management (e.g., independent and franchised restaurants)

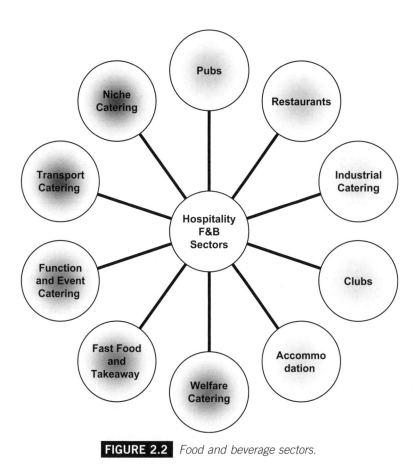

FIGURE 2.2 *Food and beverage sectors.*

Restaurants

The primary function of restaurants is the provision of food and beverages to customers. The food and beverages on offer are likely to act as the main motivator for visiting a restaurant, though other factors including ambience, atmosphere and clientele will also determine type and choice of restaurant to visit. Like hotels, the restaurant sector is broad in scope and encompasses a number of different types of outlet. This includes haute cuisine restaurants where the offering is classical in preparation and presentation. The food is served with a high level of service with close attention given to the detail of presentation to the customer. Ethnic restaurants provide food and beverages that are tailored towards foods from a particular country or place of origin. Indian, Chinese and Italian are examples of ethnic-based restaurants that are commonplace in many towns and cities.

Example: Nando's Restaurants

Nando's is a fast food chain which first originated in 1987 in South Africa and launched five years later in the UK. The chain has 213 restaurants in the UK and specialises in its Portuguese, Peri-Peri chicken delicacy. The philosophy of Nando's is based on a core set of values which includes pride, passion, courage, integrity and family.

Source: www.nandos.co.uk, http://www.restaurant-guide.com/uk+restaurant-chains. htm?chain=nandos-restaurants.

Themed restaurants are based around a particular theme. The theme may be based around a country such as an American Diner (e.g., TGI Friday's), an aspect of popular culture such as a character (e.g., Mickey Mouse Restaurant) or film and music (e.g., Planet Hollywood and Hard Rock Café) or a concept such as a jungle theme (e.g., Rainforest Café). Themed restaurants are developed to match the character of the theme on offer. This will include the detail of the furnishings, the music and the food and beverages available on the menu.

Example: Hard Rock Café

Hard Rock Cafe is a themed bar restaurant chain which was founded by Isacc Tigrett and Peter Morton in 1971. The restaurant chain is renowned for furnishing is restaurants with rock 'n' roll and music memorabilia. Food and beverages have an American style theme and include steaks and burgers.

Source: www.hardrock.com, http://en.wikipedia.org/wiki/Hard_Rock_Cafe#Expansion_into_other_businesses.

Cafés and brassieres as a sector of the restaurant trade have become increasingly popular particularly amongst previously underrepresented markets such as women. The café culture has emerged alongside a more European approach to dining.

Industrial catering

Industrial catering is the provision of food and beverages within the work environment. The principle of this is based on the acknowledgment that the provision of food maintains a more motivated and satisfied work force. This may come in the form of the canteen or restaurant that provides meals and

Example: Apollo Sindoori Hotels Limited (ASHL)

Apollo Sindoori Hotels Limited is an Indian company which has an industrial catering section. This specialises in serving catering products to staff canteens, cafeteria, guest-houses and so on.

Source: http://www.sindoori.com/IndustrialCateringServices.html

beverages for those working in the business. These operations can be run in-house or by a contract catering company. The latter is a popular option with many businesses as it transfers the cost and responsibility of production and service to a third party.

Clubs

Clubs are outlets which provide food and drink to members and their guests. The scope of clubs includes social clubs, working men's clubs, sports clubs and political party clubs. Clubs often have a defined membership and this influences the target market and the products that are on offer. The atmosphere and common social bond of the core membership have been key components to the longevity of many clubs. However, in a highly competitive marketplace, many traditional social clubs have had to demonstrate innovation in their product offerings so as to accommodate emerging and growing target markets.

Example: Birdland Golf & Country Club

The Birdland Golf & Country Club is based in Bükfürdő, a popular holiday resort in the west of Hungary. It offers golfing facilities alongside accommodation services which are operated in partnership with Radisson SAS Hotels and Resorts.

Source: http://www.birdland.hu/indexf.html.

Pubs

Pubs are licensed premises with the primary focus of serving food and alcoholic beverages to the consumer. Pubs have to adhere to strict licensing laws and are only granted licenses if they are able to conform to strict conditions. This includes opening hours, age limitations and conduct in the premises. The pub market is wide ranging and includes high street and rural pubs and bars. Pubs have had to evolve quite significantly in recent years. The impact of enforced smoking bans across many countries in Europe has meant that public houses have had to adapt their product and cater to new markets. Extended opening hours in the UK has provided opportunities for public house providers to broaden their customer base. Many new pub concepts now exist including Gastropubs that serve high-quality food and drink in up market public house surroundings.

Example and Activity: The Wortley Arms

South Yorkshire master chef, Andy Gabbitas, has reopened the Wortley Arms located between Barnsley and Sheffield. Major restoration has restored the beautiful eighteenth century inn to its original state.

What is it? Visit http://www.wortley-arms.co.uk/ and think through the offer.

It is a pub – selling real ales.

It is a gastro pub – serving traditional food and several very special specials.

It is also a restaurant – Montagu's promises the very best in fine dining, with private dining rooms and meeting rooms.

How do you characterise this offer?

Welfare catering

Welfare catering is where food and drink is provided in colleges, universities, the armed forces, prisons and hospitals. It is also provided to those who may have particular social needs and may have difficulty in producing their own meals. In welfare catering, the government provides for a budgetary allowance on what should be spent on food provision. This is often based on an allowance per head that welfare caterers have to budget to when formulating their costing plans. Though profit is not necessarily the main focus of welfare caterers they have to ensure that the food provided meets certain nutritional values and standards. This is to ensure that those consuming the foods have a healthy balanced diet.

Example: Jamie Oliver and School Dinners

Jamie Oliver is a celebrity chef who has been influential in changing governmental policy on school dinners and nutrition. Since 2005, his 'Feed Me Better' campaign has been changing perceptions away from what he describes as in nutritious school meals. This has culminated in new standards being introduced by the ruling labour party of the British government. The new standards, introduced in September 2006, require the following:

- high-quality meat, poultry or oily fish regularly available;
- at least two portions of fruit and vegetables with every meal; and
- bread, other cereals and potatoes regularly available.

Additionally, there are controls on the following foods:

- deep-fried food limited to no more than two portions per week; and
- fizzy drinks, crisps, chocolate and other confectioneries removed from school meals and vending machines.

Source: www.direct.gov.uk

Fast food and takeaway

This segment sees food and drink produced quickly so that it can be sold immediately and consumed either on or off the premises. The focus is on systems and processes that enable the quick turnaround of customers through the fast food and takeaway outlet. The food served is often simple in nature requiring minimal preparation and serving time. The standardisation of the service enables customers to be dealt with quickly as there is limited scope for elaboration during the service encounter. The scope of the fast food sector is broad and includes high street fish and chip shops, specialist takeaway outlets such as Chinese and Indian restaurants and established branded fast food outlets such as McDonalds and Burger King. All are based on similar principles of ensuring that the food and drink is served in the optimum time possible.

Example: Wendy's

Wendy's/Arby's Group, Inc. is the third largest fast food restaurant company in the United States. The group comprises the Wendy's® and Arby's® brands and franchises over 10,000 restaurants. The company states its central purpose as to 'maintain aligned, people-driven culture and values; attract, retain, and develop top talent; offer performance-driven compensation and rewards'.

Source: http://www.wendys.com/

Function and event catering

Function and event catering is based on the large-scale provision of food and drink. This is often at a particular time and place and for a specified number of people. Though it can be a feature of a hotel's operations this is not exclusively so and many independent event operators will provide services of this nature. The arrangements for the food and beverages will be negotiated with the client who is requesting the service and a set price for the event will be agreed. Function and event catering has become significant in the hospitality industry. Corporate organisations often request specialised functions to entertain their business clients and to act as a reward for employees. In addition, the growth of the conferences and events industry has promoted the need for a range of services to be provided by hospitality enterprises. This can range from large-scale outdoor catering to small-bespoke wedding functions.

Example: Events Catering

Events Catering was founded by Brian Hyde and Michael Hyde and provides on-site or off-site catering. This includes Corporate Functions, Backyard Barbeques, Graduations, Weddings and Parties.

Source: http://www.eventscateringcompany.com/home/

Transport catering

Transport catering is the provision of food and beverages to those in transit. The mobility of people from place to place requires catering facilities that can be accessed easily to enable customers to dine in comfort whilst also facilitating the transit experience. Transport catering is broad in scope and includes the full range of travel methods including road and railway services, airport terminals and shipping ports. Catering facilities may be large scale in the form of airport catering or small in the form of roadside cafes and diners. Many travellers now perceive the journey to a destination as part of the overall experience and this has contributed to the continued growth of the transport industry. It has also required transport catering operators to reposition their offerings to ensure that customers are receiving an enhanced experience when visiting.

Example: Ambassadors Sky Chef

Ambassadors Sky Chef is part of the Indian-based Ambassador Group. It offers in flight catering services to airlines including Lufthansa, Swiss International, Saudia Airline, Air India, Kenya Airlines, Jet Lite and Indian Airlines.

Source: http://www.ambassadorindia.com/skychef.asp

THE HOSPITALITY PRODUCT

Hospitality products are made up of a number of constituent parts and hospitality managers need to determine how these parts compare with competing offers. The product can then be adapted or modified so as to gain a positional advantage over others in the marketplace. Kotler (1994) identifies three levels or components of a product: core, tangible and augmented. The *core product* is the fulfilment of the consumer's primary need. This will act as the main driver for the product purchase. In terms of hospitality products this may be for food, accommodation or social interaction. The *tangible product* is the physical benefits offered. This includes aspects of the product including packaging, quality, features, design and the brand name. The *augmented products* are elements that differentiate them from competitors through the inclusion of perceived added value. This may consist of speed of service, payment options, after sales service and so on. It is the augmented aspects of the product that can enable it to gain an advantage over competitor offerings. The broad core, tangible and augmented aspects of the hospitality product are illustrated in Figure 2.3.

In the fast food industry, for example, the core product will be the consumption of food quickly to satisfy a basic hunger need. On the basis of a branded fast food chain competing with a small independent fast food outlet the choice will be based on tangible product issues concerning location, quality, brand and so on. However, if the consumer's choice was between the leading branded fast food establishments, due to similarities in the core and tangible aspects of the product, the final purchase decision would be influenced by the augmented aspects of the product. This may include the speed of service, the alternative nutritional food options offered and so on. It is on this basis of the augmented product that branded hospitality organisations often compete. This example raises a number of issues when considering the core, tangible and augmented aspects of hospitality products.

First, there will be differences between the sectors of the hospitality industry as outlined earlier in this chapter. The core hospitality product

FIGURE 2.3 *The hospitality product.*

will often distinguish what this difference is. A stay in a luxury five star hotel may be driven by relaxation and need for fulfilment of self-esteem, whereas a night out at a nightclub may be driven by excitement and social interaction. Second, there will be differences in the categories that make up the sectors. It will be the tangible aspects of the product that will differentiate between these categories. Third, it will be the augmented element of the product that will differentiate between operations offering similar core and tangible products. It is on this basis that organisations will gain an advantage. Fourth, changing customer expectations will impact on the different product levels. Changing trends, fashions and consumer tastes will influence the adaptations that hospitality businesses make to the different product levels. This may require, for example, adaptations to the design, décor and furnishings of the tangible product or the repositioning of the brand to meet current consumer trends.

Activity

1. Select a hospitality business within a sector of the industry.
2. Analyse the products constituent elements in relation to Kotler's model.
3. Identify similar organisations that the hospitality business is competing against within the same sector category. What possible adaptations can the hospitality business make to the tangible or augmented aspects of the product so as to offer an advantage over these competitors?

SUMMARY AND CONCLUSIONS

This chapter has introduced the scope of the hospitality industry and attempted to explore some of the complexities in thinking of the sectors and sub-sectors as an industry. We have highlighted the specificities of the offerings but we have also demonstrated that the market is competitive and the consumer choice may be decided by elements within the augmented product rather than simply based on the product core. It is possible for a hospitality business to operate within a number of sectors of the industry – by offering accommodation and food, by offering dining and takeaway facilities or by offering conference facilities in an airport hotel. It is therefore worth remembering that these categories are helpful for analysing the market but they may not be sufficient for exploring the specific detail of a hospitality business. The following chapters will explore the complexities of those relationships more fully.

REVIEW QUESTIONS

1. Explain why hospitality is a service industry. Critically discuss the implications of this for hospitality operations.
2. Define the two main sectors of the hospitality industry.
3. Explore the complexities of the augmented hospitality offer, working through one example from a hospitality business which you think has the potential to develop further.
4. Why does it make sense for hospitality businesses to operate across sectoral boundaries?
5. Think about your favourite pub and explain its offer. What sort of theme does it have? What sort of drinks do they offer? What sort of food – if any – do they provide?

Case Study: Holiday/Vacation Rental Properties

When making a decision to book holiday accommodation, the customer will be confronted with the decision of either choosing a hotel or rental accommodation. A hotel may be part of a larger corporate entity whereas rental accommodations are often individually owned houses, flats, apartments or villas. A vacation rental is a fully furnished outlet which is rented to the customer for a specific length of time, normally based on weekly hire. The term holiday or vacation rental differs around the world and can be described alternatively as self-catering rentals or holiday cottages in the UK, condominiums in the US, Gites in France or Casaa Rurales in Spain. Rental properties can be based in a variety of urban, rural or coastal locations and can include lakeside cottages, mountain top cabins, beachfront villas, luxury townhouses, ski chalets, farmhouses and so on. Properties can be provided by private owners or run by property management companies. Property management companies can provide for 24-hour customer service contact, concierge services, housekeeping and partnerships with local businesses. A rental property which is part of a management company will often provide for its maintenance and booking and marketing facilities so as to ensure consistency of service quality and standards across the portfolio of properties. Rental providers can also offer additional services including grocery shopping, massage delivery and in-home chefs.

A number of factors have driven the demand and supply of holiday rental properties. From a demand-side perspective there has been an increased desire for short breaks. These breaks are often wanted in more adventurous and exclusive locations where private hotel companies are unable to develop. From a supply-side perspective there has been the increased supply of second home ownership and the ease of booking directly through the Internet.

The decision to choose a holiday rental will be based on a number of criteria. This includes the length of stay that is required. For a single night's accommodation, booking a rental property can be uneconomical if a minimum stay is required from the accommodation vendor. The party size will influence the type of accommodation required. If it's a large group the cost of the rental can be shared amongst the whole party. The type of facilities that are required will also influence the decision. This includes the provision of a kitchen, laundry equipment, balconies, barbeques, private patios, swimming pools, beach access and so on.

From a customer perspective, there are a number of advantages for selecting a rental property. First, the availability of properties and the different types that can be accessed is vast. Second is value for money when compared to hotel outlets. This is further promoted by the provision of self-catering, and if staying in a rental complex, on-site facilities including entertainment and swimming pools. Third, the provision of space can be far greater than in traditional hotel accommodation. Fourth, extra facilities like DVD and video game players can be provided. Fifth, rental properties may also allow pets to stay in the accommodation. Sixth, there can be far greater privacy in rental accommodation and staying in a private property can provide a greater cultural experience with the local area and residents.

However, there can be a number of disadvantages involved in the provision of rental properties. First, if a client books a property independently he/she is still required to book the additional services which may include flights and taxis to and from the destination of the property. Second, the level of service can be sporadic and inconsistent due to limited housekeeping services. These services may incur additional charges or the client may be required to clean the accommodation before he/she leaves. Third, the holiday rental can lack the level of flexibility of hotel accommodation when wanting to arrive at alternative times during the week. Furthermore, cancellation of the accommodation can incur the loss of the full cost of the rental fee.

Sources

Karpinski, C., 2008. How to Rent Vacation Property by Owner, second ed. Kinney Press, Pollack.

http://popularvacationrentals.net/homes-vs-hotels?format=pdf.

http://www.findrentals.com/vacation-rentals-vs-hotels.html.

http://www.discovervacationhomes.com/vacation-rental-advantages.asp.

http://www.destinationvillas.com/travel-tips/Vacation-Rentals-vs-Hotels.html.

http://www.destindining.com/a204167-vacation-rentals-vs-hotels.cfm.

http://newsblaze.com/story/20061212084035tsop.nb/topstory.html.

http://www.vacationrentalscommunity.com/wikis/vacationrentalwikipedia/definition-of-vacation-rentals.aspx.

http://www.wisegeek.com/should-i-opt-for-a-vacation-rental-or-hotel-when-im-traveling.htm.

Questions

1. Explain the similarities and differences between holiday/vacation rentals and hotels.

2. Search the Internet for different property management companies. Review the advantages and disadvantages of using a property management company.

3. Discuss the present and future impacts of vacation rentals on other hospitality sectors (hotels, motels and guest lodging).

GLOSSARY

Augmented product   The way the core offer is presented to the market with 'extras' that mark the offer out from competitors by making it more accessible, more desirable and easier to consume.

Core product   The offer of the hospitality business, stripped of any of its dressing or positioning. It may also be a service.

Heterogeneity   Hospitality services are heterogeneous in that the experience of the service will be different each time it is delivered.

Inseparability   The hospitality industry is inseparable as customers have to go to the place where the product is being produced for it to be consumed.

Intangibility   The hospitality product is intangible in that it cannot be seen, touched, smelled or tasted prior to purchase.

Lack of ownership   The customer does not own the hospitality product or service.

Manufacturing   The process by which a company produces a tangible product which it offers to the market.

Perishability   The hospitality product is perishable and cannot be stored or stockpiled for later use and sale.

Tangible product   The physical benefits offered. This includes aspects of the product including packaging, quality, features, design and the brand name.

CHAPTER 3

The Hospitality Environment

Learning Objectives

Having completed this chapter you should be able to:

- Consider the different layers of the external hospitality environment.
- Determine the external environmental influences on hospitality businesses.
- Evaluate different models and concepts for understanding the external hospitality environment.

INTRODUCTION

The hospitality business has to be fully aware of how the environment in which it competes can influence its development decisions. It also has to be flexible enough to adapt to the ever-changing and dynamic nature of the hospitality environment. The hospitality business needs to be able to understand those factors that can have an impact on its future development and consider how it can position itself to be able to react to changing environmental forces and competitive activities. This chapter will discuss a range of concepts for analysing the environment of the hospitality business. These concepts can be used as a basis for the decision-making activities of the hospitality business.

SWOT ANALYSIS

An initial starting point for analysing the hospitality business within the context of the external environment is via a SWOT (strengths, weaknesses, opportunities, threats) analysis. Johnson et al. (2008: 119) define SWOT as summarising 'the key issues from the business environment and the strategic capability of an organisation that are most likely to impact on strategy development'. Strengths and weaknesses are analysed internally to the organisation, whereas opportunities and threats are analysed externally to the organisation. The SWOT analysis can be illustrated in table format (see Table 3.1) and can quickly establish the extent to which the hospitality business has areas of strength, which it can capitalise on, whilst also acknowledging areas of weakness that it needs to develop further. The SWOT analysis therefore enables the hospitality business to understand and make decisions about its future development.

Sources of strength and weakness will be driven through an appraisal of the hospitality business's resources and capabilities. This can include, for example, brand and reputation, the human resources, quality of service, methods and systems of operation, access to financial capital, the physical makeup and location of the hospitality business and so on. Determining the hospitality business's resources and capabilities is discussed in greater detail in Chapter 8.

Table 3.1 Example SWOT Analysis for a Hospitality Business

Internal

Strengths	Weaknesses
■ Brand recognition and reputation	■ Staff turnover
■ Market share	■ Declining profitability
■ Specific expertise (e.g. research and development of new products and services)	■ Poor quality service
	■ Poor location
■ Gaining economies of scale	■ Lack of differentiation
	■ Declining sector life cycle

External

Opportunities	Threats
■ New product or service opportunities	■ Economic factors (e.g. global recession, deflation)
■ Market expansion opportunities	■ Rising customer expectations
■ Geographic markets (e.g. China, East Europe)	■ Rising supplier and distribution costs
■ Demographic markets (e.g. ageing population)	■ Growing competition
■ Competitors leaving the marketplace	■ Threat of substitute products ad services

Understanding the hospitality business's strengths, weaknesses, opportunities and threats is based primarily on the strengths and weaknesses of competitors. A number of other criteria also influence the application of the SWOT analysis as follows:

- Emergence of new competitors and competitor offerings.
- Complexity of factors in the external environment (i.e. are there a high number of factors that can impact on the business).
- Rate in which factors change in the external environment (i.e. is it a fast moving industry or sector).
- Trends in the marketplace (e.g. food trends, demographic shifts in the population).
- Emergence of new resources (i.e. technologies, food products, etc.).

It should also be noted that as the hospitality environment changes, strengths could turn to weaknesses. The changing nature of food tastes towards healthy alternatives impacted greatly on those hospitality businesses that were perceived to be selling unhealthy-related food products. This was particularly the case amongst fast food outlets. However, environmental conditions can also bring about opportunities. For example, the global recession has impacted on household expenditure resulting in opportunities for fast food outlets that sell items that are within the discretionary income of households. In this respect the hospitality business needs to develop strategies that maximise its strengths within the context of opportunities that are apparent and emerging within the external environment.

When understanding the influence of threats, Henry (2008) also notes the importance of acknowledging 'discontinuities'. Discontinuities are 'threats faced by organisations that have the potential to undermine the way they compete' (Henry, 2008: 42). For example, the Internet has impacted on the way in which transactions and bookings are carried out between hospitality businesses and customers. It has also influenced the means in which customers seek out pre-purchase information about the quality of the hospitality product. An analysis of the external environment, which is discussed in this chapter, will more closely reveal those factors which may act as threats against the hospitality business.

The limitations of the SWOT analysis

Though a SWOT analysis offers a broad appraisal of a hospitality business's current situation it is limited in its potential to more narrowly classify those factors that can impact on the development of the business. Furthermore, as it is based on an analysis of competitors' own strengths and weaknesses it is a relative, and to some extent subjective, assessment of a hospitality business's current situation. It is important to acknowledge which factors are of most importance (Henry, 2008; Johnson et al., 2008). Therefore, prioritising the factors is a task which the hospitality business needs to undertake when conducting a SWOT analysis. The hospitality business also has to ensure that they do not overgeneralise the factors (Johnson et al., 2008). It can be overly simplistic to list a range of factors and it is important to explore deeply why a particular factor may be a strength or weakness (Grant, 2008). For these reasons some caution needs to be raised in the model's application. Nevertheless, a SWOT analysis can offer an efficient review of the organisation's current business development situation.

Activity: SWOT Analysis

1. Using Table 3.1, conduct a SWOT analysis of a hospitality business of your choice.

2. What factors have influenced your decisions when identifying the business's strengths, weaknesses, opportunities and threats?

3. How can the hospitality business use the SWOT analysis to understand its future development?

BUSINESS ENVIRONMENT LAYERS

The hospitality manager has to be fully cognisant with those factors in the external environment that may impact on their business decisions. The aforementioned discussion of the SWOT analysis has already acknowledged the importance of addressing external threats and opportunities that can impact on the hospitality business. These factors emerge from the different layers that make up the external environment and influence the strategic direction of the hospitality business. These layers are called the macro and micro environments as illustrated in Figure 3.1. An understanding of the external environment of the hospitality industry is crucial in determining the future development of the business.

MACRO-ENVIRONMENTAL ANALYSIS

The macro environment is the broad business environment that is made up of a number of factors that can impact on the hospitality business. These factors can often be unpredictable, volatile and fast moving and the

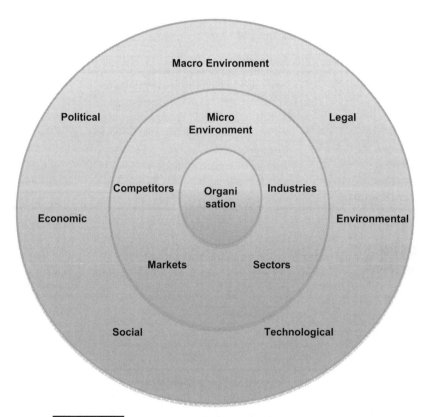

Macro Environment

Political

Micro
Environment

Legal

Competitors

Organi
sation

Industries

Economic

Environmental

Markets

Sectors

Social

Technological

FIGURE 3.1   *The layers of the external hospitality environment.*

hospitality business has to not only consider those factors which can generate opportunities but also those which may pose threats to the business. The hospitality business also has to prioritise those factors to determine which may have the most impact and influence on the business. There are many models which can be used to analyse the external environment. These models are often associated with acronyms which Table 3.2 illustrates.

Essentially, these models are used to analyse the range of factors that may impact on hospitality businesses at any given time. However, they are limited by their generalist application and fail to fully acknowledge how factors may impact on organisations from local, national and global perspectives. Hospitality businesses operate in a variety of different contexts depending on their product markets and the customer segments that they target. Not all the factors will therefore have the same degree of impact on the business and these need to be distinguished further. In this respect, Capon (2004) forwards an extended framework known as LoNGPEST (see Table 3.3).

Table 3.2	Environmental Analysis Models
Acronym	**Explanation**
PEST	Political, economic, social, technological
PESTEL	Political, economic, social, technological, environmental, legal
STEEP	Social, technological, economic, environmental, political
SPECTACLES	Social, political, economic, cultural, technological, aesthetic,
(Cartwright 2001)	customer, legal, environmental and sectoral
SCEPTICAL	Social, cultural, economic, physical, technical, international,
(Peattie and	communications, administrative, legal
Moutinho 2000)	

Table 3.3	LoNGPEST Analysis (Capon, 2004)			
	Political	Economic	Sociocultural	Technological
Local				
National				
Global				

The LoNGPEST framework enables organisations to understand and differentiate the issues from a local, national and global perspective. According to Capon, the local level encompasses the town, city or region in which the business competes, the national level is the organisation's home country and the global level is anything that is beyond the local or national level. When analysing hospitality, this is a relevant model to use as firstly, hospitality is a global industry and secondly, hospitality managers need to consider the impact of the different levels on their product decisions. The following discussion will present the PEST factors from the context of these different levels and assess the influence they have on hospitality product decision-making.

Political factors

Political factors are those which are influenced by the government that is in power at any particular time. This will be further influenced by the underlying objectives and policies of the political party that is leading the country. These policies may be based on the development of social capital and the well-being of the population or on free-market enterprise and entrepreneurialism. The values of the political party will determine the agenda of nation states and the policies that are subsequently developed and implemented. As governments will have overarching power over the legislative landscape within the countries where they are in power, legal factors are also included in this analysis.

At a local level, the hospitality business will be impacted on by political decisions that may emerge from within local government who will be influential in determining by-laws and planning decisions. For example, if a decision was made to build a by-pass around a town, for those local restaurateurs and hoteliers whose target markets are based on drive through trade, this has the potential to have a negative impact. The political leaning of the local government may be different from that of the national government that has overarching power in terms of national policy and legislation. This can give rise to competing political values and objectives at the local level and can slow down decision-making on key issues impacting hospitality businesses.

At a national level, governments determine legislation which can influence the product decisions of hospitality businesses. Laws concerning health and safety, disability access, smoking bans and so on have meant that hospitality businesses in the UK have had to adhere to strict controls or face stiff penalties if prosecuted. The national government will also be responsible for determining macro-economic policy which includes ensuring fair competition between companies. In the UK the Competitions Commission is responsible for investigating sectors and industries where anti-competitive practices may become apparent. This can occur as a consequence of merger and acquisition activities between hospitality businesses.

Example: Competitions Commission and the Rail Food Services Industry

On-train food services are concerned with the procuring and supplying of food and beverages to passengers on the trains. This is classified in two ways. The provision of full meals and buffet and trolley service on long routes or just a trolley only service. In 2002, the Competitions Commission produced a report on the rail food services industry. This was in response to the acquisition by Compass Group PLC of the companies Rail Gourmet Holding, Restorama and part of Gourmet Nova. This had the potential to be anti-competitive and the combined market power that Compass would ultimately have in that industry could prevent new companies being able to enter the industry. However, following their enquiry, the Competitions Commission considered that the acquisition would not discourage new companies into the industry or be anti-competitive in nature.

Source: Competitions Commission Website.

From a global perspective, political issues including trade relations between nation states and war, conflict and terrorism will all influence the product decisions of hospitality businesses. Multi-national hospitality businesses that operate on a global basis will need to adhere to regulations that operate in that host country. This includes employment, planning and health and safety regulations. Issues concerning climate change and global warming have also encouraged worldwide policies and initiatives on sustainability and energy conservation. This has led many hospitality businesses to review product decisions based on ethical and sustainable principles and any potential impact that they may have on the environment.

Activity: Marriott Hotel Bombing

Marriott International is a global brand and has approximately 3000 properties worldwide. On 20 September 2008, a bomb blast hit the Marriott Hotel in Islamabad, the capital city of Pakistan, killing over 50 people. The blast was caused by a vehicle packed with explosives driving into the security barriers at the front of the hotel. On the night of the attack the city was staging a significant event where the country's newly appointed President, Asif Zardari, was giving his first parliamentary speech. The hotel is seen as a major landmark and was the first five star hotel to be built in Islamabad and attracted many government officials and foreign visitors. The bomb blast caused massive damage to the hotel devastating the front façade of the building and leaving a 60-feet wide crater where the impact occurred.

1. What political impact does this example have from a local, national and global perspective?

2. In what way would this situation influence the product decisions of Marriott International?

Economic factors

Economic factors are concerned with fiscal and monetary-related issues that can have a major impact on hospitality businesses. There is a close relationship between the political and economic factors as governments will be responsible for economic policy and regulation. Economic factors determine the extent to which the population has the ability to spend money on goods and services and there will be different levels of influence on the hospitality business.

At the local level, hospitality businesses and consumers will be liable for taxes that they owe to local government. This may come in the form of council tax and local congestion charges. The latter can influence the mobility of people in and around towns and cities and impact the potential target markets that hospitality businesses attract.

At a national level, rises in interest rates and inflation can generate extra expenditure on loan repayments and household essentials, respectively. This can lead to a decrease in levels of disposable income and expenditure on luxury items such as holidays and eating out. Governmental policy on taxation will also influence hospitality businesses and consumers.

At a global level, macro-economic factors such as monetary policy and trade relations between countries are governed at a supranational and international level by organisations such as the European Union and the World Trade Organisation. The global credit crunch has been a symptom of the internationalisation of the global economy and has had a major impact throughout the world. There are many international hospitality enterprises that have representation in a number of countries and therefore can be impacted on by trading and economic factors that may arise. It is the objective of supranational and international organisations to ensure that good trade relations are fostered between nation states, so as to ensure the continued viability of businesses operating in those environments.

Socio-cultural factors

Socio-cultural factors are concerned with the demographics of society and changes in the age, structure and culture of the population. These factors will have an impact on the way in which the hospitality business develops its products and the target markets that it is aiming to attract.

At a local level, hospitality businesses have to be culturally sensitive to the provision of food and beverages that meet the tastes and needs of the local population. Further issues concerning anti-social behaviour can also impact at a local level. This can occur when excessive consumption of alcohol leads to a concentration of fighting and abuse in towns and city centres. Hospitality businesses therefore have to take an ethical and socially responsible approach to product development.

At a national level, the creation of extended opening hours for licensed premises by the UK Government was introduced to adapt the nation's alcoholic drinking habits towards a more leisurely continental approach and to curb a binge drinking culture. The growing rise of obesity, particularly amongst the young in many western nations, has also encouraged many governments to introduce policy measures on healthy eating.

At a global level, a number of demographic shifts are occurring. In many western countries there is a growing ageing population but a decreasing younger population. For hospitality businesses this is a significant factor if they target a particular age demographic which is either declining or growing, though it also presents opportunities for hospitality businesses for developing new products or repositioning existing products to markets that are growing. Further, at a global level, international hospitality businesses have to be sensitive to the values and norms of the host culture. This is in terms of the language, religion and behaviour. Therefore, when developing products, hospitality businesses have to be aware of factors that can either cause offence or dislike towards the brand due to a lack of cultural sensitivity.

Technological

Technological factors are pervasive across local, national and international levels and therefore not exclusive to any particular perspective. Technology has always been a feature of hospitality businesses. This is in the widespread use of computerised reservation systems (CRS), global distribution systems (GDS) and property management systems (PMS). Hospitality businesses use these systems at a local level to manage their operations and distribution networks.

The Internet has generated a process of disintermediation and reintermediation in the distribution of hospitality goods and services. Hospitality businesses can sell directly to customers through their own Websites or use online eMediaries who can do this on their behalf. The impact of social networking has already been mentioned earlier in this chapter, but this is an important technology that is impacting hospitality businesses and the promotion of their products. The impact of Web 2.0 technologies such as Podcasting and Weblogs enables hospitality businesses to more innovatively communicate with their target markets about their product offerings. The rapid adoption of mobile phones across the globe has enabled hospitality businesses to communicate directly with their customers about product offers and availability.

Activity: LoNGPEST Analysis

1. Choose a hospitality business with which you are familiar and conduct a LoNGPEST analysis of the sector within which it competes.

2. What are the priority factors for the business? What factors from the analysis present themselves as opportunities and which are threats that the business needs to counter?

MICRO-ENVIRONMENTAL ANALYSIS

The micro-environmental analysis is an analysis of the competitors, industries and markets within which the hospitality organisation competes. This analysis enables the hospitality business to understand who its competitors are and the factors that influence competition in an industry. In respect to analysing the micro environment it is important to differentiate between industries, sectors and sector categories. Industries are broad in scope and encompass a diversity of sectors and organisations. These sectors and organisations may not necessarily compete with one another and offer complementary products that target different markets. This chapter has already acknowledged that the hospitality industry is broad in scope and consists of a number of different sectors and categories within these sectors. These can be classified into the following:

- **Direct sector analysis**

Competitors within direct sectors offer the same goods and services and target similar markets. An example of direct sectors includes the branded budget hotel or the fast food burger sectors. Organisations operating within these sectors will be competing directly with one another.

- **Indirect sector analysis**

Indirect sector analysis is based on competitors that operate in a different category of the same sector. For example, the branded budget hotel sector operates vis-à-vis the five star hotel sector. Though they essentially target different markets they are both fulfilling the same need and therefore, in many respects, are competing with one another.

It is important to analyse the micro environment by different sectors as closer attention can be paid to those factors that influence competition. The bases on which competitive advantage is gained can also be more closely assessed.

SECTOR LIFE CYCLE

All sectors will have a life cycle as illustrated in Figure 3.2. This is the cycle that each sector will go through and is a process of four stages. First is the introductory stage where sales are relatively small and competitors may be few in number. Competitors in the sector will incur high costs due to inexperience and the focus being on product innovation. Second is the growth

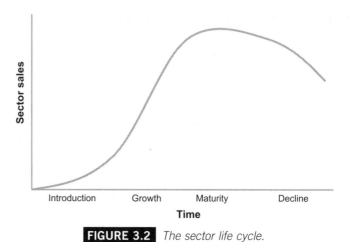

FIGURE 3.2 *The sector life cycle.*

stage where competitors begin to enter the market on prospect of increased sales in the sector. Third is the maturity stage where the sector begins to become saturated with competitors. At this stage sales plateau and a 'shakeout' of the sector occur. This often comes in the form of consolidation within the sector as stronger competitors acquire the weaker competition or mergers and alliances are formed amongst organisations. The final stage of decline occurs when sales decrease significantly and competitors either reposition themselves to target new markets or withdraw from the sector completely.

It is important not to confuse the industry life cycle with individual products. For example, the life cycle of the branded fast food industry has been in existence since the 1950s. However, individual burger products within the fast food sector can have a life cycle. For example, the Quorn Premiere was a vegetarian option which was introduced by McDonalds in 2004. Due to poor sales the product was withdrawn from its menus meaning that the life cycle of the product was a relatively short one.

It can be challenging to determine where a sector actually is in its life cycle. A judgement has to be based on factors including the number of new entrants to the sector, sales and customer growth and sector profitability. Furthermore, there is no set pattern to sector life cycles and external factors such as the introduction of new substitutes, changes in consumer tastes, demographic shifts and economic influences can all impact on the rate of change and the length of a sector in the life cycle. It should also be noted that instead of going into decline, industry sectors might actually go through a process of rejuvenation where new product innovations are introduced that stimulate sector growth.

COMPETITOR ANALYSIS

Porter's (1980) model of competitive structural analysis (Figure 3.3) enables an understanding of the factors that form the basis of competition within an industry. Porter argues that there are five competitive forces that influence competition within an industry and it is the collective strength of these which determine the profit potential of the industry. By determining the relative importance of each of these forces, Porter contends that an organisation can identify where to position itself to take advantage of opportunities and overcome or circumvent threats. The model is broadly

FIGURE 3.3 *Competitive structural analysis.*
(Adapted from Grant, 2008).

applied to industries. However, the scope of the hospitality industry is very broad and, as has been noted, encompasses an array of different sectors. It is advisable, therefore, that the model be applied to a sector within the context of the hospitality industry. The different forces are outlined as follows.

■ Threat of new entrants

A number of barriers can prevent new entrants from entering an industry or sector. If a hospitality entrepreneur decided to open a boutique hotel, they would require a large amount of capital to develop the premises and access to distribution channels to market the goods and services. If this is a single entity, the extent to which the entrepreneur is able to gain economies of scale through purchasing in bulk would also act as a barrier. Another barrier is the extent to which the hotel is able to differentiate its goods and services from other competitors in the boutique hotel sector. This can be influenced by the number of competitors in the sector and similarities they have in characteristics. A further barrier is the extent to which the hotel is able to meet government regulations such as health and safety, licensing laws and so on. If the sector is highly regulated, conforming to the different laws and legislation can act as a barrier to the competitor entering the sector.

■ Power of suppliers

The extent to which suppliers have power within the sector needs to be established. Who the suppliers are will depend on where in the supply chain the organisation is. For example, a nightclub will have as its suppliers, brewers, maintenance, security contractors and so on. These suppliers will be powerful if they are few in number and the costs of switching to alternative suppliers are high. This can be due to contractual arrangements where the organisation is tied into a contract for long periods of time. There may also be brand associations that the organisation wishes to have with the supplier, such as the supply of a certain type of food or beverage. Suppliers will also be powerful when there is the threat of forward integration from suppliers and they have the potential to acquire the hospitality enterprise or the suppliers' products are differentiated and therefore difficult to obtain from alternative sources.

■ Power of buyers

Who the buyers are will depend on where in the supply chain the buyers are. For example, a licensed premises will act as a buyer to the brewers it purchases the beverages from. The customer will act as a buyer when purchasing the beverages from the licensed premises. Buyers will have power if they are few in number, they are able to switch easily between alternative sellers, there is the threat of backward integration or products are undifferentiated.

■ **Threat of substitutes**

Substitutes are goods and services that are either identical or can satisfy the same need. Substitutes can therefore be separated directly and indirectly. Direct substitutes are those that offer the same, or a variation of the same, good or service. For example, the need to satisfy hunger can be offered by a variety of hospitality enterprises. However, if the buyers have a particular food preference in mind then this will determine the choice of outlet they ultimately purchase from. If there are many similar outlets which sell this food preference then the threat from direct substitutes will be high. Indirect substitutes will be other providers that sell food products such as high street retailers and supermarkets which can satisfy the same need. Substitute goods and services are threatening when the switching costs for buyers are low and there is a high propensity for the buyer to purchase substitute products. The product brand will therefore act as a key factor in determining the propensity of the buyer to purchase from substitute providers.

■ **Competitive rivalry**

The central force of the model is rivalry amongst competitors. This will be based on the amount and intensity of competition in the sector and influenced by the amount, size and diversity of the competitors. Competitive rivalry will also be determined by the life cycle stage of the industry sector and the rate in which it is growing. The relative exit and entry barriers to the industry sector will also influence competitive rivalry as will the degree of product differentiation between competitors.

■ **Alternative forces**

It should be acknowledged that Porter's model does have its limitations and has been criticised for analysing industries holistically and within a bounded context (Dale, 2000). It should also be recognised that industry sectors are not static and the forces that influence competition can evolve over time. Indeed, when applied to different industry sectors, other forces may emerge that influence competition. For example, when applied to the

UK tour operating sector, Dale (2000) has argued that a number of alternative forces are apparent which include the threat of new entrants, the threat of customer expectations, the influence of synergistic alliances, the threat of regulation, the threat of alternatives and the influence of digital information technology and organisation reinvention.

Grant (2008) forwards 'complements' as an additional sixth force to the model. Complements are those goods and services that in contrast to substitutes can actually increase value. For example, music played in hotels is a complementary product that can enhance the value of the customer's overall experience. However, the supply of music is dependent on licensing and copyright agreements which, for example, in the UK, have to be agreed with the Performing Rights Society.

Activity

1. Select a hospitality business. Conduct a five forces analysis of the sector in which the hospitality business competes.

2. To what extent is there the threat of new entrants? To what extent do suppliers and buyers have power? To what extent is there the threat of substitutes? What factors influence rivalry between competitors?

3. Identify alternative forces which may be influencing competition in that sector.

4. Evaluate to what extent the hospitality business is positioned to take advantage of the competitive forces that are influencing the industry?

SUMMARY AND CONCLUSIONS

The hospitality business has to fully acknowledge the influence of the external environment. This chapter has explored the external environment of the hospitality industry and the challenges that this presents to hospitality managers and their business decisions. This chapter has discussed the different layers of the external macro and micro environments. In doing so, an appraisal of the different models and concepts that can be used to analyse the external environment has been addressed. This has included SWOT, LoNGPEST, the sector life cycle and competitive structural analysis. Whilst recognising their limitations, hospitality businesses should use these concepts as a basis for understanding the environment within which they are competing. They will then better understand complexity of the hospitality environment and be able to make more informed business development decisions.

REVIEW QUESTIONS

1. Select a hospitality business. Using the models discussed in this chapter, conduct a macro- and micro-environmental analysis of the business.
2. What are the priority factors in the external environment that the organisation needs to pay closest attention to?
3. How might these factors influence the development of the hospitality business in the future?

Case Study: The Coffee Sector

It is estimated that over 2 billion cups of coffee are drunk worldwide. In terms of its trade as a commodity, coffee is second to the oil industry. In the UK alone, sales of coffee generate over £1 billion. The coffee industry consists of a number of major coffee shop operators who have expanded rapidly in recent years. The sector includes coffee shop chains such as Starbucks, Costa Coffee (owned by Whitbread), Caffe Nero as well as a number of other independent high street coffee shops. According to Mintel data, in 2008 Costa Coffee had the largest market share at 27%, followed by Starbucks at 25% and Cafeé Nero at 13%.

The coffee sector of the hospitality industry has been confronted with some challenging times in recent years. After massive expansion of many of the large chains sales, profitability has begun to decline. This has been due to a number of external and competitive factors.

External Factors

First, the global recession has impacted on consumer disposable income and spending power. Discretionary expenditure on items such as eating out and beverages in coffee shops has been particularly affected. In April 2009, Starbucks announced that global profits were down by 77% and over the course of 2008/2009 the chain closed nearly 1000 stores with the loss of almost 7000 jobs worldwide. The Starbucks chairman Howard Schultz even commented on the spiralling impact of the UK economy and how this was a reflection of the fall in the chain's overall coffee sales.

Second, rising supplier costs have impacted on coffee shop operators. Rising dairy prices have led operators to increase their prices. These costs have been driven by increased demand globally from the likes of China and India. In China the demand for powdered milk in particular rose by 20% during 2008. Under investment in the dairy industry in the UK has also impacted on the ability of farmers to maintain demand.

Despite falling oil prices, energy costs have also been rising, though the large chains attempt to control their costs through negotiating fixed price contracts with the energy companies. Though there has been a price rise in coffee beans, this to some extent has nominal impact as coffee beans only marginally make up the cost of a cup of coffee. Furthermore, like energy costs, coffee operators often tie themselves into long-term fixed price deals with coffee bean producers.

Third, due to the economic downturn customers have become increasingly fickle and price sensitive. Any slight fluctuation in price impacts on customer perceptions of the product. Furthermore, going to a coffee shop is often viewed as an occasional treat as opposed to an everyday experience and this has driven down sales.

Fourth, environmental factors including fluctuating weather systems and climate change can impact on the supply chain of products to coffee outlets. This can also impact on the consumer choice of beverage and where to purchase this.

Continued

Competitive Factors

Due to healthy sales growth prior to the global economic downturn, the major coffee shop operators all initiated on rapid expansion plans. Where Starbucks and Cafeé Nero pursued growth organically, chains such as Costa Coffee have used a strategy of franchising. Expansion has enabled the coffee shops to gain economies of scale thus driving down supplier costs. There has also been a strategy to cluster sites together so as to generate greater brand awareness. However, there has been the contention that overexpansion has led to diseconomies of scale where the cost of running so many outlets actually raises the cost of the end product. Clustering stores within close proximity also has the potential to cannibalise the sales potential of outlets.

Overexpansion of outlets globally has also been argued to have impacted on Starbucks in particular. What was originally viewed by its core customer base as an aspirational and exclusive brand has become diluted by the opening of so many outlets. The business model of coffee outlets has also been very easy to replicate, leading to a lack of distinctiveness and differentiation amongst competitors.

The major coffee chains have also had to contend with hospitality businesses in other sectors entering the market. For example, pub operators such as JD Wetherspoon and fast food operators such as McDonalds have both introduced their own gourmet coffee lines and free WI-Fi access. This is in addition to supermarkets and in store restaurants also selling coffee products.

Customers also have the potential to bring their own refreshments to work or to make coffee on site. Coffee manufacturers such as Nescafé and Kenco have both been producing their own gourmet brands of coffee.

Development Opportunities

The coffee shop operators have been seeking out new business development opportunities. For example, in February 2008 Starbucks began to sell an instant coffee which it intended to launch into supermarket chains. This capitalises on the price sensitivity of customers in addition to differences in consumption habits. Instant coffee granules account for over two-thirds of coffee consumption in Britain and Japan. This is in contrast to the United States where fresh coffee is most popular. Promotions such as offering free refills and 'breakfast pairings' where customers get a lower price if they purchase a latte or coffee with a food item has also been seen as a method for increasing shop visits.

According to Mintel data, though visits to coffee stores during 2007–2008 began to stagnate, trends in the market suggest that there has been a decline in sit-in customers but a rise in takeaway users. The population of 20–34 year olds who are traditionally high coffee drinkers is also forecast to grow.

Though operators such as Starbucks have embarked on a rationalisation of coffee shops, there is argued to still be potential for openings in areas where there is a lack of presence and where there is a concentration of customer flows. For example in supermarkets, motorway services, train stations and retail parks.

Questions

1. Conduct a detailed SWOT analysis of a coffee shop operator.

2. Further review the external environmental factors that are discussed in the case study. Classify these as per LoNGPEST analysis. What are the priority factors that the coffee shop operators should pay closest attention to?

3. To what extent are McDonalds and JD Wetherspoon direct or indirect competitors to the coffee shop chains and why is this an important factor to consider?

4. Where is the coffee shop sector in its life cycle? What implications does this life cycle stage pose for coffee shop operators?

5. Apply Porter's Five Forces model to the coffee shop sector. Are there alternative forces operating in the sector? What factors influence competitive activity in the sector?

Sources

www.guardian.co.uk.

www.bbc.co.uk.

www.telegraph.co.uk.

www.mintel.com.

GLOSSARY

Direct sector Competitors within direct sectors offer the same goods and services and target similar markets.

Indirect sector Indirect sector analysis is based on competitors that operate in a different category of the same sector.

Macro environment Broad business environment which is made up of political, economic, social and technological factors.

Micro environment Analysis of the competitors, industries and markets within which the hospitality organisation competes.

SWOT Strengths, weaknesses, opportunities, threats.

CHAPTER 4

Hospitality Business Positioning

Learning Objectives

Having completed this chapter, readers should be able to:

- Introduce the concept and significance of positioning and repositioning in the hospitality industry.
- Explore the relationship between positioning and hospitality business development.
- Explore the different types of strategies and tools used for positioning.
- Discuss the different elements and process of positioning in the hospitality industry.

CONTENTS

Introduction

Why Positioning/ Repositioning?

Business Positioning Components

Hospitality Business Positioning Analysis

Summary

Review Questions

Glossary

INTRODUCTION

There is little doubt that the changing market environment is forcing marketing experts to reconsider how they approach their tasks. These macro- and micro-environmental changes include all social, cultural, economical, political–legal, technological, consumer, market and competition changes. Such critical changes are already beginning to reshape the marketing concept. For example, consumer tastes, wants and needs change from time to time, as do new competitive patterns and developing technology. Also, it reflects the fact that mature markets and aggressive competitors are seeking opportunities for profit and growth which have eroded existing positioning. Hence, the attractiveness and power of yesteryear's position begin to fade, prompting a constant appraisal and review of products.

Marketing activity is a dynamic process that demands an understanding of shifting cycles and the timing to react instantly to those changes or trends. This reaction or adaptation of a business or a product to our changing environment is an inevitable process that reflects the interaction between marketing strategies and those uncontrollable variables mentioned previously. Meanwhile, the main aim of any new hospitality business is to establish and maintain a distinctive place and image in the market for an organisation and or its individual product offerings so that the target market/prospect understands and appreciates what the organisation stands for in relation to its competitors. In simple terms, the main goal of any hospitality organisation is to properly position or reposition itself in the market. However, there are no magic formulas that could be applied to fit each and every situation. Furthermore, to apply positioning principles, concepts and techniques within the boundaries of an individual hospitality business requires a tremendous amount of creativity and differentiation. In other words, no business positioning programme could fulfil the needs of all hospitality operations for all times and under all circumstances because positioning is a sophisticated process that comprises so many uncontrollable and dynamic variables. Also, each hospitality organisation is a unique separate entity that needs a specifically developed business positioning plan.

In addition, Kotler (1994) argues that, regardless of the initial success of the brand position in the market, existing firms may be forced to reposition it later. Similarly, Trout and Rivkin (1995) state that today is a time for more repositioning than positioning. This is normal due to the changing marketing environment that influences any organisation. Along the same lines, Brassington and Pettitt (2005) note that repositioning has a number of serious implications. It might involve redefining or enlarging segments or reshaping a whole marketing plan. These essential implications are expected to apply to a mature product when its quality commences to diminish. Also, the term 'repositioning' was derived from the term 'positioning'. Accordingly, the broad scope of hospitality business positioning in this chapter will cover: (a) the positioning on new operations and (b) the repositioning of existing ones.

The basic objective of this chapter is the presentation and the comprehensive description of the hospitality business positioning and identifying its importance and significance within the hospitality industry. Additionally, an explanation of positioning tools will be discussed, as well as a presentation of the strategies used for positioning. Furthermore, an overview of the positioning process is discussed to build a fully descriptive picture of all aspects of positioning. It should be noted that the main focus of this chapter is on hospitality positioning and repositioning at business unit level, although positioning, as well as repositioning, can be experienced at different levels such as industry positioning, organisation positioning, product line positioning and/or single product positioning.

Definition and importance

A recent examination of the available literature seems to support the viewpoint that there is no single universally approved definition of positioning or repositioning. As mentioned by Wind (1982), *positioning means different things to different people*. The major part of this confusion may be attributed to the gap between hospitality academics and practitioners in terms of their different utilisation and applications of the concepts. However, the most suitable definitions for the purpose of this book are indicated below.

As a concept, positioning can be defined as: 'the act of designing the company's offer and image so that it occupies a distinct and valued place in the target customer's minds.' (Kotler, 1997: 301). Along the same lines, repositioning can be defined as being: 'the marketing management process of changing, partially or totally, the perception of the public about a firm through any modification or addition to one or more of its controllable variables (marketing mix) to comply with its changing uncontrollable variables (e.g. customer, competition, technology, corporate, etc.) in order to retain, expand, or change its target market(s).' (Hassanien and Baum, 2002).

Thus, positioning is considered the product's reason for being and the reason why consumers buy it. In addition, Ries and Trout (1986) mention that market positioning means creating an image in the consumer's mind and therefore it should deal with the prospect's mind. Based on this, marketing activity is to move consumer perception as close as possible to management's intended position (Powers, 1997). Loudon and Bitta (1993) also revealed that positioning involves determining how consumers perceive the marketer's product and also developing and implementing marketing strategies to achieve the desired position in the market.

Substantially, a product's position involves the complex set of perceptions, impressions and feeling that consumers hold for the product compared with competing products (Kotler and Armstrong, 2007). Therefore, a product's position is the place that it occupies relative to competitors in a given market as perceived by the target market segment (Loudon and Bitta, 1993). In other words, it can be viewed as an image and value by consumers of the target segment through understanding what the company or brand stands for in relation to its competitors (Evans et al., 1996).

WHY POSITIONING/REPOSITIONING?

Lovelock (1984) argues that the marketer should control the positioning and not just 'let it happen'. This is because failure to plan for, implement and retain a successful position in the market might direct the organisation to one of the next unpleasant positions:

1. The organisation (or one of its products) is pushed into a position where it faces head-on competition from stronger competitors.

2. The organisation is pushed into a little customer demand position.

3. The organisation's position is so fuzzy that nobody knows what its distinctive competence really is.

4. The organisation has no position at all in the marketplace because nobody has ever heard of it.

Consequently, we can assume that the effect of increased competition might be regarded as the key factor which assigns business positioning its fundamental role in the hospitality industry.

Through positioning, the desired product's position is conveyed to consumers so as to establish a competitive advantage over its competitors by emphasising its important attributes that are perceived by customers. Thus, a product's position is an important determinant of its competitive strength. A product's design and marketing strategy must be consistent with its intended position (Ansari et al., 1994; Kotler, 1994; Urban and Hauser, 1980; Wind, 1990). Furthermore, an essential aspect of effective positioning is that it must assure the values or benefits that will be obtained by the consumer. In other words, a position must be chosen on which the organisation can, in fact, deliver. Otherwise, positioning can backfire if what is promised is not what is delivered.

In the hospitality industry, positioning should exist in the core of any business development. That is because it has an effect on the numerous inter-related management activities that make a hospitality experience. For example, it influences all of its marketing decisions, operations management, strategic management, human resources management, facilities planning and so forth.

Based on the above, positioning has a vital role in guiding strategy development of the organisation and this should be evident from all of the activities of the organisation. The reason is because any of these activities can have an impact on the image of the organisation that is being portrayed to its current or potential customers.

Along the same lines, Kotler (1994) argues that it is irrelevant how well a brand is originally positioned in the market as the firm may be prompted to reposition it at a later stage. This is normal due to the changing environment that forces companies to cope with these requirements to stay ahead in the market. Some marketing academics (Trout and Rivkin, 1995; Kotler, 1994; Bohan and Cahill, 1993; Jain, 1997; Palmer, 1998; Lewis et al., 1995) raise different reasons, which make positioning and repositioning an essential need for the success of hospitality operations and other businesses. These different reasons include the following examples:

- To keep up with the competition or to avoid a competitive entry positioned next to the brand with an adverse impact on its market share;
- To appeal to a new segment, to hold onto an old one and or to increase the size of the current segment by satisfying current or potential customers by meeting their wants and needs;
- To comply with new trends and technology in the market (e.g. the green consumers);
- To correct previous positioning mistakes (confused positioning, over-positioning and under-positioning) when the company fails to signal its competitive advantages sufficiently and loses a clear positioning for its product;
- To maintain corporate image and standards in the case of affiliated hotels;
- Owners might want to change the hotel's affiliation to one better suited to the hotel's facilities and market orientation; and
- To cope with the political/legal requirements [e.g. The American People with Disability Act (ADA) in the United States].

Example

The management of the Holiday Inn at Disneyland Paris was taken over by Vienna International Hotelmanagement AG. The group undertook a repositioning exercise of the hotel and rebranded it as 'The Magic Circus Hotel'. The hotel group acknowledged that the circus theme had been apparent since its opening in 2004 but this needed to be made more explicit and communicated more clearly to the hotel's family target market. As part of the repositioning exercise the hotel was renovated to fit in with this theme.

Source: http://www.hospitalitynet.org.

BUSINESS POSITIONING COMPONENTS

The main components of business positioning are segmentation, differentiation and internal and external analyses. Segmentation and differentiation are mentioned in most of the published positioning approaches. On the other hand, little attention is paid to internal and external analyses.

For some researchers, the starting point of positioning is the customer or segments of customers. They are the most important instance in the whole positioning process for whom marketing instruments are designed. The main purpose of segmentation is to identify groups of customers who have the same or very similar aspirations, expected benefits, perceptions and attitudes towards a product. Within each group the product can have a specific position.

The position depends on a second market aspect, which is the relative position of the competitors. Therefore, the second important underlying concept of positioning is differentiation. In a differentiation strategy, 'a firm seeks to be unique in its industry along some dimensions that are widely valued by buyers' (Porter, 1985: 14). The ultimate goal of differentiation is to obtain a long-term competitive advantage. Some authors focus strongly on competitor analysis and their positioning development approaches start with the competitor (Aaker et al., 1992; Aaker and Shansby, 1982; Hooley and Saundres, 1993). However, some marketing scholars argue that 'Highly competitor-centred approaches may have the disadvantage of a too high preoccupation with costs and controllable activities that can be compared directly with corresponding activities of close rivals' (Day and Wensley, 1988; Lovelock, 1996; Porter, 1985).

Example

Marriott International positions the Fairfield Inn by Marriott to target the lower–moderate lodging segment. To further leverage the purchasing power of the mid-tier target market, the group introduced a new product called 'Fairfield Inn & Suites by Marriott'. This included renovating larger sized guest rooms into suites with extra guest amenities including an ergonomic desk chair, coffee maker, hair-dryer and second telephone.

Source: http://www.hospitalitynet.org.

Another important source of information having a decisive impact on the positioning process is internal analysis. Before making a decision about a position, a business has to 'identify its resources (financial, human labor and know-how, and physical assets), any limitations or constraints, and the values and goals (profitability, growth, professional preferences, etc.) of its management. Using insights from this analysis, the organization should be able to select a limited number of target market segments which it is willing and able to serve' (Lovelock, 1996: 113).

Competitors and the company itself are the main influences of a position in consumers' mind. But these two are not the only forces driving the positioning process. External forces and stakeholders play an important role in implementing positions for products or companies. They can decide the rise and fall of product positions because they have the necessary resources for the establishment of a position. Surprisingly, only a few researchers mention the importance of stakeholders and even less insert internal analysis in their positioning approaches.

To sum up, Figure 4.1 summarises the main components of hospitality business positioning. However, the deployment of these components within the context of hospitality businesses will be further explained in the hospitality business positioning process section below.

Student Activity

1. Apply each of the positioning components in Figure 4.1 to a hospitality business of your choice.
2. To what extent is the hospitality business maximising its current position in the marketplace?
3. To what extent should the business undertake a repositioning exercise? Discuss how it might do this using the positioning components.

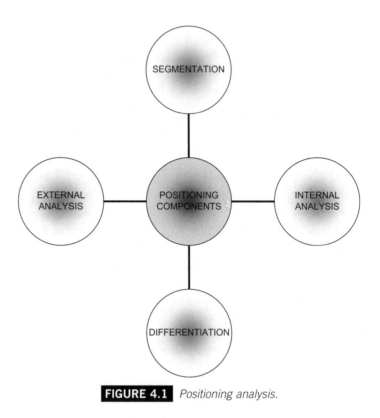

FIGURE 4.1 *Positioning analysis.*

HOSPITALITY BUSINESS POSITIONING ANALYSIS

This framework commences with both external and internal analyses. External analysis of different uncontrollable elements (e.g. customers, markets and competitors) is undertaken to identify the opportunities and threats in the market. On the other hand, internal analysis of the hospitality business's resources (i.e. financial, performance, human resources and physical assets) has taken place in order to identify its strengths and weaknesses. For existing businesses in the market, another essential output of external and internal analyses is the current position specification that should be implemented before taking any action towards the desired position (Hill and Fay, 1992; Lewis et al., 1995; Boyd et al., 1995). In other words, before any hospitality business launches a positioning strategy, accurate, inclusive and detailed internal and external analyses of company resources, competition and market should be undertaken. The following sections explore these variables in detail.

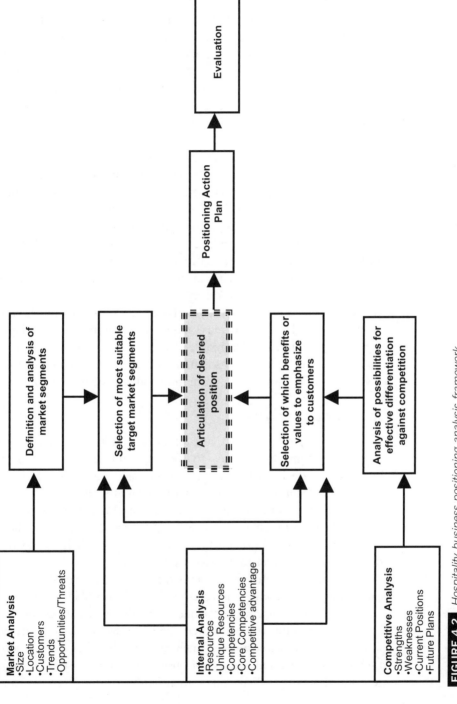

FIGURE 4.2 *Hospitality business positioning analysis framework.*
Adapted from C. Lovelock, services Marketing, Prentice Hall, 1984.

Internal analysis

For any hospitality organisation, the main purpose of positioning is to create a competitive advantage over its rivals by emphasising its important attributes as perceived by its customers. That is because the real significance of positioning lies in its impact on the target market. In other words, organisations compete successfully by offering superior products to meet consumers' needs. This is done through identifying their own competitive advantages and understanding consumer's perceptions. Therefore, it is necessary for an organisation to have full awareness of its own strengths and weaknesses, and also the threats and opportunities represented by its micro and macro environments (i.e. SWOT). It means that the basis of analysis should be the internal resources and competencies, competitors, market and consumers. The results of these key analyses are the main components for the formulation of a desired positioning strategy.

Company analysis is important to assure the existence of the resources needed to change the marketing mix and also to evaluate how positioning allows the company to reach its objectives. Analysis of competitors is essential to identify opportunities for differentiation and ensure that the company's strategy will not be copied by its rivals. For example, by knowing the strengths of the business, and if any of them is unique, the property can capitalise on it to be strategically positioned in the market. Hooley et al. (1998) argue that a company can differentiate itself from its competitors through using different elements such as brand, product, price, promotion and/or distribution differentiation.

Competition analysis

In order to exploit competitive edge in its markets, competition analysis allows hospitality businesses to identify and assess their competitors' objectives, strategies, strengths and weaknesses. Also, it is very important to find out which competitors you wish to appear different from (Ries and Trout, 1986). Competition analysis gives hospitality businesses opportunities to: (a) improve their products and services; (b) prevent them from falling behind the times; (c) differentiate their products from their competitors; and (d) attack their competitors' market positions.

Unlike the internal analysis, competition research is a challenging task since specific data about competition are not usually accessible and where, in many cases, requesting information about competition is banned by trade laws. Consequently, competition research should be based on both secondary and primary sources of information such as travel bureaus, convention centres, disclosed statistics and the use of observation and personal inspection. For example, knowing where and when competitors advertise can provide information about their unique characteristics and target markets. Overall, competition analysis is an essential activity which should not be overlooked by any hospitality business. Nevertheless, it is worth mentioning that successful competition should not always be regarded as a threat. On the contrary, competition's success might indicate that it is a healthy market that provides adequate demand. However, it is up to every management to capitalise on its available resources, competencies and market opportunities to secure a reasonable market share. In other words, it is the 'poor management', not the 'saturated markets', that negatively affects the growth and development of organisations.

Market analysis

Another significant element of the hospitality business positioning process is market analysis, which helps in understanding the market in terms of its size, growth, geographic distribution and profit opportunities, as well as identifying the market segments. It is also concerned with analysing the market in order to identify the profile of the typical guest a property primarily serves, and more importantly, that of the potential customer who could be motivated to patronise the establishment being marketed.

As mentioned before, customer attraction, satisfaction and retention should be the primary goals of the hospitality business. It is indisputably true, since customers generate the revenues that keep the organisation in existence and deliver its profits. Given the variety of people in the world, there must be a wide diversity of consumers' demand in the hospitality market. Trying to satisfy all consumers' demand in the market is not cost-effective (Bowie and Buttle, 2004), the concepts of market segmentation, target marketing and positioning try to address this issue. Segmentation is related to the division of a market into distinctive clusters of consumers with similar wants and needs according to different types of factors (e.g. demographic, geographic, psychographic and behavioural). Segmentation is very important for hospitality operations because it identifies and analyses the current and potential demand for a hospitality business. Moreover, the rationale of market segmentation is to 'divide a larger market into smaller segments with different preferences and subsequently adjust a product to preferences in different segments, then one can reduce the overall distance between what a product offers and what the market requires' (Hanson, 1972). By doing this, marketers improve their competitive position through focusing on a few segments of the market in order to avoid the creation of a vague image of the product. Certainly the option for some market segments and for the competitive position to reach in each market segment must also be guided by internal analysis of the company resources and competencies. In fact, there are many techniques that can be used for segmentation in the hospitality industry.

Example

It can be the case that religious and cultural norms can require the separation of genders. For example, in some Muslim countries, if a woman is unaccompanied then she must produce a document that gains approval from her male guardian. If a woman is therefore travelling alone, it can therefore be difficult to find hotel accommodation. With this in mind, The Luthan Spa and Hotel in Saudi Arabia was created by a group of 26 business women and caters specifically for women.

Source: www.muslimnews.co.uk.

Example

Surveys have noted how consumers are increasingly becoming more environmentally conscious. This reflects a need for hospitality businesses to reflect these values on their product offerings. For example, the Hotel Tritone which is situated in Lipari, Sicily is a five star hotel that is also recognised as having five green stars as certified by ecohotelsoftheworld. com. To meet these requirements the hotel provides low-energy light bulbs, motion detectors, water flow regulators in the bathroom and makes use of biodegradable detergents.

Source: www.ecohotelsoftheworld.com.

Target marketing

Once the market is segmented, it helps a company to identify the demand characteristics of each segment. Then a company can select which segment(s) it aims to serve on the basis of the segment(s)'s attractiveness to the company. This process of selecting one or more market segments is defined as *target marketing* (Lynch, 2000).

There are three alternative target marketing strategies that are widely used by hospitality companies (Bowie and Buttle, 2004):

a. Mass marketing

In this strategy, a company recognises the similarities of consumer's needs and wants in a large market, thus an individual marketing mix is offered to satisfy all customers.

b. Differentiated marketing

In this strategy, a company identifies the differences between the needs and wants of various market segments, and develops an individual marketing mix to satisfy the needs and wants of each market segment.

Table 4.1	Major Segmentation Variables for Consumer Markets

Variable	Typical Breakdown
Geographic	
Domestic	Cities, counties, states, regions
International	American, British, Japanese, Egyptian
Demographic	
Age	Under 6, 6–11, 12–19, 20–34, 35–49, 50+, 64, 65+
Gender	Male, female
Family size	1–2, 3–4, 5+
Family life cycle	Young, single; young, married, no children; young, married, youngest child under 6; young, married, youngest child 6 or over; older, married, with children; older, married, no children under 18; older, single; other
Income	High, medium, low
Occupation	Professional and technical; managers, officials and proprietors; clerical, sales; craftspeople, foremen; operatives; farmers; retired; students; housewives; unemployed
Education	Grade school or less; some high school; high school graduate; some college; college graduate
Religion	Catholic, Protestant, Jewish, Muslim, Hindu, other
Nationality	American, British, French, German, Italian, Japanese
Ethnicity	White, Black, Asian
Psychographic	
Socio-economic class	Lower lowers, upper lowers, working class, middle class, upper middles, lower uppers, upper uppers
Lifestyle	Straights, swingers, longhairs
Personality	Compulsive, gregarious, authoritarian, ambitious
Behavioural	
Occasions	Regular occasion, special occasion (honeymoon market)
Benefits	Quality, service, economy, speed
Buyer needs	For example: convenience, luxury, children-friendly accommodation, improved health facilities
User status	Nonuser, ex-user, potential user, first-time user, regular user (light, medium and heavy users)
Usage rate	Light user, medium user, heavy user
Loyalty status	None, medium, strong, absolute
Readiness stage	Unaware, aware, informed, interested, desirous, intending to buy
Attitude towards product	Enthusiastic, positive, indifferent, negative, hostile
Purpose of travel	Business, non-business (e.g. leisure and holiday travellers),visiting fiends and relatives (VFR)
Price sensitivity	High, medium, low
Rate	Rack rate, conference rate, corporate rate, leisure rate, group rate, walk-n rate

Adapted from Kotler et al. (2003) and Bowie and Buttle (2004).

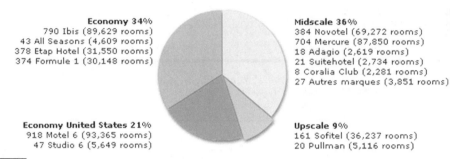

Economy 34%
790 Ibis (89,629 rooms)
43 All Seasons (4,609 rooms)
378 Etap Hotel (31,550 rooms)
374 Formule 1 (30,148 rooms)

Midscale 36%
384 Novotel (69,272 rooms)
704 Mercure (87,850 rooms)
18 Adagio (2,619 rooms)
21 Suitehotel (2,734 rooms)
8 Coralia Club (2,281 rooms)
27 Autres marques (3,851 rooms)

Economy United States 21%
918 Motel 6 (93,365 rooms)
47 Studio 6 (5,649 rooms)

Upscale 9%
161 Sofitel (36,237 rooms)
20 Pullman (5,116 rooms)

FIGURE 4.3   *Hotel portfolio by brand – Breakdown by number of rooms (on June 30, 2008).*
Source: http://www.accor.com/gb/groupe/activites/hotellerie/chiffres/chiffres_hotellerie.asp#.

c. Focused, concentrated or niche marketing

In this strategy, a company concentrates their marketing mix on a single market segment.

For example, most of the international hotel companies adopt either differentiated or niche marketing. The differentiated marketing strategy is used by hotel companies to attract more target markets, which then enables them to gain more market share, and offer specific products/services in accordance with demand characteristics from each market segment. For instance, Accor Hotels Group developed many specific international brands each catering to distinct market segments, from budget (economy) to luxury (upscale). Accor Hotel portfolio is illustrated in Figure 4.3.

Similar to Accor Group, InterContinental Group Hotel PLC developed many distinct brands in the European market, which cater to demand for business and leisure accommodations from midscale market to upscale. Their target marketing variables are the length of stay, socio-economic class and purpose of travel. Each hotel brand is described in Table 4.2. For each targeted market, the company developed unique products in accordance with the demand characteristic for each market segment.

Student Activity

1. Review the discussed Intercontinental brand names in Table 4.2.

2. What are the main differences between these brand names in terms of their target markets?

3. Why did Intercontinental label each product or brand with a different name?

Along the same lines, examples of hotel companies which adopt niche marketing include Whitbread PLC and Permira. By adopting niche marketing strategy that means those hotel companies only focus on a single market

Table 4.2	Hotel Portfolio by InterContinental Group Hotel PLC				
		Hotels open		Pipeline Size	
Brand	**Overview**	**Hotels**	**Rooms**	**Hotels**	**Rooms**
INTERCONTINENTAL. HOTELS & RESORTS	High-class facilities and services aimed at the discerning business and leisure traveller.	157	53,630	69	21,566
CROWNE PLAZA HOTELS & RESORTS	One of the world's fastest growing upscale brands, for business and leisure travellers who appreciate style.	331	90,775	131	40,293
HOTEL indigo.	Design-led hotels for people who value design at an affordable price.	19	2445	56	6979
Holiday Inn	One of the world's most recognised hotel brands, which is undergoing a $1 billion re-launch announced in October 2007.	1352	250,207	379	61,485
Holiday Inn Express	Convenience, comfort and value, ideal for people who are on the road – also part of the $1 billion Holiday Inn re-launch.	1889	169,227	728	70,482
STAYBRIDGE SUITES	High-end residential style rooms and suites for extended stays.	142	15,656	178	19,360
CANDLEWOOD SUITES	Midscale rooms and suites for extended stays of a week or longer.	196	20,024	230	20,842
Total* as on 30 September 2008		**4108**	**608,225**	**1773**	**243,509**

Source: http://www.ihgplc.com/files/pdf/factsheets/ihg_at_a_glance.pdf.

segment, thus enabling them to really understand the needs and wants of their customers in that market segment. Whitbread PLC and Permira in this case, with their brands respectively are Premier Travel Inn and Travelodge. These are budget hotel operators which only focus to serve the midscale market, specifically business travellers.

Positioning strategies

Having identified the current position, opportunities and threats in the market, and the strengths and weaknesses of the hospitality operation, the positioning statement or the desired position can be determined. So, the SWOT analysis approach discussed in the previous chapter forms the basis for articulating the desired position, which should effectively reflect and communicate a clear meaning of the business to the market. This desired position could be achieved through modifying one or more variables or sub-variables of the marketing mix.

The final step of the positioning process is to determine the positioning strategy which is a critical step to decide how the firm competes in the market successfully. Effective positioning strategy is to achieve best possible product positions in the market. Actually, many ways exist for positioning a product or service. Aaker and Shansby (1982) suggest the six most popular major positioning approaches. It should be noted that combinations of these approaches are also possible. They are the following:

(1) Positioning by attribute feature and customer benefit;

(2) Positioning by price/quality;

(3) Positioning with respect to use or application;

(4) Positioning according to user or class of users;

(5) Positioning with respect to a product class; and

(6) Positioning vis-à-vis the competition.

The first approach is the most frequently used by associating the product with an attribute, a product feature or a customer benefit. Quality/price positioning strategy is commonly used by using high price as a signal of high quality (Evans et al., 1996). Also, some brands may emphasise the best value for money (Kotler, 1994). User/application positioning is to associate a product with use or application. By using this approach, a product is positioned in terms of the consumer usage situation (Loudon and Bitta, 1993). Sometimes it represents a second or third position designed to expand the market (Evans et al., 1996). User positioning approaches associate the product with a user or a class of users. Often some products use different package sizes to target different classes of users, such as light, medium and heavy users. Product class positioning is the one that involves product class associations. For instance, Dove positions itself as a beauty and cosmetic product rather than a soap. Also, a product class dissociation is particularly effective to position a new product to differ from the typical products in an established product category (Evans et al., 1996). A competitor positioning approach is to persuade consumers to compare with competing brands on important attributes directly or indirectly. It involves looking for weak points in the positions of its competitors and then launching marketing attacks against these weak points (Brown, 1985). Kotler (1994) added another approach to the previous ones, called benefit positioning. It links a product's benefits with individual's values and lifestyle aspects. It is also considered transformational positioning.

After searching alternatives, the next step is to evaluate and select the most appropriate strategy. For evaluating alternative strategies, one should consider market dynamics. These include the growth of market segments, evolution of a segment's ideal points, changes in positioning intensity, evolution of existing brands' positions, emerging attributes, development of new segments and introduction of new brands (Boyd et al., 1995).

Finally, the process should be evaluated to see how the actual repositioning looks when compared with the desired one (Lewis et al., 1995: 356–358; Boyd et al., 1995: 207–218). This evaluation should be based subjectively in terms of customer feedback and objectively in terms of hotel performance and profitability.

SUMMARY

This chapter contained a comprehensive discussion of the concept of repositioning in the general marketing literature and in hospitality marketing in particular.

While this section has discussed some of the major aspects of the hospitality business positioning, its definitions, significance, types and its decisions, there is a considerable lack of accurate information and understanding about the issues involved. It is argued that these issues make a significant contribution to hospitality marketing, planning and strategies, but the nature and extent of this contribution is somewhat vague. Also, there is a clear need for empirical detailed studies on the repositioning concept within the hospitality context.

Finally, this chapter has concluded with an analysis of the positioning process. Building on the literature analysis, an inclusive model is designed to show the different phases involved within the positioning process. As argued, it differs fundamentally from previous approaches in three respects. First, it includes some other forces of positioning (such as chain standards, technology and governmental requirements) as well as customers. Second, it concentrates on the role played by each marketing mix variable or sub-variable in the positioning process. Third, it considers the positioning process as a cycle since it is an ongoing process in hotels.

As mentioned before, the process should start with external and internal analyses. The internal corporate analysis necessitates the businesses identifying the scope and range of their resources, products and services. The conclusions drawn from these exercises should guide the business decision-making processes and help in the identification of viable target markets that will respond positively to the existing offer or the proposed modifications or enhancements.

The external analysis must include some attempts to analyse the market and competitive positions of the business and its offers. Statements of strengths and weaknesses should be tested against the state of the market, the performance of the competitors and the perceptions of the customers. The suggested model makes market analysis an integral part of the process, as this is where the business can make itself aware of the value of attributes amongst the customer base. The decision-making process should evaluate the different opportunities for product and service development and differentiation. Market location, along with other factors such as the overall categorisation of the offer, quality standards, trends in customer behaviour, demographic, psychological and other characteristics of sources of demand can be seen as important attributes. These discussions will also necessarily examine any alternative approaches to the market and of segmenting the customers, with the decisions informed by a full critical analysis of the impact of adopting any new proposals – especially in terms of how they reshape the overall size and potential for maximising the markets that are most likely to be profitable for the business. By integrating all the forms of analysis that have been discussed, the business can produce a definitive 'positioning statement', which identifies and specifies where the business sees itself wanting to be in the market. Having clarified that the book now turns to explore and discuss another concept that is considered to be of great importance to the development of any hospitality operation, which is customer-centricity.

REVIEW QUESTIONS

1. Explain what you understand by the terms positioning and repositioning?
2. Discuss the four components of positioning analysis.
3. Choose a hospitality business and by applying the principles that you have learnt in this chapter to:
   (a) evaluate the business's current position; and
   (b) develop a revised positioning strategy for the business.

Case Study: Repositioning at McDonalds

McDonalds is a global fast food chain with over 31,000 restaurants worldwide. It operates in 119 countries and serves more than 47 million customers a day. The first McDonalds fast food outlet was opened by the brothers Dick and Mac MacDonald in 1940 in San Bernardino, California in the United States. The chain was then taken forward in the 1950s as part of a franchising arrangement by Ray Kroc, upon which the company's foundations were primarily built. Throughout the 1970s, 1980s and 1990s, McDonalds embarked upon a strategy of rapid expansion. This was driven through a combination of direct ownership, franchising or joint ventures. However, this expansion was mirrored by a growing apathy towards the McDonalds brand and a high level of negative press. This included the McLibel Trial of the mid-1990s in the UK where David Morris and Helen Steel were sued for libel against McDonalds. The pair produced a pamphlet that was critical of the company's operating practices and the trial generated a wealth of bad publicity for McDonalds.

In 2003, McDonalds recorded its first ever quarterly net loss of £212 million. Poor sales growth, particularly in its largest market the United States, had impacted upon the chain. Furthermore, there had been rising competition from both indirect and direct sectors. As well as competing directly with other burger-based fast food outlets such as Burger King there was also the emergence of indirect competitors offering alternative fast food products including sandwich bars such as Subway and from coffee shops such as Starbucks and Costa Coffee selling snacks in addition to beverages. Competitive pressures resulted in McDonalds introducing a 'Dollar Menu' creating a price war amongst its main rivals and further undermining profitability.

Rising obesity levels in Western Europe were also argued to be as a consequence of fast food consumption habits and this was having an impact upon the McDonalds brand. The association of fast food with unhealthy lifestyles was reinforced in the 2004 documentary 'Super Size Me' by Morgan Spurlock. The film documented the impact on Spurlock's psychological and physical health after eating McDonalds food, three times a day for thirty consecutive days. The film generated further negative publicity for McDonalds.

In light of these factors, McDonalds embarked upon a repositioning strategy which entailed becoming more customer focused. The repositioning strategy took a number of forms. First, McDonalds changed to a café style menu introducing options which were perceived as being healthier. This included salads and snack wraps. On the children's menu carrot sticks could be chosen in place of fries with the Happy Meals. These perceived healthier options had a reciprocal effect across the product range. However, this perception was initially based upon an assumption. For example, selected salads such as the Chicken Caesar were argued to have a greater fat and calorie content than the burger-based products. To counter this, McDonalds introduced low fat dressings to its salad range. McDonalds also introduced an alternative drinks range including bottled mineral water and juices. McDonalds also formed partnerships with ethically orientated brands. This included the Smoothie company, Innocent Drinks, to trial its drinks in its North East England outlets. McDonalds also decided to source its coffee from 'eco-friendly' farmers who were certified as part of the Rainforest Alliance.

Second, McDonalds began to renovate many of its stores as part of a 'Forever Young' philosophy. This included removing the red and yellow plastic chairs and tables and replacing them with more natural colours such as terracotta and olive greens. The furnishings were also replaced with brick and wood designs and they introduced free Wi-Fi into their stores.

Third, McDonalds made use of marketing tactics to reposition the brand. By sponsoring pop acts such as Justin Timberlake and Destiny's Child, McDonalds aligned the brand with opinion leaders that their key markets would aspire to. In March 2005, McDonalds embarked on an advertising campaign under the slogan of 'It's What I Eat and What I Do'. The focus of this campaign was to

Continued

emphasise a balanced diet amongst its key target markets. McDonalds also sponsored major sport events such as the Olympics and the FIFA World Cup.

In terms of sales and profitability, the result of this repositioning exercise for McDonalds has been significant. In comparison to the previous year, profits rose by 80% in 2008 and percentage sales increased across the United States, Europe and the Asia/Pacific, Middle East and Africa regions. The brand also announced further store openings in growing markets including Russia and China.

Sources: Adapted from Choueka, E. Big Mac fights back, BBC Money Programme, 8th Jul., 2005, http://news.bbc. co.uk, www.McDonalds.com.

Questions

1. To what extent did environmental and competitive factors impact upon the positioning of the McDonalds brand?

2. Why did McDonalds have to become more customer focused?

3. Using Figure 4.1, evaluate the different components of McDonalds positioning strategy.

4. Who are McDonalds key target markets? Develop a positioning action plan for these key markets based upon the Hospitality Business Positioning Analysis Framework in Figure 4.2.

GLOSSARY

Differentiation   A firm can obtain a competitive advantage through being unique in its industry along some dimensions that are widely valued by buyers.

External Analysis   It refers to the analysis of the macro environment (e.g. PEST) and the micro environment (e.g. competition analysis) of a company in order to identify the opportunities and threats in the market that may have an impact on the business.

Internal Analysis   It refers to identifying the strengths and weaknesses of a business through the analysis of its resources (financial, human labour and know-how and physical assets), any limitations or constraints, and the values and goals (profitability, growth, professional preferences, etc.) of its management.

Positioning   The process by which the business, based on its competitive advantage, tries to differentiate its offering(s) in a specific target, in order to occupy a unique or distinctive place in the consumers' minds when compared to its competitors.

Repositioning   'the marketing management process of changing, partially or totally, the perception of the public about a firm through any modification or addition to one or more of its controllable variables (marketing mix) to comply with its changing uncontrollable variables (e.g. customer, competition, technology, corporate, etc.) in order to retain, expand or change its target market(s).

Segmentation The division of a market into distinctive clusters of consumers with similar wants and needs according to different types of factors (e.g. demographic, geographic, psychographic and behavioural).

CHAPTER 5

Developing Customer-Centred Hospitality Businesses

Learning Objectives

Having completed this chapter you should be able to:

- Understand the concept of customer-centred business
- Explore the issues surrounding customer attraction, satisfaction, retention and loyalty
- Evaluate the processes involved in hospitality businesses becoming customer-centred operations.

INTRODUCTION

Hospitality businesses cannot succeed without their customers and moreover without satisfying their customers' needs. In this chapter we introduce the idea of customer-centred business development and review the importance of understanding customer behaviour. We see this trend as being at the heart of a new approach to hospitality business development, but recognise that many of the issues have been long debated (Dick and Basu, 1994). Although we are part of a debate about introducing this as a new idea, Shah et al. (2006) note that the debate has been going on for more than 50 years. Undoubtedly we can point to a great deal of research that supports the benefits for businesses that come from introducing the processes that we will refer to as becoming customer-centred (Buzzell and Gale, 1987; Zeithaml, 2000). As Clarke and Chen (2007) observed, the focus on the firm itself concentrated management thinking on production and internal administration, but putting the customer at the heart of business necessitates a much broader concern. In the increasing competitive environment of global competition, hospitality businesses value customers more than as a simple source of revenues. Within these contemporary competitive markets, Scott (2001) has identified that the approval and loyalty of customers has been recognised as one of the key success factors for hospitality businesses (Scott, 2001) and the service offer has been shown to be one of the main determinants of customer satisfaction and loyalty (Gronroos, 2000). As McDougall and Levesque (2000) have observed, these factors now mean that from the position of hospitality managers the service offer has become central to the business model and must thus be seen as a vital strategic function within the business.

Customer-centred business models mean that hospitality businesses have to address how the internal functional areas, such as marketing, operations and human resources, are developed. In customer-centred businesses these functions operate markedly differently from the way they are constructed in more traditional models, such as those evidenced in production and manufacturing businesses. We can see that this reconfiguration is a product of the distinctive features of services – inseparability of production and consumption, intangibility, and perishability – but it is more than this. It has long been recognised that in hospitality businesses, production and consumption of services occur simultaneously. There is therefore a necessary and direct contact between the service deliverers and their customers. This had been seen as a problem for the service sector and for hospitality in particular but now it is recognised that these interactions are not only unavoidable, but are also actually the most important elements in generating a sense of value for the hospitality customers. The service encounter depends upon the interpersonal interactions between the customers who experience the so-called 'moments of truth' (Carlzon, 1989) and the hospitality businesses' front-line employees who deliver the service that the experience depends upon. Indeed as we shall show later in this chapter, these interactions are at the heart of hospitality and are now seen as one of the most crucial elements supporting or determining customer satisfaction and perceptions of service quality. The 'moments of truth' are particularly important with the close proximity of production and consumption within the hospitality exchanges and this encourages the management to think about ways in which these situations can be constructed to engender trust. In modern hospitality businesses, the customer-centred rationale means that operations, marketing and human resources should be carefully managed not as isolated and separated functions of the business, but as interrelated internal functions, where every employee should have a strong sense of their responsibilities not only for their narrowly defined job function, but also for how they contribute to both the operational and marketing functions of the business. As we shall demonstrate, it is important for the waiter who delivers food services to recognise that they are actually and simultaneously acting as a crucial personal 'part-time marketer' (Gummesson, 2002) for the hospitality business that employs them as a waiter.

For all hospitality businesses, it is especially important to develop your knowledge of your customers, both in terms of their expectations and their potential levels of demand. As early as 1996, Gummesson was observing a slow but definite switch in management practices and in the journals of management research away from the concerns with, and of, the supplier towards those of the customer. This opens up new pressures on the businesses and means developing knowledge about the customers, through market research and developing some meaningful form of two-way communications, through marketing communications systems, with those customers who use your services; and, even more difficult, reaching those who might potentially use your service. This is the basis for an ongoing process, where the customers influence the choice of new product development and influence the launch strategies and attributes emphasised in the business development. What we see is a need to undertake market research to know the market(s) and to constantly review your communications strategy to ensure that your business becomes and remains aware of what it is that the customers want in what you bring to the market. The successful adoption of customer-focussed business models should see the businesses improving both their market share and their profitability.

Activity

Think through a successful hospitality encounter and note in how many ways the business touched you as a consumer. All these points of tangible and intangible contact create a business environment that impacts on the consumer as well as those involved in the business organisation. The diagram on the following page might help you identify some of those points of contact.

Meeting the needs of customers is never as simple as it sounds. As we noted earlier, there are significant differences between service exchanges and the consumption of products. These differences mean that the production, delivery and quality-control systems that are utilised in manufacturing industry may be inappropriate for the hospitality industry. Those factors that seemed to guarantee business success in the past are no longer seen to be as

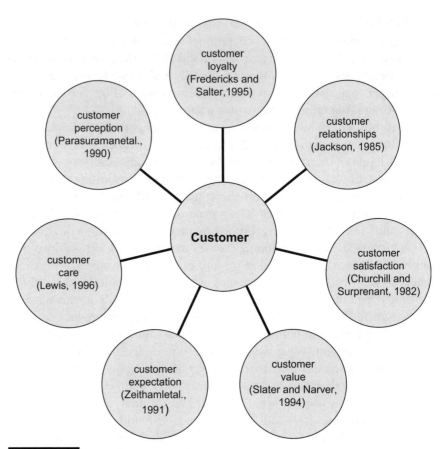

FIGURE 5.1   *Approaches to customer research.*
Source: Adapted from Kandampully, 2006. The new customer-centred business model
for the hospitality industry.

relevant today as managers have realised that traditional approaches to management and marketing are inadequate in an increasingly competitive market (Vargo and Lusch, 2004a,b).

We believe that the only basis for successful business development is solid and comprehensive market research. Knowing your customers – actual and potential – and your competitors is essential to the development of strong businesses and testing the new product development proposals. If a traditional business model is adopted, it is all too easy for the businesses not to be aware of how their customers are changing in buying behaviour and perceptions of the market. The more the companies' existing business models maintain a strong base of customer-centredness, the greater the likelihood they will be sensitive to any, positive and negative, changes in their customers, priorities, attitudes and expectations. Businesses need to be aware of what customers actually experience. This awareness is critical, especially as it should be remembered that often the current customer experience is the result of emergent or unplanned development. Even in the pages of this text it would be naïve to assume that customers always get the best experience from hospitality businesses and this dissatisfaction has consequences for both the customers and the businesses which disappoint them.

There is plentiful evidence, both in the journals and anecdotally from talking with hospitality managers, that there are almost always considerable cost and revenue gains to be made where businesses make improvements to the customer experience. This reinforces the need for the initial mapping of the potential customer and also the current customer experience. In the spirit of two-way communication, it is not enough to take notice but businesses should then seek to validate this with the customers. This testing helps managers to identify the 'touch points' that customers' actually value and dislike and improve the sense of where the overall engagement with the business falls short of customers' expectations. The perception of managers can be very different from that of the customers, so it is important to ensure that the true feelings of the customers are built into the feedback that shapes the business decision-making. Customer-focussed businesses have begun to hold regular meetings with particular groups of customers to rapidly check the meaning of the feedback and what the reactions to the comments will mean. There is now a feeling that innovations can flow from these meetings with the customer groups, rather than just validating suggested changes.

Managers can gain a great deal by looking at other businesses that are operating in similar markets or with similar business models. Increasingly, networking is seen as an integral part of senior management roles as the observation of best practice is becoming more important. Some aspects of best practice can be identified through formally benchmarking with other businesses. Many areas, both geographic and sectoral, now provide entre-preneurs with opportunities to network and this can lead to executive benchmarking clubs. Benchmarking also helps to build a view of the readi-ness of an organisation to move towards a more customer-centred business model and where customer-centred values have to be highlighted or intro-duced. It is important to recognise that formal benchmarking can be sup-ported by informal benchmarking, where casual observations are brought back to the businesses and put into the decision-making processes. One such example comes from a chain of Danish steakhouses that operate a child friendly restaurant policy and have added extra dimensions because of recommendations of best practice they have received from their staff who have taken their own children out to eat and found interesting stories to bring back. This has led to the introduction of table games for the children and a direct link with Cartoon Network for the use of their characters, many of whom are popular with the children.

RITZ-CARLTON

Ritz-Carlton has become a regular feature of case studies. We are aware of all sorts of things about their operations because they continue to be an object of fascination. From general accounts, such as the two part case study entitled 'My Pleasure' (http://www.expertmagazine.com/EMOnline/RC/part2.htm) or the 'Ritz-Carlton Case Study' (http://www.oppapers.com/essays/Ritz-Carlton-Case-Study/191116) and particular hotel developments such as *Case Study:* The Ritz-Carlton, Marina Del Rey (http://www.afproducts.com/resources/case-study/ritz-carlton-marina-del-rey) or the $144.5 million Ritz-Carlton & Residences at Battery Park, located just five blocks to the south of the World Trade Center site in New York (www.gamewell-fci.com/casestudies/ritzcarlton.html). We can learn about their branding, for instance in 'Branding, a job well done' http://www.brandchannel.com/features_effect.asp?pf_id=286. And their management practices have been documented in 'Ritz-Carlton's Human Resource Management Practices and Work Culture: The Foundation of an Exceptional Service Organization (http://www.icmrindia.org/casestudies/catalogue/Human%20Resource%20and%20Organization%20Behavior/HROB100.htm), which brings us much closer to our focus here. The story is well told in the account of the Portman Ritz-Carlton in Shanghai (*media.ft.com/cms/5aa22940-74a7-11db-bc76-0000779e2340.pdf*), describing how the hotels operate to provide exceptional customer satisfaction. Their policy is to satisfy every need of their customers and they have given every employee the authority to commit up to $2000 (including even the low-paid, hourly workers), encouraging them to do 'whatever it takes' to make their customers happy.

The impact this commitment has on the profitability of the business has been the subject of less comment. This may be partly because it is not easy to establish the profitability of the individual hotels. The Ritz-Carlton brand is part of the Marriott Corporation and they have never reported on profits individually. However, the situation is even more complicated as, although the brand is owned by Marriott, the hotels are not owned by them, they help to manage them for the owners of the specific properties. Therefore the contribution to the Marriott corporate accounts comes from the management fees they charge rather than the operating profits of the hotels. In this way the Ritz-Carlton brand can make money even if its hotels do not. There is no formal requirement for individual hotels to make public their operating performance so it is difficult to comment in detail. What has been observed is that there have been a number of disputes between the owners and Ritz-Carlton, with the owners claiming that Ritz-Carlton puts the commitment to the customers' satisfaction ahead of operating profits. Some commentators have pointed to several high-profile lawsuits, an increasing number of bankruptcies, the conversion of properties to other brands and the switching of the management contracts to other management companies as evidence that the return to the owners is not the highest priority for the Ritz-Carlton brand (www.brandchannel.com/brand_speak.asp). They suggest that there is little evidence that links the strategic commitment to high levels of customer satisfaction with profitability, suggesting rather that what the examples demonstrate is the opposite as the commitment to customer satisfaction can have significant negative impacts on short-term operating costs and therefore on the profitability of the hotels.

The Ritz-Carlton story has been built on reversing several conditions which were taken for granted in the hospitality industry. The long time president of the Ritz-Carlton, Horst Schulze, argued that in the 1980s the industry was 'a lousy lot' but he argued that his company – and by extension, the whole of the industry – could be transformed by moving towards what we have called a customer-centred approach. He did this by rejecting the traditional big business models and refocusing the company. He recognised the dire conditions of the industry, seeing the vicious circle for what it was – a low pay environment with little by the way of fringe benefits for the workforce, that contributed to very high levels of labour turnover because there was no reason to develop any loyalty to any particular hotel company – especially if another hotel offered you a little bit more. Management reaction to this turnover was to ignore training, as the training would be lost when the worker left and even worse would benefit a rival if they went to work for someone else ... as they surely would in the double bind of the vicious circle. If the workforce were not treated well, how could the management expect them to treat the customers properly, with courtesy and friendliness? Schulze argued that when customer satisfaction is at stake, the front-line workers had to be empowered to feel good about the organisation and to respond to customers helpfully. It was seen as a long-term strategy but one which he saw as being totally within the control of management.

That Schulze was successful is now almost the stuff of legend – and it is possible to see the huge transformation of the industry as the results of the initiatives of this one man. The learning point here is not to underestimate what the effects of one deeply committed entrepreneurial leader can be even in the difficult circumstances surrounding the hotel industry. A shift towards a customer-focussed business strategy could be introduced and the results could be so successful that other players in the industry had to take note. It was the start of what could later be seen as a customer revolution!

The organisation we see today has developed from 1983 when the historical Ritz-Carlton of Boston and the rights to the brand name were acquired by the Marriott Corporation. It is now an independent division of Marriott International, managing 45 hotels on five continents. Its success has been recognised by awards for service quality and customer satisfaction in all five continents. The model is simple with the approach that all of the Ritz-Carlton's 22,000 staff are, in the words of the company, *'Ladies and Gentlemen Serving Ladies and Gentlemen'*. The message is straightforward, with over 85% of the workforce engaged in front-line employment the mantra means that the basics of customer-centred business are led from the front. The essence of the approach to quality service is based around:

1. a warm and sincere greeting using the customer's name if possible;
2. a constant anticipation of the customer's needs; and
3. a warm goodbye, again using the customer's name when ever possible.

The company has broken the old vicious circle of low salary and high turnover by refocusing all of its processes on the customers – including recruitment and training, where there are now 250 hours of training for first-year front-line associates. The ladies and gentlemen are now offered a wide range of opportunities for professional development, and encouraged to think in terms of careers in the Ritz-Carlton. A survey in 1999 revealed that more than 80% of their guests claimed to be 'extremely satisfied'. The Ritz-Carlton Hotels have established a policy of 'defect-free' experience for its guests, that has led the management along a journey that removes all customer problems. This has seen detail-oriented procedures for quality improvement and problem solving being developed and documented. These processes have identified many areas where problems can arise and the systematic analysis of the data has identified how these problems can be addressed and the customer experience made a more positive one. Through this systematic research, the company established that there are 1,071 potential instances for a problem to arise during interactions with Meeting Event Planners. As a result of adopting this systematic customer-centred approach in 1998, over 80% of Meeting Planners reported that they were 'extremely satisfied' with their overall experience, up from fewer than 70% a year earlier.

Since the success of the Ritz-Carlton revolution, it has become apparent that successful hospitality firms have recognised the value of meeting the customers' expectations and developed customer-centred processes that help to ensure that this happens. The two-way communication with customers about the business and about the customers' own views has helped hospitality offers to be shaped around the customers and the customer service issues. This is not to say that the tangible elements of the hospitality package are not important, but that the ways that they are presented and delivered to the customers makes a significant difference.

What we have tried to demonstrate is that the strategic commitment to customer satisfaction does not always sit easily with profit generation in the short term and should not be confused with shareholder satisfaction. The costs incurred in implementing customer-centred business processes require a delicate balancing act by the managers. All the elements of customer-centred business come at a price to the business – training, increased staffing levels, more products; higher service levels all incur costs. Unless the introduction of these elements produces increased business, justifies higher prices or generates higher levels of occupancy, the business's profits will be reduced. Increasing customer satisfaction does not always translate into greater profit – the changes have to be validated in the market and valued by the customers.

ATTRACTING CUSTOMERS

It is worth remembering that over 40% of new businesses set up in the UK each year fail within their first two years of business. Prior to starting a business, it is imperative to carry out research to determine which sector(s) of the market(s) the offer should be aimed at. Once a business has identified its target demographics, it is then necessary to determine the best ways of reaching them. There are many ways to achieve this and the most appropriate way will vary from business-to-business. Targeting the wrong sectors with promotional activities is a waste of valuable time and money.

Activity: Lunch at the World's Best Restaurant

http://in.rediff.com/news/2006/may/29spec.htm

Please read the article which is reprinted at the site listed above. It is one journalist's account of his trip to the Fat Duck Restaurant. Heston Blumenthal is becoming a very famous chef but read through this mouth-watering account of a visit to his restaurant and think about how he first attracted customers to the restaurant and how he manages the demand for his restaurant now. We would also like to know if what you read makes you want to visit the restaurant or to avoid it and eat something you might recognise!

We have selected just one section to give you a flavour – but please read the whole account if you want to see just how the experience worked for the journalist. We normally paraphrase our sources but here we want you to read the original because the sense of the experience is conveyed by the author's use of language and their rapport with the whole experience. You join the account a little way into the afternoon:

> 'I am amazed by the magic of the nitro-tea lime and vodka mousse. Not just remarkable for the way it seems to burst and dissolve in a tangy sharpness on the tongue, this ball of flavour had science and logic that actually made sense. Besides that are the wonder, awe and drama of its creation. Blumenthal has set the stage for the next 3.5 hours of delight, intense flavour, surprise and sheer joy.
>
> As we break small pieces of bread and spread on the creamy butter, the next appetiser appears. On a clean white plate are two postage size squares of jelly. One deep red and the other brilliant orange.
>
> "Orange and beetroot jelly", the European accent pronounces and leaves after asking us to begin with the orange jelly.
>
> We (obviously) take a bit of the orange-colored jelly and the intense, distinct flavour of beetroot bursts through. Concentrated and clean. The next bite of the red-colored jelly brings all the wonders of citrusy, sharp orange. There is a genius in that kitchen who is having a lot of fun surprising naïve would-be-gourmets like us. Nothing is what you expect it to be.'

The last sentence raises an interesting question. How many people (and therefore what size of market) do you think would eat in a restaurant where nothing is what you expect it to be?

Customer communications

Marketing has in the past focussed on getting the message from the business to the customer but a customer-centred approach calls for something more than this. We have stressed the importance of attitudes and values in the business models we are focussing on. A hospitality business must establish these attributes as a central part of its business image. How businesses capture these intangible elements is part of the image and identity building processes, building upon the market research that has helped to specify what those positive attributes are in the eyes of the potential customers, in terms of both the core and augmented products and services to be offered. This then forms the basis for constructing the identity of the business, which is at the heart of raising awareness and interest in the business activities.

Identity can be promoted in a variety of ways, some of which involve major investment whilst others cost little or nothing. Using the available budget to the best possible results has to be carefully managed and evaluated. We have seen very successful identities created in airlines through the choice of corporate colours – everyone recognises easyJet's orange, which is a basic approach, but Cathay Pacific and Singapore Airlines have also built up their reputation with cabin crew uniforms of great distinction, although they probably cost more than easyJet's! We are told by the texts that a regular small presence creates more awareness than less frequent big splashes. In general this principle holds but there are exceptions which help to challenge the thinking behind such an easy assumption. EasyJet have a policy of regular small adverts but their fierce rivals use eye catching one offs to great effect. They have been helped by a number of these campaigns being halted by legal objections – they were threatened by the advertising standards agency over an advertisement featuring a supposed school girl and by the French President Sarkozy for featuring his wedding arrangements without his permission. The lesson to be drawn from this is that there may be no single best way to launch an image and to maintain it – but you need to conduct your market research in order to be able to say whether the communications were successful. You also need to hear from your customers about why they were – or were not – successful and what attributes they were developing in terms of your business identity.

A business can use a variety of means to reach its target markets – you might consider these methods outlined in Figure 5.2.

Activity

Businesses should not underestimate the value of word-of-mouth recommendations but they are harder to control and indeed are not directly controllable by the business managers. This does not mean that it should be neglected – it has to be influenced positively to build up the image and reputation of the offer. Think back through your own experiences of hospitality offers – which stories do you tell to your friends and family? As always customer service is important and the adage that 'the customer is always right' should be remembered – a happy customer is more likely to recommend your business to their contacts. However, the literature says contented customers tell one person for every ten that dissatisfied customers complain to.

Is this true for you? What sort of stories do you tell when you return?
A close friend has recently returned from Canada professing deep love for the countryside but after one and a half hours of listening to stories, only had bad things to say about the quality of the service offered. Waiting over an hour for the starters in a restaurant was a top story – only made better by the fact that they ran out of chips as well. Given that over 80% of main courses on the menu came with chips, this is staggering for all sorts of reasons. Which part of this will you remember? That Canada is beautiful or that restaurants can be difficult places?

To bring the point home, highlight what makes good service for you and then think through when you have passed the good news on. It may be harder than you first imagine!

The Internet has added an extra dimension to this, which has been exploited by Dave Carroll of the Canadian band Sons of Maxwell. He found that his guitar had been damaged during a United Airlines flight and when he did not get any positive response from the company exacted this poetic revenge. The song, 'United Breaks Guitars has become a cause celebre, featuring on news programmes as well as being very popular on i-players and music channels. Please watch it – at (http://www.youtube.com/watch?v=5YGc4zOqozo&NR=1) and it has made the customer

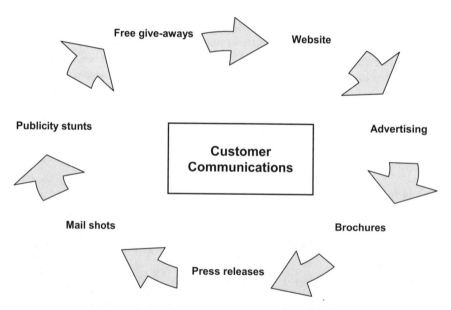

Source: adapted from Business Advice from the Business Experts
(http://www.enetrust.com/Communications/PressReleases/PressReleases2006/2006_02_24.asp)

FIGURE 5.2 *Customer communications approaches.*

relations officer Ms Irlweg famous, or should that be infamous. Carroll has since added a response which shows how far he has moved the company, even if he has taken over 12 months to do it and makes the point that, although she has been heavily criticised, Ms Irlweg was only following company policies at the time. (http://www.youtube.com/watch?v=Ay7hFIYQFnw&feature=related). United Airlines have seen their share prices drop by 10% in the first two weeks and market share drop, which you may feel is no coincidence.

This is not the end of the story though. Taylor Guitars have issued a clip which sympathises with the guitarist and also offers guidance on how to travel safely with your guitar (http://www.youtube.com/watch?v=n12WFZq2__0). Moreover, the incident has triggered further story telling, as North western Airlines now know to their cost – http://www.youtube.com/watch?v=6v3NgxGKqCE.

CUSTOMER PERCEIVED VALUE

The communications strategy needs to be sophisticated enough to gather information about the customer to ensure that the offer is correctly matched. As we have observed already, improving customer satisfaction does not always lead to improved profitability. We have to recognise that the relationship should be rephrased to properly capture the connection and suggest that profits come only from actual sales to customers and, therefore, increased profitability requires more sales at a price that covers the service quality offered. The problem for the business decision makers arises if they make the assumption that increasing customer satisfaction will automatically increase sales. It should also be noted that increased demand without sufficient capacity can affect the perceived value of the offer and there is a likelihood that customers' perception will register the poorer service quality that follows. In one of the first studies of its kind, Heskett (1986) reported a study in a restaurant in which customers' perceptions of service quality changed dramatically once the restaurant reached 75% of its capacity. Anywhere below 75% of capacity and there was an increase in the levels of perceived service quality but after 75% the customers' perceptions of service quality declined quite rapidly. Therefore hospitality businesses which want to develop any notion of a customer-centred strategy have to maintain an appropriate balance between demand, capacity and the quality of services at the same time. The number – 75% – may not be magical and it will need to be established for every specific hospitality offer individually as the combination of location, circumstance and context will be unique.

Market research can tell us many things but it does reinforce the idea that customers operate with a keen sense of value within the markets. It appears that customers buy whatever appears to be of the greatest value to them, with this sense of value coming from many different elements of the transaction. Budgets, available time, taste, fashion and experience all add to the construction of a customer's sense of the value that the purchase will contribute to them. This is known as customer perceived value. The difference between customer satisfaction and customer perceived value is centred on the very important notion of the willingness to pay for the benefits offered by the seller. It is all too easy to be misled by customers who talk up customer satisfaction as they will always say they like better products, and more services, and fewer problems. However, as we have observed, these improvements only work for the business if the customers are willing to pay for them. Offering improvements that the customers are not willing to pay will only drive down profits.

One of the problems in dealing with customer satisfaction is that the best information is always historical, even if it is recent history, as the reports are based on consumption that has already happened. This means not only the conditions of the offer but also the conditions surrounding the consumption – and changes in either could reinforce or challenge the sense of value in the prospect of undertaking a future purchase. The data for customer perceived value are based on information about how the customer feels now and how they are contemplating purchases in the future. The idea is designed to allow market research evaluation of what the likely uptake of proposed product and service developments would be, in terms of how they would be valued by the potential customers.

CUSTOMER SATISFACTION

We have so far used the term customer satisfaction as if it is an easily understood notion, but the drivers of satisfaction are many and varied. As with our approach to hospitality, satisfaction must include both tangible and intangible elements of the experience. Some argue that the benefits gained from hospitality exchanges lead to satisfaction through the satisfaction of functional needs. However, there are also important emotional elements involved in customer satisfaction in the hospitality industry and trust constructs are very important in assessing satisfaction. It is possible to construct a six-dimensional categorisation which includes:

- material provision,
- technical operations,

Processing

P00VU2GP7

Wigan and Leigh College

Customer Number: 15499001	ISBN: 9781856176095
Budget/Fund Code	hehos
Loan Type/Stock	Standard
Site / Location	pw1
PL Category	General
Order Date	05/21/2010
Order Type	orders
PL Intellect. Level	Adult

Hand Notes:

Order Spe
Coutts c
Local
Loan 1
Fun
P

- staff adaptability,
- staff/customer relations,
- image and
- value.

It must also be recognised that the drivers of satisfaction will vary across customer groups such as leisure versus business guests, and amongst users of different categories of hotel or services. We are also sure that customer satisfaction should also encompass employee satisfaction, using Heskett's Service-Profit Chain. It became popular to refer to the employees as internal customers to capture their importance in the construction of the hospitality offer. However, we believe that the argument is that employees need to experience quality service from the business before they can be confident in offering it to the – external – customers.

Parasuraman and Grewal (2000) have linked the notions of satisfaction and perceived value and argued that the offer of a unique or distinctive perceived value can lead to a competitive advantage that competitors find it difficult to challenge. They argue that this is the basis of customer loyalty, one of the important ways of measuring customer reactions in the hospitality industry. Since the 1990s we have seen studies (Zeithaml et al., 1996) that have shown that loyalty is based upon the customers' sense of perceived value and of the quality of the service delivered (Kangis and Zhang, 2000). This has now even become a concern for politicians and political parties as they seek to build long-term relations with the voters (Brennan and Henneburg, 2008).

Example: Frequent-Stay Programmes on the Rise

Members of hotel loyalty schemes are nearly twice as likely to return to a hotel compared to non-members. Industry reports in 2003 suggested that guests are finding frequent-stay, or hotel loyalty, programmes increasingly important. The numbers involved in frequent-stay programmes grew by nearly 12% in 2003. The number of guests who indicated that membership in a hotel's frequent-stay programme was 'very important' in selecting their most recent hotel stay rose steadily throughout 2003, with a 25% annual increase. Features like the transferability of points and instant redemption, combined with no blackout dates and no point expiration, are making it faster and easier for members to redeem their points for hotel and merchandise rewards and are helping drive guests to join such programmes in greater numbers. Beyond the repeat business that these programmes encourage, club members typically spend more per room, are less sensitive to price increases and are more satisfied with their hotel experience.

Source: http://www.hotel-online.com/News/PR2004_1st/Feb04_MarketMetrix.html.

As we are often told, hospitality customers are an increasingly sophisticated clientele and there is evidence that these sophisticated customers may be more influenced by a sense of style and design. It is argued that there is a shift with increasing experience from functional benefits to emotional ones. This is best seen in the popularity and placing of the boutique hotels and their individualised offers, which compete effectively on a small scale with the much larger and established brands. It is apparent that the customers of today are unwilling to compromise on the quality of service they receive, and therefore the quality of service has become the key to customers' approval of a hospitality organisation. This basis in the customers' perceptions can be hard to shift and thus make it very difficult for businesses to create loyalty, even if customers are satisfied. However, if we examine the relation between customer satisfaction metrics (i.e., behavioural loyalty, attitudinal loyalty, etc.) it is possible to see the intangible or emotional elements outweighing the functional and tangible ones in consumers' decision-making processes. This may mean that loyalty may be more important than satisfaction.

CUSTOMER RETENTION

Loyalty brings us to the arguments surrounding customer retention. We have seen retention strategies developed into customer relationship management (CRM) in many larger organisations but the lessons are valid for small- and medium-sized enterprises (SMEs) too. The bottom line is simple – market research shows that marketing to new customers is much more expensive and less effective than retaining existing customers. Retaining a customer only costs something like 10% of the costs of attracting a new customer. Implementing a CRM with a retention policy will lower marketing costs as the full costs are only experienced when acquiring the new customers. Indeed the longer the relationship, the lower the overall and average costs. This means looking at the elements of both behavioural loyalty and attitudinal loyalty to ensure that the business processes highlight and emphasise the positive value sets that will appeal to customers. Sivadas and Baker-Prewitt (2000) go further, claiming a direct correlation between the customers' perceptions of service quality and their subsequent loyalty. This also extends to their willingness to refer the business to others. With this in mind we can begin to formulate a chain of understanding for the hospitality relationship.

All of these stages are worthy of research and understanding of the complex constructions in terms of specific businesses and particularly in testing new business proposals.

> Customers' expectations   ->customers' perception of service quality ->
> customers' perceived value -> customer satisfaction -> customer retention and
> loyalty

Source: Authors own design

FIGURE 5.3   *Critical stages in the customer relationship.*

We can also note that retention brings other benefits as long-term customers demonstrate characteristics that are supportive of the business. They have been identified as being:

- less inclined to switch,
- less price sensitive,
- more likely to introduce new customers,
- more likely to purchase additional products,
- less expensive to service because they are familiar with the process,
- require less 'education' and
- more consistent in their buying behaviour.

All these factors make them 'good' customers and therefore they should be valued not just because they are there but because they offer advantages to the business. They are also difficult for your competitors and their loyalty and retention makes it harder for other businesses to enter the market or increase their market share. If we look at the internal and external customer dichotomy again, we can also see that increased 'external' customer retention and greater customer loyalty leads to more satisfaction for the internal customer as well. Satisfied employees provide for better customer satisfaction in a virtuous circle. We can also identify the positive side of the word-of-mouth relationship we mentioned earlier as the verbal referral of the existing customers is very powerful in forming new customer relations.

CUSTOMER CARE: BENEFITS AND IMPORTANCE

Sheth et al. (2000) argued that a service-oriented focus is a customer-centred focus. We would like to highlight this by tracking another aspect of customer-centred approaches and explore how you can establish the ways in which customers see and position a business. We should try to stand in the shoes of our customers. The following seven habits (http://www. strategicmarketingmontreal.ca/newsletter-13.htm) distinguish the truly customer-centric organisation from a business that merely thinks a lot about its customers.

1. We have a promise for our customers, not just a mission for ourselves.
2. We bundle services in with our products.
3. Our Website is a welcoming door, not a magnificent edifice.
4. The customer finds it easy to contact us, by whatever method is convenient.
5. Our telephone system is 'customer-friendly' and not just cost-effective.
6. Our customer has one main contact who makes everything happen.
7. Our customer service gives the service the customer really wants.

Activity

Evaluate a company that you know and think through how you would rate them on the basis of the seven habits.

How easy is it to identify this customer-centred approach from outside a business?

A CUSTOMER CENTRED BUSINESS MODEL

In one of the most important articles in this field, Kandampully (2006) presents a three-phase strategic orientation plan that provides both theoretical and practical directions for businesses in the hospitality industry, so as to effectively reorient the hospitality companies into customer-centred businesses. We will present this model to you as it is one of the most clearly elaborated workings of what we believe is the most significant challenge in the hospitality industry. Kandampully's research has identified factors that are essential to support hospitality firms to operate effectively within the new business model.

The context for his argument will be familiar as we have already worked through many of the arguments in this book. He sees the customer-centred model becoming more important for three reasons to do with the competition and the competitive advantage of businesses, the customer and changes to and within the customer base, and the importance of the service quality challenge. As we have seen customers are becoming more sophisticated and experienced, the search for competitive advantage has placed greater emphasis on the augmented product (highlighting the service elements) and the hospitality businesses have had to reconsider their core competencies. We will now elaborate the arguments underpinning these three areas.

1. Customer

The customer is no longer merely the person who makes purchases and therefore generates revenues for the business. For Kandampully the concept of 'customer' becomes an icon that serves to focus and orientate the sense of direction of the entire business. Market-driven companies continuously collect and evaluate information about their customers and their competitors. Market research means that businesses can develop their own business practices to focus on the service offer. Lifestyle changes, based on economic growth, higher disposable incomes, technological advances and globalisation mean that services are an integral part of the customers' social needs and indeed their identities.

2. Competitive advantage

Competitive advantage is often attributed to a firm's core capabilities. By developing these core capabilities that are valued and difficult to match, hospitality business firms can create the basis for a sustainable competitive advantage and superior profitability. Knowing the markets and understanding the customer are core capabilities that are considered to be some of the most distinctive and valuable features for customer-centred businesses organisations.

Businesses striving for competitive advantage in the field of hospitality have recognised that the intangible components of their offers are very important and that customers are coming to expect more and more from the companies they do business with. As globalisation and increasing competition have come to the hospitality markets, it has been observed that there is little to differentiate many of the products brought to market and therefore the service offer has become increasingly important to the claims for competitive advantage. Customers' perceptions of the firm's service quality, and their perceived value, not only offer the businesses their most sustainable basis for differentiation but also their most powerful competitive advantage.

3. Service offer

Traditional core offerings of food and accommodation do not reach the level of the competition or the expectations of the customers. The focus of successful businesses is moving away from emphasising the tangible component of their offers to the intangible component of their offers and a customer-centred and service-oriented focus has thus emerged as the prerequisite for gaining market dominance in the hospitality industry. Services are therefore no longer merely additional extras but represent an essential component of any hospitality business.

Other strategies do exist for businesses but they may encounter more constraints. For instance the decision to react to increased demand by providing more may hit real constraints in terms of capacity – in the physical limitations of the premises, the ability of staff to cope with the extra demand or the demands of the new offer. If this is added to the perishability of service offers, the risks of expansion can be seen as enormous. Demand may be restricted through pricing strategies that price customers out of the market or into the market. These pricing strategies are short term and may not deliver long-term solutions for the business. These strategies sit oddly with the emphasis on customer perceived value as the context is artificially manipulated. Customer-centred strategies have more respect for the customer and seek to increase the perceptions of value, not decrease it.

Customer-centred businesses recognise the interconnections between the functional departments, such as human resource, operations and marketing and the delivery of the service offer (Lovelock et al., 2001). Within the customer-centred business model, every employee in a hospitality business must assume an active front-line role, as the customer relationship constitutes the most important contribution that can be made by any employee. The customer-centred business model assumes that there is regular and meaningful communication between all the relevant stakeholders and the central management functions of the business and this is essential for the successful development of hospitality businesses. Given the lessons already learned about the changing patterns of hospitality businesses, the prospects of developing the business through the recognition and critical evaluation of these interactions offer the business the opportunity to achieve market share, customer loyalty and market leadership.

A CUSTOMER-CENTRED BUSINESS MODEL

The rapidly changing businesses environment has driven businesses to look at the established business models and give serious consideration to alternative models that make use of new technologies to enhance businesses' efficiency and improve the customers' perceived value. The combination of the new technologies with new knowledges and new business processes (Li et al., 2009) has produced the operational basis for the implementation of new processes to deliver effective strategies for dealing with the range of new business challenges. These new business models can suggest different ways forward to provide alternative approaches for firms to consider (Chapman et al., 2002) – not only in terms of what the businesses are going to do but also in the ways the businesses will behave to achieve their aims. Kandampully (2006: 182) proposes a model in three phases:

Phase 1: corporate intent,

Phase 2: strategic direction and

Phase 3: core capabilities.

The first phase sees the hospitality businesses reinventing themselves and their business models to place the customer at centre stage. This means centring the customer at the heart of the long-term business strategy of the business, linking together its service offer with the management functions. There has to be tangible corporate intent to bring the change of focus into effect and ensure that the involvement of the customer is all embracing. This will ensure that the business offer, including both tangible and intangible elements of the offer, will reach the market in such a way that it satisfies the customer more completely than any of the competition.

As the business moves into the second phase, we can see that there has to be a business-wide commitment to the strategic direction. This sense of strategic commitment means the businesses bringing the functional departments, what Kandampully refers to as the internal mechanisms of the business, into line with the re-centring of the business practices to ensure that the customer remains at the heart of the whole operation. The business model brings together three elements that can be used to test this commitment as the hospitality offer should be functionally efficient, create an operational distinctiveness in the market and enhance the sense of perceived value amongst the customers. Ultimately success will be judged by the customers' perceptions of the value of the new offer, both in its own terms and when compared to the offers of the competitors.

The third phase of the model is orchestrated around the four core competences in the businesses, identified by Kandampully as technology, networks, relationships, and empowered employees and the ability of the business to maximise the synergy across and between these four interdependent elements. The success of the businesses' customer-focussed strategies will mainly be determined by the abilities found within the businesses, that is to say the range and extent of their core capabilities.

The businesses' ability to deliver service quality effectively and to address service delivery problems creatively depends on their core competencies. The perception of excellence will be judged by the ways in which the businesses adjust to and anticipate the needs of their customers. Old fashioned notions of productivity cannot capture this sense of the dynamic relationship, encapsulating product, service and customer relationships (Verhoef et al., 2008). The degree to which they contribute to a specific service is decided by the requirements of the customer and the business must develop the flexibility to alter the offer for the benefit of individual customers (Wang and Lo, 2003).

SUMMARY AND CONCLUSIONS

In this chapter we have seen some of the ways in which hospitality businesses have shifted towards customer-centred strategies that enhance the sense of the customers' perceived value and help to retain those customers. Kandampully has one last image which is worth sharing with the description of the way, in less turbulent times, firms were able to rely on the 'flywheel of momentum' to sustain their progress. This is a lovely image which fits with the classic approaches to management and their commitment to measurement and incrementalism. The pressures involved contemporary business development, and the globalised nature of competition means that successful hospitality companies must be able to respond rapidly to changes in the attitudes and expectations of their customers. The shift moves customers from being the last link in the supply chain and places them at the centre of the business and the strategies for its development.

Hospitality businesses need to recognise and respond to both internal and external drivers. This means being aware of the pressures on the businesses' core and that all the important internal functions, operations, marketing and human resource management, are geared to working together to enhance the quality of the customer experience. The emphasis we have placed on market research and the relationship with the customer should ensure that the businesses will be aware of the market conditions and can shape their offer to the changes identified in the market. We have seen that knowing markets is essential to business planning and business success, as that solid knowledge and two-way communication create the conditions for greater customer satisfaction and increased customer loyalty. The strength of this relationship and the ability of the businesses to utilise such dialogue effectively are what will mark out the most successful customer centred businesses from those that are less successful.

REVIEW QUESTIONS

1. Define the concept of customer-centred business and give examples from hospitality businesses.
2. Customer satisfaction is not enough to attract potential customers – discuss.
3. Customer perceived value is a better guideline to business success than satisfaction research – elaborate the linkages between profitability, satisfaction and perceived value.
4. 'Why is it better to retain customers than to find new ones?'

Case Study: 'And You Think Strawberries are for Eating...'

The following are excerpts from a speech first delivered as the keynote of the AMERICAN MARKETING ASSOCIATION annual meeting in New York City in 1973. It was published in the Saturday Evening Post in 1974, October issue.

We make no apology for the date of the piece or for the length of the example. Please read the extracts carefully, it puts much of the chapter into perspective.

James Lavenson owned a marketing and advertising company before being invited to become a senior management executive with Sonesta International Hotels. He was given responsibility for the company's hotel and food interests and some non hospitality businesses, including the famous Mad Magazine and Hartman Luggage. For the last three years of that period he was president and chief executive officer of the chain's 'flagship', the famous Plaza Hotel in New York City. Unprofitable in the year before his assumption of the hotel's direction, the Plaza was profitable each year of his tenure until it was sold in February 1975 to Western International Hotels.

This is what he had to say – try to read this approach from the 1970s in the light of the work you have just done on the customer-centred business. You will see many of the antecedents of that approach spelt out in terms of the changes introduced in the Plaza. You will get a feel for what the challenges of change management are in the hospitality industry – and it may even make you smile!

'One day early in my career there I got a little idea what I was up against with professional staff when, in walking through the lobby, I heard the phone ring at the bell captain's desk, and no one was answering it. So to give a demonstration to my staff that there was no job too demeaning for me I went over and I picked up the phone and said, "Bell captain's desk. May I help you?" The voice came on the other end. "Pass it on, Lavenson's in the Lobby."

... At the Plaza Hotel, "Think Strawberries" has become the code words for salesmanship. Actually, a team approach to what I consider to be the most exciting profession in the world selling. But hotel salesmanship is salesmanship at its worst. So it is with full knowledge that I was taking the risk of inducing cardiac arrest on the hotel guests if they heard one of our staff say a shocking thing like "Good morning, Sir" or "Please" or "Thank you for coming" or "Please come back"

I decided to try to turn the 1400 Plaza employees into genuine hosts and hostesses who, after all, had invited guests to our house. Secretly, I knew I didn't mean hosts and hostesses; I meant sales people. But before the staff was able to recognise my voice over the phone, a few calls to the various departments in the hotel showed me how far I had to go. "What's the difference between your $85 suite and your $125 suite?" I asked the reservationist over the telephone. The answer you guessed it. "Forty dollars."

Continued

"What's the entertainment in your Persian Room tonight?" I asked the bell captain.

"Some singer" was his answer.

"A man, or a woman?", I wanted to know.

"I'm not sure," he said.

It made me wonder if I'd even be safe going there.

Why was it, I thought, that a staff of a hotel doesn't act like a family of hosts to the guests who have been invited, after all, to stay at their house? And it didn't take long after becoming a member of that family myself to find out one of the basic problems. Our 1400 family members didn't even know each other. With a large staff working over 18 floors, a thousand guest rooms, six restaurants, a nightclub, a theatre, three levels of sub-basement including the kitchen, a carpentry shop, a plumbing shop, an electrical shop, and a full commercial laundry, how would they ever know all the people working there? Who were the guests? Who was just a burglar smiling his way through the hotel while he ripped us off?

I can assure you that in the beginning if he smiled and said "Hello", he was a crook. He certainly wasn't one of us. Even the old time Plaza employees who might recognize a face after a couple of years would have no idea of the name connected to that face. It struck me, that if our people who worked with each other every day couldn't call each other by name, smile at each other's familiar face, say good morning to each other, how on earth could they be expected to say astonishing things like "Good morning, Mr Jones" to a guest?

A short time after my arrival there, the prestigious Plaza staff were subjected to uncouth blasphemy. The Plaza name tag was born, and it became part of the staff's uniform. And the first name tag appeared on my own lapel, on the lapel of God Himself. And it's been on the lapel of every other staff member ever since. Every one, from dishwasher to general manager at the Plaza Hotel, wears his name in large letters where every other employee, and of course, every guest, can see it.

Believe it or not, Plaza people began saying hello to each other by name when they passed in the hall, or in the offices.

At first, of course, our regular guests at the Plaza thought we had lost our cool and we were taking some kind of gigantic convention there. But now the guests are also able to call the bellmen, and the maids, and the room clerks, and the manager, by name. And we began to build an atmosphere of welcome with the most precious commodity in the world, our names and our guests' names.

When someone calls you by name, and you don't know his or hers, another funny thing happens. A feeling of discomfort comes over you. If he calls you by your name twice, and you know you're not world famous, you have to find out his name. And this phenomenon we saw happening with the Plaza staff name tags. When a guest calls a waiter by name, because it's there to be read, the waiter wants to call the guest by name. Hopefully it will drive the waiter nuts if he doesn't find out the guest's name. The waiter will ask the maitre d'. And if the maitre d' doesn't know, he can see if they know at the front desk.

Why this urgent sense of mission? What makes calling a guest by name so important? I am now about to tell you a secret which is known only in the hotel industry. The secret is calling a guest by name, it is a big payoff – it is called, and you can write this down if you want, a tip.

At first there was resistance, particularly on the part of the executive staff, to wearing name tags. The old-time hotel managers liked being incognito when wandering around the hotel. It avoided hearing complaints and, of course, if you don't hear complaints, there are none. Right?

About 500, almost a third of the staff of the Plaza, are Hispanic. That means they speak Spanish. That means they understand Spanish. It also means that they don't understand English, and they don't read English. But all our communications to the employees were in English. The employee house magazine, with all those profound management messages, and my picture, were in English.

It seems to me that to say we had a language barrier at the Plaza would be an understatement. Before we could talk about strawberries, we first had to learn Spanish and put our house magazine in both English and Spanish. We started lessons in Spanish for our supervisors, and lessons in English for the staff. It was interesting to me to note that the staff learned English faster than our supervisors learned Spanish. With 1400 staff members all labelled with their name tags, and understanding why in both Spanish and English, with all of them saying "Good morning", and smiling at each other, we were ready to make sales people out of them.

There was just one more obstacle we had to overcome before we suggested that they start selling: asking for the order. They had no idea what the product was that they were supposed to be selling. Not only didn't they know who was playing in the Persian Room and they didn't know that the Plaza had movies, full-length feature films without commercials, on closed circuit TV in the guest rooms. As a matter of fact, most of them didn't know what a Plaza room looked like unless they happened to be a maid or a bellman who checked in guests. The reason that registration thought that $40 was the difference between the two suites was because he had never been in one. Of product knowledge, our future salespeople had none, and we had our work cut out for us.

Today, if you ask a Plaza bellman who is playing in the Persian Room, he will tell you, Jack Jones. He will tell you its Jack Jones because he has seen Jack Jones and heard Jack Jones, because in the contract of every performer there is a clause requiring that performer to first play to the staff in the Employees' Cafeteria, so that all the staff can see him, hear him and meet him. The Plaza staff now sees the star first, before the guests. And if you ask a room clerk or a telephone operator what is on TV closed circuit movie in the guest rooms, they will tell you because they have seen the movies on the TV sets which run the movie continuously in the Staff Cafeteria.

Today, all the room clerks go through a week of orientation which includes spending a night with their husband, or their wife, or just like a guest. They stay in a room in the Plaza. The orientation week includes a week of touring all the guest rooms, a meal in the restaurants and the reservation room clerk gets a chance to actually look out the window of the suite and see the difference between an $85 and a $125 suite, because the $125 suite overlooks beautiful Central Park, and the $85 suite looks up the back of the Avon building.

The Plaza, as you may know, is a dignified institution. It was so dignified that it was considered demeaning to admit that we needed the business, no matter how much money we were losing. And if you didn't ask us, we wouldn't ask you. So there! We weren't ringing our doorbell or anybody else's. You had to ring ours. And this attitude seemed to be a philosophy shared by the entire organisation, a potentially large sales staff of waiters, room clerks, bellmen, cashiers, doormen, maids, about 600 guest-contact employees.

If you wanted a second drink in the Plaza's famous Oak Bar, you got it with a simple technique-tripping the waiter, and then pinning him to the floor. You had to ask him. You'd think, wouldn't you, that it would be easy to change that pattern of Oak Room waiters. After all, they make additional tips on additional drinks. Simple sales training. Right? Right?

I had our general manager for the Oak Room the maitre d' learn my new policy. It was inspirational. When the guest's glass is down to one-third full, the waiter is to come up to the table and ask the guest if he'd like a second drink. Complicated, but workable. Couldn't miss, I thought.

About a month after establishing this revolutionary policy I joined the general manager in the Oak Bar for a drink. I noticed at the next table there were four men all with empty glasses. No waiter was near them. After watching for fifteen minutes my ulcer gave out and I asked the general manager what happened to my second-drink programme? And the manager called over the maitre d' and asked what happened to the second-drink programme. And the maitre d' called over to the captain, pointed out the other table and said, "Whatever happened to Lavenson's second drink programme?" And the captain called over the waiter, and he broke out into a wreath of smiles as he explained that the men at the next table had already had their second drink.

So we started a programme of all our guest contact people, along with all of our salespeople, using a new secret oath "everybody sells". And we meant everybody – maids, cashiers, waiters, bellmen, assistant manager, general manager, and me – everybody!

We talked to the maids about suggesting room service, to the doormen about suggesting our restaurants, not the one

Continued

at the Pierre, to our cashiers about suggesting return reservations to the parting guests. And we talked to the waiters about strawberries.

Now I don't know how it is in Chicago, but in New York the waiter at the Plaza makes anywhere from $12,000 to $20,000 a year. The difference between those figures, of course, is tips. I spent 18 years in the advertising agency business, and I thought I was fast computing 15 per cent. I am a moron compared to a waiter.

Our suggestion for selling strawberries fell on very responsive ears when we described that part of our Everybody Sells Programme to the waiters in our Oyster Bar Restaurant. We had a smart controller, and he figured out that if with just the same number of customers already patronising the Oyster Bar the waiters would ask every customer if he'd like the second drink, wine or beer, with his meal, and then dessert given only one out of four takers we would increase the Oyster Bar Restaurant sales by $364,000 a year.

The waiters were well ahead of this lecture. They had already figured out that was $50,000 more in tips, and since there are 10 waiters in the Oyster Bar, I, with the aid of a pocket calculator, could figure out that that meant five grand more in tips per waiter. And it was at this point that I had my toughest decision to make since I'd been in the job, which was whether to stay on as president, or become a waiter in the Oyster Bar. But while the waiters appreciated this automatic raise in theory, they were very quick to point out the negative: "Nobody eats dessert any more," they said, "everybody is on a diet. If we served our specially, the Plaza chocolate cheesecake to everybody in the restaurant, we'd be out of business because they'd all be dead in a week." "So sell them strawberries," we said, "but sell them!"

Then we wheeled out our answer to the gasoline shortage. It is called a dessert cart. It has wheels. And we widened the aisles between the tables so that the waiters could wheel the cart right up to each table at dessert time without being asked. And not daunted by the diet protestations of the average guest, the waiter goes into raptures about the bowl of fresh strawberries on the top of the cart. There is even a bowl of whipped cream for the slightly wicked. And by the time the waiter finishes extolling the virtues of luscious strawberries, flown in that morning from California or Florida or wherever he thinks strawberries come from you, the guest, not only have an abdominal orgasm, but one out of two of you orders them.

We showed the waiters every week what happened with strawberry sales. The month I left the Plaza they doubled again, and so had the sales, incidentally, of second martinis. And believe me, when you have a customer for a second martini, you have a sitting duck for a strawberry sale, and that is with whipped cream. The Plaza waiters now ask for the order. They no longer stare at your waistline and say, "You don't look like you need dessert".

"Think Strawberries" is becoming the Plaza's sales password. The reservationist thinks strawberries and suggests that perhaps you would like a suite overlooking Central Park rather than a twin-bedded room. Bellmen are thinking strawberries. Each bellman has return reservation forms with his own name imprinted on them as the addressee, and he asks you, in checking you out and into your cab, can he make a return reservation for you?

The room service operators were thinking strawberries. They ask you if you'd like to watch the closed circuit TV film in your room as long as you're going to be there. No trouble, "We put three bucks on your bill and you never notice it compared with the price of the sandwich". Our telephone operators think strawberries. When you leave a wake up call, they suggest a Flying Tray Breakfast sent up to your room. 'You want the light breakfast, no ham and eggs; how about strawberries?'

We figured we added about 400 salesmen to the three-man sales staff we had before. Additional salesmen, at no extra expense, didn't exactly thrill my Board of Directors. But I will tell you what did tickle their fancy. The Plaza sales volume my last year there went from $27 million to a nice round $30 million. And our controller was seen giggling in his cage where we kept him, since our profits were double the year before's.

I'll tell you what pleased me most. The Plaza sold $250,000 worth of strawberries in the last six months alone – $250,000 worth of strawberries!

We created the Order of the Strawberry Patch. It's a little strawberry insignia worn on the employee's name tag, and any staff member, except those, naturally, in the Sale Department, who gives the sales manager at the Plaza a lead, just a lead, for rooms, or banquet business, gets to wear the little strawberry patch. He has joined the sales staff. And if that lead is converted into a sale, a savings bond is given to the person who suggested it.

Let me tell you what happened with that strawberry patch programme. There's a captain in the Oak Room, his name is Curt, and he likes savings bonds. He also has a wild imagination, and he imagined that if a Plaza salesman would call on his wife's friend's daughter, who was getting married, the wedding could be booked at the Plaza.

Obviously he was insane! The Oak Room captain's wife's friend's daughter, who lived in Brooklyn, with a wedding at the famous Plaza. The Plaza salesman was persuaded to call the lady in Brooklyn. At first he didn't want to go. But he was given a powerful incentive like keeping his job. And, of course, you can guess the result, or, can you? Would you believe a $12,000 wedding?

And that's not all. Just before I left the Plaza, Curt told me that his wife's friend's daughter had a sister, not yet married.

I believe I mentioned there's a laundry in the Plaza. Thirty ladies work in that laundry, three levels below the street. When they are working, these ladies don't exactly remind you of fashion models. They wear short white socks and sneakers, no make-up, and I suspect, although I have never been able to prove it, that three of them chew tobacco.

You can imagine the scepticism which greeted one of those ladies when she asked if she could earn a strawberry patch for a lead on a luncheon of her church group. How many members? Only 500! At least 500 showed up for lunch at the Plaza dressed to the heavens and paying cash. That laundry lady is papering her walls with savings bonds.

An Oak Room captain, and a laundry lady, like hundreds of other Plaza staff members, they wear the strawberry patch on their name tag.'

Thank you for reading through this – it is an account of an experience which still carries value into the globalised industry we work in today.

Source: Taken with kind permission from http://www.strategicmarketingmontreal.ca/newsletter-13.htm.

Questions

1. How do you feel when you are making a purchase and the company you are dealing with know your name?

2. Do you think empowerment can really be introduced throughout a company?

3. Is the time it takes to build a relationship with a customer worth it?

4. Do you agree that if customers do not say anything to the staff there cannot be any problems?

GLOSSARY

Consumer relation marketing   Processes designed to maintain a long-term relationship with customers and develop a deeper commitment with your offer. This often involves two-way communications as the customers can express opinions and attitudes that businesses can use to tailor the development of their business to ensure that they maximise customer satisfaction.

Customer attraction   The processes involved in bringing your hospitality offer to the market and gaining the interest and action of potential customers.

Customer-centred business   The business model that places the customer, knowledge about the customer and an ongoing relationship with the customer at the heart of all the business planning decisions.

Customer perceived value   The calculation made by customers after experiencing your offer and judging it against the price charged.

Customer retention   The business processes involved in ensuring that customers return to the business or place it high in their list of recommendations to others.

Customer satisfaction   What happens when your offer meets the needs – expressed and emergent – of your customers. Best established through both quantitative and qualitative approaches to ensure that you find out what your customers actually thought about the experience and the elements within the experience.

CHAPTER 6

Hospitality Business Planning and Feasibility

Learning Objectives

Having completed this chapter, you should be able to:

- Introduce the concept and scope of the hospitality business plan.
- Evaluate the characteristics of the hospitality offer in terms of its feasibility.
- Outline the research necessary to evaluate project proposals.

CONTENTS

INTRODUCTION

Every individual business proposal will require a unique specification but there are common concerns that all business development proposals should consider. In this chapter we will introduce a framework for a business plan and then work through the testing of that plan with the exploration of a feasibility study of the development. According to both Ransley and Ingram (2004) and Swarbrooke (2002), the business plan and feasibility studies are similar, but we would argue that there are significant differences between the two in the ways they are used and implemented in the business development processes. The processes of the business plan and the feasibility study are often seen to be similar but they serve different purposes and different audiences. The business plan takes the idea for a new offer and works through it so that it can be presented in the best possible way for potential supporters. The feasibility study is concerned with testing those claims and checking how far they are likely to be achievable. This is not to suggest that the business plan will not be honest or realistic but it may not be tested as

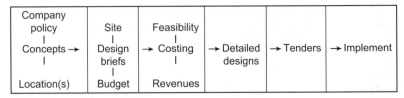

Source: adapted from Ransley and Ingram (2004: 46)

FIGURE 6.1   *The (hospitality) design process.*

rigorously. This is because it is primarily intended for internal use, where the feasibility study will often be conducted by outsiders.

We need to begin with a consideration of the business design process, where the business ideas are first shaped and brought forward for discussion. Ransley and Ingram (2004) suggested a simple process model which we have summarised in Figure 6.1. This demonstrates some of the factors which affect the way business ideas are put forward and the factors which shape them. The whole venture is shaped by the company's policies. This is not to say that the company's policy could not be challenged and changed, but proposals must be set within a context and it is important that the champions of the proposal know whether they are suggesting which sits easily within the company or will challenge some of its values and policies. A few years ago, many pub chains debated the morality and business costs of operating 24-hour opening and found that this challenged both their business models and their sense of corporate social responsibility (you can use your imaginations and think through the dilemmas involved in developing lap dancing clubs!).

The one thing everyone knows about hospitality development is that location is the key – but do not believe that it is ever that simple. Locations have to be specified and evaluated. They are not always what they seem. On the west coast of Barbados you will find a hotel on a promontory offering an ideal location for guests to enjoy sea views from every room in the hotel. The pricing of the rooms shows that rooms facing south carry a premium price compared to those looking north along the coast. At first glance this seems odd, until you take the second glance and see that the rooms looking north actually look out onto the main oil terminal for the island. It is a prime location but you still need to check!

The other observation we would make of this model is that it is too simple to account for the complexity of the processes it outlines. The main reason for this is that it is a linear model, with the assumption that the logical process is to move from left to right. This is correct but we would argue that it is not a simple movement as many of the considerations of budget and revenues, for instance, can force you to move backwards as well as forwards. We would propose that the model requires a series of feedback loops to make it more appropriate.

All projects have to begin with a definition of the concept or a project brief. This should take the idea and present it in a fairly detailed form, usually written, although some architects work visually, and explain the new elements of the project with a clear operational philosophy and an explanation of how this suggestions matches or exceeds the operating standards found in the area and other competitor offers. Ransley and Ingram (2004: 4) summarise the hospitality concept as 'an idea with definition and identity that defines an image'. It is this concept that drives the rest of the development, the setting of objectives and the strategies that allow it to happen. The design or project briefs are very important documents that elaborate the details of the project's parameters. You would expect them to clearly set out the objectives of the project, in terms of both the whys and the whats are the most important aspects of the project. Alongside a specification of the timeframes, usually specified into phases for design, build and operationalisation, it will also outline the key aspects of the budget, establishing the limits on the required resources and also setting out the required rate of return. The project brief must be comprehensive, realistic, clear, specific and flexible. It should also address the quality issues around the project in terms of the standards required and the durability of the venture. This is summarised in Figure 6.2. The elements of the hospitality concept can be brought into the process as outlined in Figure 6.3.

The conceptual process should also include a critical review of the proposals by looking towards evaluating the concept design proposals. This would be expected to include evaluation in relation to:

- Organisational strategy
- Corporate marketing objectives
- Sound commercial design practice
- Funding, resourcing and delivery.

Katsigiris and Thomas (1999), cited in Ransley and Ingram (2000), listed the key attributes of 'good' concept design as:

- An appropriate mix of 'hard' and 'soft' elements
- An appropriate balance between 'form/style' and 'function/durability' in order to maintain flexibility.

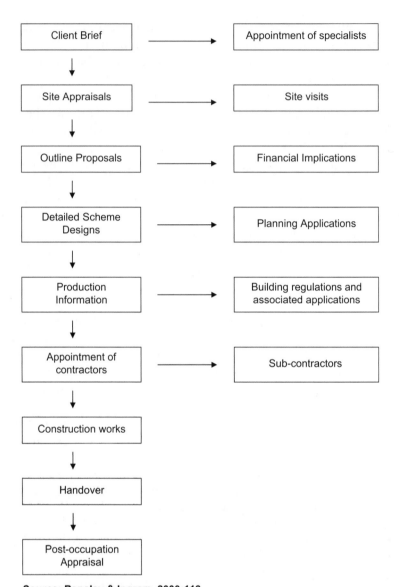

Source: Ransley & Ingram, 2000:112

FIGURE 6.2   *The design to building process.*

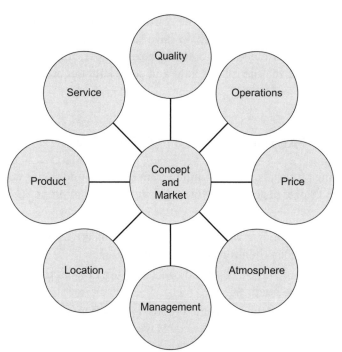

Source: adapted from Lundberg & Walker (1993) as cited in Ransley and Ingram (2004: 4)

FIGURE 6.3   *The hospitality concept.*

Activity

Think about two hospitality businesses and identify the elements that allow you to complete the matrix that this approach suggests.

Hard	Soft
Function/durability	Form/style

Then you should attempt to put a value on these elements in order to be able to add them to the business plan. This will allow you to see the similarities and the differences in the two businesses and help to highlight the basis for the business case to develop further.

Again the difficulty here is in the contextualisation and the specification of what is meant by appropriate. We have seen in the previous chapter how the augmented offer has come to be as, or even more, important as the core offer and here we see the mix of hard and soft elements being built into the design process.

GENERAL FACTORS AFFECTING DESIGN

By reviewing proposals, Ransley and Ingram (2004) found that it was possible to identify a range of general factors affecting the design proposal. These key factors are:

- Company policy – what are the strategic objectives of the company and how does the proposal fit within these?
- Concept – is there a clear and concise vision of what the proposal will bring to the business?
- Location – are there specific proposals for where the new development should be located? Have these been subjected to market testing?
- Function – does the proposal have a clear functional message?
- Aesthetics – how does the proposal fit with lifestyle and customers' expectations of perceived value?
- Budget – what are the demands on the business and what are the projected returns on that investment?
- Business – what levels of business can be expected both in terms of volumes and pricing?
- Logistics – how easily does the proposal sit within the existing offers and how can it be maintained by the company alongside those offers?
- Legislation – put simply is the proposal legal? But more seriously what legal constraints are there on the development, such as licensing and food safety for example?

TRENDS RELATING TO HOSPITALITY DESIGN

We now want to look at some of the trends that impact on the development of hospitality businesses by highlighting some of the factors that we have observed impacting on the new business proposals in the hospitality industry. These can be grouped into a number of areas and we will turn first to locational factors.

- Increasing land and property prices – we can see that developments are being limited by increasing land and property prices. Looking back we can see how development was diverted to out of town or destination fringe locations because the price of land and property was cheaper there than in the centre.

- Increasing shortage of green field sites – locations that are untroubled by previous history or usage are becoming harder to find and planning designations are also limiting the number of places where hospitality businesses can be developed.

- Availability and cost of space – these factors can be summarised as the balance between the availability and cost of space. Location is important but the costs of acquiring a particular location have to be balanced with the possibly lower developmental costs of an alternative, initially less attractive location. This also draws attention to the type of design put forward – where land is expensive then more intensive use of the site can be expected. Where tourism resorts are designed to spread along a beach front using large amounts of land, city centre and especially capital city centre developments will look to utilise high-rise building techniques on small parcels of land.

The second group of factors clusters around financial issues and management concerns. We would note:

- The increasing separation of property ownership and operation – this has seen a growing number of property management companies operating in hospitality.

- The need to build in greater flexibility to the developments – but this flexibility comes at a greater cost as the design must be more complex to allow for the flexibility.

- The inherent risk pertaining to increasingly shorter product life cycles – it is noticeable that developments are being proposed with shorter investment return periods as the impact of fashion and lifestyle issues has made the investment community more sensitive to the changes in demand that could follow from a change in fashion.

- The increasing difficulty in achieving effective differentiation within an ever more mature and competitive market – this works both in terms of supply and demand analyses of the market. Globalisation has become both an asset and a liability in developing new hospitality products as there are new markets for a diverse range of products but the competition has increased and the expectations of the customers have also changed dramatically.

■ The increasing use of prefabricated/modular materials – this advance in the technology of construction impacts on the range and diversification of the hospitality offer.

■ The changes in working practices within the design and construction industries – these practices tend to increase the costs and legal constraints on the development process and hospitality businesses must find ways of working within these conditions.

All of these factors should be borne in mind when devising and elaborating a project proposal as they will certainly be in the mind of those who will be testing and questioning the proposals. It is unusual for all of the financing of a project to come from a single source and therefore convincing financial supporters has become a key factor in hospitality business development.

When we consider the way proposals can be brought to the market, it is possible to identify three broad categories of development. These can be presented as:

■ Internal (or organic): where the business adds the new proposal to its existing portfolio.

■ Acquisition or merger, or disposal: where the proposal requires some change to the existing portfolio.

■ Some form of strategic alliance: where the proposal requires extended working with another business or agency.

Strategic alliances are normally seen as formal linkages between two or more businesses but they may also be negotiated through informal networks. It is possible to identify two broad types of strategic alliance. The first is based on equity and can be seen in the operation of joint ventures and the variety of management contracts in the hospitality industry. However, there are significant alliances that develop on a non-equity basis. This second form of alliance can be seen in the growth of partnership or network arrangements, collaborations and licensing/franchising arrangements to be found in hospitality developments.

FUNDING SOURCES

We now want to turn to the sources of financing available for developers. It is necessary to think in terms of funding which is from direct or indirect sources. We can see direct funding coming from a variety of sources. According to Swarbrooke (2002), the usual sources of direct financing can be seen to come in the following forms:

- Private sector
  - e.g. bank lending; venture capital; and equity
- Public sector
  - e.g. European Commission; central government; and local authorities
- Voluntary sector
  - e.g. conservation or educational trusts

There are also significant indirect sources of funding for hospitality projects and these can be captured in terms of:

- Private sector
  - e.g. leasing; franchises; and sponsorship
- Public sector
  - e.g. land/buildings; infrastructure provision; and tax allowances
- Voluntary sector
  - typically through the provision of labour.

In reality the majority of project finance comes from the private sector from two fundamental sources of debt capital or equity capital. Debt capital comes mainly from banks, whilst equity capital can come from the public market, real estate funds or friends and family. These funds will broadly be used to support four business activities:

- Project development: creating new or redeveloping existing facilities (e.g. the project can be a new built or an extension).
- Acquisition financing: purchasing buildings.
- Refinancing: lowering the costs of the finance and/or releasing value from the premises.
- Renovation and refurbishment: using the finance to maintain income generating potential by ensuring that the perceived value of the offer is not eroded.

LEGISLATIVE CONSIDERATIONS

Alongside the financial considerations, proposals must also ensure that they conform to the legislative frameworks that apply to the operation, both in the home state of the parent company and in the jurisdictions of the specific operations.

Even the ownership of land and property is not straightforward. Many countries still impose restrictions on the nationality of people who can be seen to own the property within the country. The basic types of ownership are freehold, where the business owns the land and property outright, or leasehold, where the ownership is specified for a fixed number of years. This ownership can be held by individuals (which legally would include groups; trustees; partnerships; and companies) or corporations (which would include the banks, investment funds, venture capitalists, property groups and other such institutions). There are many restrictions that can impact on ownership and the rights to develop businesses. These include the lenders' terms and conditions and residents' covenants.

There are also significant considerations that impact on the design elements of the proposal. This begins with the initial terms and conditions of the contract that will normally bind the processes of development. Developers need to be aware of the conditions required to secure planning permission and ensure regulatory compliance, which can vary significantly from project to project and location to location.

There may be important considerations about the tendering actions and the remit of professional services. This could lead to an unintended exposure to claims of negligence and it is important to remember that ignorance is no defence to these accusations. Client liabilities, licences, permissions and so on, should be explored fully before any commitments are entered into. It is also important to ensure that any dealings with contractors or sub-contractors are dealt with appropriately and that legally approved and binding 'letters of retainer' are in force. This actually protects both the parent company and the contractor as both could lose out if the specific legal conditions have not been met.

When looking at developing building, hospitality companies must guarantee that they have satisfied all relevant local construction standards. Building regulations vary greatly in different locations – including such important issues as site safety and the different versions of Occupiers Liability Act that can be found in various parts of the world. Businesses must always make sure that they are aware of all the relevant Local Orders, temporary closure notices and other constraints on their development proposal and on their development site.

There is an opportunity to use the architect as the project manager but the issues of responsibility still remain. The appointment and the specification of the responsibilities of the lead and any sub-contractors are matters of great significance. These issues should remain central to the business and the parent company management rather than being simply delegated to local agents. Even the mighty Disney Corporation had to learn this lesson the hard way – as the opening of the theme park in Paris saw one crisis after another, the management learned that when they were going to open the Chinese park in Hong Kong they needed a greater presence in the market and hence had a very senior manager dedicated to the new market and the new development (Clarke and Chen, 2007).

Businesses need to make certain that the financial considerations of the development are clearly and unequivocally specified at the outset of the project. There are many issues surrounding the payments that fall due during the development which should be transparent at the beginning of the operations. If there are staged payments then these should be obvious to all the parties involved. What penalties are involved for late completions – and who is to be held responsible for contractors' and sub-contractors' performances? Penalties are difficult but contracts can also specify bonuses and these are just as difficult if they are not properly managed! Not only should the proposal specify the working assumptions for payments, delivery standards and expectations, but they should also make clear the arbitration framework for any disputes. It is too late to try to do this when the need becomes apparent and the dispute resolution framework should be clarified before any contracts are signed.

STRUCTURE OF A TYPICAL BUSINESS PLAN

We will take you on a journey through the development of a business plan for a new development and show how we have elaborated a simple model of the business plan suggested by the Royal Bank of Scotland (RBS, 2005). This suggests that the business plan should contain the following steps:

- Summary
- The business idea
- Target market
- People
- Marketing and advertising strategy
- Premises and equipment
- Financing and assets
- Financial projections.

The next part of this chapter is structured differently to the others in this book as we are going to use an elaborated case study to demonstrate the different nature of the business plan and the feasibility study. The rest of the

	Section	Topics to be covered
1	Introduction	- Business description - Business formation - Directors - Management team - Business goals/mission - Business philosophies/identity - Geographical markets - Vision of the future
2	Executive summary	- Main objectives - Sales summary - Strategic positioning - Strategic alliances - Licenses - Key advantages - Funds required
3	Marketing	- The product mix - Sales estimates - Analysis current product mix - Competitive research - Market analysis - Marketing goals & strategies - Pricing policy - Advertising & promotion - Sales management - SWOT analysis
4	Historic analysis	- General view - The market position - Balance sheet historic if available
5	The organizational structure	- Administrative organization - Management and personnel - Contingency planning
6	Operations	- identity - location - layout
7	Financial plan	- The investment budget - Statistical data (ratios) - The return on investment - Financial projections
8	Risk management	- Risk reduction - Exit strategy
9	Appendices	- Personal income statement - Other

Source: Vonzerő 2005 BT business consultants

FIGURE 6.4 *Hotel Business Plan template.*

chapter is therefore focussed on the presentation of a business plan drawn up by two of the authors for a small hotel by Lake Balaton in Hungary, which you are invited first to study and then to test with the application of the feasibility study. You should question the assumptions as well as the financial projections – the success of the business proposal will come from the combination of the quantifiable and the qualitative in the development of the hospitality offer.

We would suggest Figure 6.4 provides a template for elaborating the simple model suggested by the RBS, particularly as the Hospitality Business Plan should draw out the specifics of the project as much as possible and these will be elaborated within the following headings.

Case Example

Let us now take you on a journey to the largest inland freshwater lake in Europe, to a peninsula jutting out into the lake and to a large rambling property offering views right along both sides of the lake. This is the introduction to a new hospitality business proposal which was carried out by Attraction and Vonzerő business consultants. The sections follow the template above and are numbered to help you follow through the process. As you read this, take notes as you think about what the owners were trying to say and why. However, you should also read through this and try to see what the owners were not saying and identify areas of the plan where you would require further clarification or additional information before you were willing to commit your own money (or your organisation's money) to the project.

THE PETRALAN BED AND BREAKFAST BUSINESS PLAN

1 Introduction

1.1 Business description

The Petralan Bed and Breakfast (PBB) will be a charming 'panzio' – this unique Hungarian form of accommodation offers flexibility and individuality. It is largely unknown outside of Hungary and therefore we will style our offer as a bed and breakfast (B&B) but it must be remembered that this does not capture the full scope of the proposal. PBB is located in Tihany, with commanding views of the Lake Balaton. The Balaton is well known for its beauty and history and Tihany is one of the recognised attractions for visitors to the Lake (http://balaton.gotohungary.co.uk/).

Hungary offers attractive investment opportunities as land prices are very low compared with much of the rest of Europe. However, it should be noted that the location selected for this proposal is the most expensive in Hungary outside of the capital city, Budapest. This is both a deterrent as there are higher initial costs to be covered by the development, but if the development fails there is a higher retained value in the property than if it had been located anywhere else and particularly anywhere removed from the Lake. Advertisements are currently in place for village property within 15 kilometres of the Lake for as little as 1 euro per square metre, where Tihany would command prices of up to 300 euro per square metre or even more. The B&B will be set up as a limited company of the owners, who will continue to live in part of the buildings as their home. Their home is the heart of the entire experience. There will be up to 14 rooms to choose from. The facility has a wonderfully welcoming sitting room where the guests can gather, private patio and gardens, and the Highwaymen Centre will also be developed on the property.

1.2 Business formation

The opportunity has arisen to convert these historic properties at a time which coincides with the owners having sufficient resources to finance the restoration and conversion of the premises. It will bring to fruition a long held dream of the owners, who have worked together in different roles for a long time and feel confident in putting their relationship to the test of this business development.

1.3 Directors

The company will be solely owned by Petra Nemeth and Alan Clarke. There is no intention at the present time to seek to extend ownership or involve other directors in the business.

1.4 Management team

PBB will be able to deliver its strong customer-centred business model because of its management. The owners have worked their way through the industry to reach the point where they can offer such an experience. Between them they have over 40 years' experience of working in the hotel and travel industries. They have academic experience – both in terms of their own qualifications and in leading training for the industry. We will also utilise our close connections to the major television production companies and invite the 'celebrity chefs' to help us develop the Highwaymen Centre – both as an eating experience also as a training institute.

PBB will be able to capitalise on its location immediately and will become profitable by month three and will return a profit by the end of the first year.

1.5 Business goals

The objectives of the PBB for the first five years are:

- To exceed customer's expectations with the excellence of our hospitality.

- To continually improve the quality of our service standards.
- To increase the number of visitor nights every week throughout the year.
- To increase our number of clients by 10% per year.
- To achieve levels of 50% occupancy in 2012.
- To develop a sustainable B&B business.
- To develop a sustainable Highwaymen Centre.
- To operate as a sustainable business accredited by Green Globe awards.

1.5.1 Mission

PBB will be the preferred choice for accommodation for discerning customers when they visit the Lake. PBB will exceed the expectations of our guests and colleagues by providing a contemporary, world class experience, through continuous commitment to the development of ourselves and product to achieve maximum growth and profitability.

1.6 Business philosophies and identity

PBB is committed to a customer-centred business philosophy. We believe that exceeding the expectations of our customers is the key to success and we will strive to continuously improve our serve quality and delivery in order to achieve this goal.

1.6.1 Business identity

PBB will have a strong identity based on both the tangible and intangible aspects of our offer. We will promote a strong image of the business and use this throughout all of our communications and marketing. Moreover we will build into this our reputation for excellence and quality. PBB will become widely recognised and the intangible qualities will support the building of this identity through direct experience and word-of-mouth reporting.

1.7 Geographical markets

PBB will attract customers from the local area (domestic visitors), travellers (near international visitors) and tourists (international visitors). The Balaton is located at the heart of Hungary and therefore makes it easy to target Hungarian markets. Hungary itself is at the heart of Hungary and has many historic connections with the surrounding countries which allow for recognition in the market. Finally the growth of international tourism has been helped by the popularity of Budapest and the growth of its airport but we have also seen the opening of the Balaton Airport, situated less than one hour's drive away from Tihany.

1.8 Vision of the future

PBB will become the destination of choice for the discerning visitor to the Balaton. We will delight our customers by meeting and exceeding their expectations. Our buildings and furnishings will be exceptional and our service quality will continue to surprise. When people talk of the Balaton experience, they will single out PBB for special mention.

2 Executive summary

2.1 Main objectives

The objectives of the PBB for the first five years are:

- To exceed customer's expectations with the excellence of our hospitality.
- To continually improve the quality of our service standards.
- To increase the number of visitor nights every week throughout the year.
- To increase our number of clients by 10% per year.
- To achieve levels of 50% occupancy in 2012.
- To develop a sustainable B&B business.
- To develop a sustainable Highwaymen Centre.
- To operate as a sustainable business accredited by Green Globe awards.

2.1.1 Keys to success

In order to succeed, the PBB will strive to achieve the following goals:

- Position the PBB as the best accommodation in the region for tourists.
- Offer unique experiences and service to our guests.
- Build strong market position among the local patrons within a 200-kilometre radius.
- Develop an international reputation for our excellence.
- Maintain sound financial management of the venture.
- Link into the strongest referral engines and Accommodation Association engines for room bookings.
- Automate our full digital calendar and room night booking system onto our Website.

2.1.2 Monitoring

- To exceed customer's expectations with the excellence of our hospitality and the quality of our service standards.
- To increase the number of visitor nights every week throughout the year.
- To increase our number of clients by 10% per year to achieve levels of 50% occupancy in 2012.
- To develop a sustainable business, surviving off its own cash flow, exceeding set data. Customer Comment Cards should score 90 or above on average.
- To develop a sustainable Highwaymen Centre which survives off of its own cash flow, changes exhibits and contributes to the Bed and Breakfast operation by increased demographic draw. Customer Comment Cards should score 85 or above on average.
- To operate as a sustainable business – spanning water, power and emissions - becoming a beacon in the region for others.
- To contribute to the community in a loving and giving manner allowing us to preserve our community. This will be measured by awards received.

2.1.3 Milestones

The PBB will have several milestones early on:

- Business plan completion. This will be done as a road map for the organisation. While we do not need a business plan to raise extended capital, it will be an indispensable tool for the ongoing performance and improvement of the company.
- Joining the different associations.
- Completion of the facility renovations.
- Our 100th client.

2.2 Sales summary

Sales forecast

The home has 14 different rooms. December will be used for furnishing rooms and adding safety features. By March 2010 the buildings will be finished and advertising will have begun. We will have joined a number of Accommodation Associations promoting online bookings.

Scenario planning suggests that we should look to first-year occupancy rates of between 10% and 25% with the median of this study at 18.5%. We do not believe that we would have lower than predicted occupancy (at the low end of 10%) or higher (at the high end of 25%). In our research we can demonstrate that we can confidently expect to be nearer the higher end of these rates. For the financial calculations, we have been cautious and predicted first-year occupancy at lower than even the median. Accordingly, our prediction starting in month one, March 2010 is based on 15% occupancy. From there we predict a 10% increase month-by-month and 10% year-by-year.

The following assumptions explain the sales forecasts for rooms and suites.

Room night @ 110 per night (5) (23 p/month) 365/15% = 54.75 × 5 rooms = 273.75 nights per yr/12=

Suite night @ 175 per night (2) (9 p/month) 365/15% = 54.75 × 2 rooms = 109.5 nights per yr/12=

Sales forecast

	2010	2011	2012
Sales			
Room night @ £110 per night	£53,653	£59,018	£64,920
Suite night @ £175 per night	£34,151	£37,566	£41,323
Museum & Tour of Mansion @ £3 pp	£6415	£6600	£6800
Total sales	£94,219	£103,184	£113,043
Direct cost of sales	2010	2011	2012
Room night @ £20 cost	£5520	£5796	£6085
Suite night @ £30 cost	£3240	£3402	£3572
Museum and Tour of Mansion	£480	£500	£520
Subtotal direct cost of sales	£9240	£9698	£10,177

2.3 Strategic positioning

The PBB is a unique offer in the Balaton market and rare anywhere in the world. The positioning requires us to establish a foothold in the elite travel markets within Hungary, throughout Europe and internationally. This competitive position is based upon excellence – excellence of location, excellence of facilities and excellence of service.

We believe that even in a recession there will continue to be a market for luxury and indulgence. PBB will become the home for those discerning customers who want to enjoy the delights of the Balaton from a base of comfort and delight.

2.4 Strategic alliances

PBB is an independent venture but we have entered into alliances with the local Chambers of Commerce and the Accommodation Associations.

We are also developing alliances with two of the finest wineries on the North Shore of the Balaton to showcase their wines. Similarly alliances will be established with food producers locally to ensure that supplies of the finest and freshest foods are available.

2.5 Licences

We will undertake all the necessary health and safety, food preparation and accommodation standard checks that are required to operate the PBB.

We will seek licenses to sell alcohol and we will apply for a performing rights license.

We will go beyond what is normally required in this section of a business plan and seek licences from Green Globe – about the sustainability of our operations – and from ISO – to assure the quality of our practices and processes.

2.6 Key advantages competitive edge

The PBB's two competitive advantages which are:

Commitment to customer-centred service

Anyone at a B&B should reasonably expect good service, but we believe that there are ways of setting yourself apart. This will be done through the unrelenting pursuit of personal attention. In the area there are no B&Bs that offer such outstanding service. The customer-centred approach adds a positive aspect to the B&B experience.

Uniqueness and beauty of the facility

The PBB will be housed in the buildings where the owners live. One unique aspect of the PBB is the setting within Tihany. To compliment this setting, the PBB will have a large outside patio allowing guests to spend relaxing time outside with the magnificent views of the lake, marina and the Balaton Highlands. The full glory of the Balaton can be glimpsed on this Website http://www.balaton-tourism.hu/public/balaton – the reality, of course, is even better and the experience of the PBB will transcend even that.

2.7 Funds required

We are seeking an additional £140,000. The money will be used to pay for the refurbishment and meet the start-up costs of the operation.

3 Marketing

3.1 The product mix

PBB offers both a simple and a complex product mix of offers:

1. Accommodation in rooms and suites
2. Restaurant covers
3. Highwaymen Training Centre

This can be further differentiated with the offer of special evenings and special events.

3.2 Sales estimates

As explored above, we believe that realistic estimates of trading are:

Sales forecast

	2010	2011	2012
Sales			
Room night @ £110 per night	£53,653	£59,018	£64,920
Suite night @ £175 per night	£34,151	£37,566	£41,323
Museum and Tour of Mansion @ £3 pp	£6,415	£6,600	£6,800
Total sales	£94,219	£103,184	£113,043
Direct cost of sales	2010	2011	2012
Room night @ £20 cost	£5,520	£5,796	£6,085
Suite night @ £30 cost	£3,240	£3,402	£3,572
Museum and Tour of Mansion	£480	£500	£520
Subtotal direct cost of sales	£9,240	£9,698	£10,177

3.3 Analysis of current product and services mix

The PBB is a small, attractive and well-resourced B&B that offers travellers and vacationers a relaxed, village setting for a weekend getaway, change of scenery, family occasions, or any other motivation that they can think of for visiting. PBB has a large central sitting room, an upstairs covered patio with a fine view of the Lake and outside gardens that will allow our guests to socialise. The customers will receive the personal attentions of the owners, who will meet any need a traveller has. We believe that the accommodation will stand out amongst the neighbouring competition and be truly remarkable. Our food and wines will be outstanding. The quality of the service which supports both the accommodation and the restaurant will be unequalled.

The romantic, the business type, the luxury seeker and the curious will be welcome to experience the delights of the PBB.

3.4 Competitive research

We have researched tourism in Hungary very thoroughly, liaising with the national tourism board (http://www.hungarytourism.hu/) and studied the Balaton even more closely. We are aware of the trends in visitor patterns and believe that they indicate that the time is right for an offer of quality and distinction by the Lake. Tihany is the most visited and most spectacular of the tourism destinations on the Balaton, and although this means that property prices are higher in Tihany than anywhere else in Hungary outside of Budapest, we believe that this is the correct location for such a development.

Although B&Bs have been firmly established in Europe for years, they were introduced in the United States in the late 1960s. There are now more than 20,000 B&Bs, up from about 2000 in 1979. A sign of a maturing industry is the increasing average number of rooms per property, increasing occupancy rates and increasing number of associations and support services; i.e., national, state and regional associations setting standards. There are now professional newsletters, travel publications, guidebooks and vendors catering to small lodges. The rewards of being a B&Bs host include meeting people, adding income, gaining independence and an enjoyable way of life, and perhaps, restoring an old building. Research suggests that personality, distinctive and personalised hospitality, standards of excellence and creative marketing can make a significant difference.

3.5 Market analysis – competition and buying patterns

Competition comes in several forms:

Other B&Bs

- Typically B&Bs have a set of unique features, something that makes them stand out.

- Some B&Bs will create uniqueness down to the level of different rooms within the B&B. We will be doing that. The size of B&Bs ranges from one or two room (traditionally called a home stay) to a country inn with 30 rooms.
- On average most B&Bs have only a couple of rooms and are often booked up in advance. Particularly during special events, demand outstrips supply for the B&Bs.
- The B&Bs differentiate themselves by personal service offerings and the general ambiance of the Inn.
- Guests of B&Bs are looking not just for a room to sleep in but the whole experience in staying in a lovely setting, with interesting people to chat with and people present to pamper them in any way possible.

Hotels/motels

- These facilities are generally bland compared to B&Bs.
- The rooms are typically the same throughout the facility (unlike B&Bs where each room is typically different). The guests of hotels generally use the hotel as a place to stay at night.
- The operator will usually see the guest when they check in and when they check out. This differs from a B&B where the guests are encouraged to spend time in communal rooms and socialise with the operators and the other guests.
- Breakfasts, if included, are sparse. The typical guests are looking for a room to stay in at night and not much more than that.

3.5.1 The market analysis

Within the hospitality industry, the PBB will be competing with hotels as there are no other similar B&Bs in the general area. The PBB facilities are certainly more distinctive than the other hotels in the area. All of the hotels in the area are either fairly standard chain hotels or very small family owned properties. The PBB is a beautiful, elegant home – on a quiet street, in a small town, with superb views over the Lake.

The PBB has different target groups it will attract. The first are people from the region that just want to get away for the weekend. They may have activities planned for the weekend around the Lake or just choose to relax in a comfortable setting. The second group are travellers who are coming from further afield and want a comfortable and elegant break. Others will seek out the quality experience promised by our premises and the reputation for fine foods and wines that will develop. Other customers will come who fall outside of these groups, but this classification depicts where we will target our marketing efforts.

3.5.2 Market analysis summary

We will target an elite market within Hungary and the neighbouring countries. We will also aim to build upon the reputation of Tihany in the Netherlands and Germany to attract those customers who have been drifting away from the Balaton because of the perceived lack of quality.

3.6 Marketing goals, strategies and market segmentation

Our customers can be broadly divided into three groups (please note it is possible to divide the customers in to much smaller groups, but we have chosen not to):

1. **Weekend-getaway customers**. These people are from the region and are looking to get away from their life so they come to the PBB to be pampered and escape.

2. **Travellers/vacationers**. These people, for whatever reason, vacationing around the Lake and prefer to stay in a B&B rather than a hotel/motel.

3. **Experience Excellent Dining**. These people will want to visit to experience the service provided. They also will be interested in the historical information, collections and other culinary items relating to the highwaymen and the history of the Balaton.

Market analysis

		2010	2011	2012	2011	2012	
Potential customers	Growth						CAGR
Travellers/Vacationers	9%	964,982	1,051,830	1,146,495	1,249,680	1,362,151	9.00%
Weekend-getaway customers	9%	241,245	262,957	286,623	312,419	340,537	9.00%
Training Centre and tour	8%	1,200	1,296	1,400	1,512	1,633	8.01%
Special evenings and events	5%	24,124	25,330	26,597	27,927	29,323	5.00%
Total	8.92%	1,231,551	1,341,413	1,461,115	1,591,538	1,733,644	8.92%

3.6.1 Target market segment strategy

The PBB intends to target these three customer groups as they make up the largest population of people who utilise B&B's. The PBB has a three pronged strategy that will work for all these groups:

- **Association membership and advertising**. A large number of visitors will look to regional B&B associations for information about the different B&Bs in the area. Most associations publish a guide to the local B&Bs and the PBB wants to be in this guide. One of the other perks of membership is visibility on the associations' Website with a link to ours. Additionally, we will be a member of many Chambers of Commerce because people will typically inquire with the local Chambers when planning a vacation and they will offer advice to potential contacts.
- **Website**. The PBB will have a full-service Website that allows the visitor to view the B&B, read details about what it has to offer, provide information on regional activities and even allow the visitor to book a reservation. With the growing use of the Internet, the Web has become an indispensable tool for planning vacations to areas that are not close enough to check out in person.
- **Other Advertising**. In many rest areas and on billboards, as well as lifestyle magazines such as food and travel journals.
- **Events**. Host Balaton history and Highwaymen themed events on the grounds.

3.6.2 Marketing strategy

The retail marketing strategy of the PBB centres on creating a strong business identity that clearly defines our market niche in terms that benefit our customer and which our customers want to see. Specific strategies that will be used include:

1. **Grand Opening**
2. **Press Releases** – The local papers and magazines have offered to run releases and/or stories concerning the opening of the PBB. We will also use the above media to run news about the monthly art events.
3. **Print Ads** – Keeping the PBB name in front of the customer while getting established will be necessary. We plan on running limited space ads in the local newspapers to keep our image, name, Website and phone number in front of the consumer. We may present

special issues within the advertisements to generate revenue from the featured partner.

4. **Gourmet Dinners and Guest Speakers** – The dining experience will be beyond compare.

5. **Monthly Events** – Focussing on Balaton history and foods. The legends of the Balaton and the Highwaymen.

6. **Special Events** – Valentine's day and other celebrations will be marked by special celebrations.

7. **Art Gallery** – The PBB will feature the work of local artists, displayed throughout the buildings. These will be for sale. Also, each month on the second Wednesday, we will host a wine (non-alcoholic), cider and cheese night with historic unveiling of 'this month's work of art.'

8. **Designer Postcard** – We will be holding a local contest for students to design a postcard for our guests to eventually buy.

9. **Apparel** – We know several people in the area who produce embroidered apparel such as robes but we see a wider line with fleeces, polo shirts and so on. A line of premium PBB apparel could be designed and produced in very small runs to reduce inventory costs. These can be sold or given away with qualifying purchases to further establish the PBB identity.

10. **Word-of-Mouth** – By giving first-time customers great service and a fair price, the word is sure to spread. Also, the many industry and business contacts that we already have in the area will prove to be most beneficial in spreading the word.

All marketing decisions with regard to specific media choices, frequency, size and expenditures will be conducted on an ongoing basis with careful considerations of returns generated.

3.6.3 Strategy and implementation summary

The PBB will be using advertising and membership in associations with drive prospective customers. They will also use their Websites as a complete source of information about the B&B. The owner will then turn these leads into customers through unsurpassed attentiveness in one-on-one phone inquiries/conversations.

3.7 Pricing policy

PBB will be one of the most expensive places to stay on the Balaton. This is a deliberate strategy as we believe this market is poorly catered for. Our prices compare with the larger hotels and the better restaurants in Veszprém and other destinations.

We believe that we can not only justify the cost of the accommodation at £110 per night with suites at £175 per night, but also that our target markets will recognise the value in this offer.

3.8 Advertising and promotion

Importance of Image, Name, and Word-of-Mouth:

We will use the already high profile and distinctive imagery of Tihany as a basis to launch the PBB. We will run the two together in promotion and advertising, establishing the distinctive logo of PBB on the solid ground that is the established reputation of Tihany.

We recognise the value of word-of-mouth advertising and we will be exploring the established networks that we belong to and which we can attach to.

In the first year we want to make sure that PBB is a constant topic of conversations and that what we offer takes this increased awareness and converts it into active interest in visiting PBB.

3.9 Sales management and sales strategy

The PBB sales strategy will be multi-pronged:

Personal attention to inquiries

It is the owner's strategy to be willing to spend a fair amount of time on the phone with prospective clients. While most accommodation providers will be pleasant on the phone and willing to answer questions, they often give the impression that the sooner they can get off the phone, the sooner they can get back to the 'real' work that the inquiry interrupted. We believe that the more time we can spend on the phone with inquiries; the more likely we will be able to turn them into customers.

Web plan summary

Using firms from Veszprém and Balatonfured, we will build an e-commerce enabled platform and Website for the PBB. This Website will encompass award winning photography and other work from local artists to create an impression of what life at PBB will be like. We aim to make the site simple yet elegant.

SuperInn will be used as the advanced room booking software with full credit card integration.

Search Engine strategies will be provided for linking into 2000+ search engines (inclusive of top shelf AOL, MSN, Yahoo!, Google, etc.) via WebPosition Gold.

Some limited Google AdWords will be used. Overture Networks SEO strategies created by Max Nevis will be employed.

Local linking will take place as will linkages with the Hungarian trade associations and tourism Websites. We will also join Websites promoting boutique hotels as we can see parallels with their target markets and ours.

Website marketing strategy

Market strategy in an Internet room-booking business depends on recognition of expertise by the consumer. For the PBB, it will start with our existing customer base, informing them of our Internet presence and encouraging their word-of-mouth recommendations to others. Further awareness will be heightened by utilising search engine marketing, banner advertising and affiliates.

We believe that over 95% of the potential clients have Web access and 80% use the Web to research their vacations and therefore we will develop a very detailed Website. This usage is compelling enough to have a comprehensive Website that offers enough information to allow the visitor to make a decision to stay at the PBB. The Website will have 3D walk-through tours, allowing people to see the different bedrooms as well as common areas. Online pricing and reservations are also available as well as a resource page that details the different activities in the area and links to the sources for more local information.

While we would like to encourage people to telephone with questions, where they do not they will be able to answer – almost – all their questions from the Website.

Sales strategy regarding food and wines

We will try to convey a sense of place at the PBB by making use of the abundance of wonderful products from in and around the Balaton, developing what the French call a 'cuisine de terroir.' We will offer many of the traditional dishes we grew up with and make them attractive to a new audience while keeping their soul intact – building a sort of culinary bridge between the past and future. We recognise that Hungarian cuisine was one of the first examples of fusion cooking with the numbers of 'visitors' that crossed through the country. We will continue that tradition in looking to offer new versions of old favourites and bringing guest chefs and recipes from around the region.

3.10 SWOT analysis

The SWOT analysis provides us with an opportunity to examine the internal strengths and weaknesses the PBB must address. It also allows us to examine the opportunities presented to us, as well as potential threats.

Strengths	Weaknesses
Location	Offer unknown to the public
Perception of area	Accessibility
Buildings	Not in Budapest
Staff expertise	Cost of service
Staff attitudes	Poor signage
Quality of foods and wines	High property prices
In-house graphics production	
Contacts with local artists	
Contacts with local wine and food suppliers	

Opportunities	Threats
Create strong image and identity	Rival accommodation developments
Create ambassadors from our visitors	Rival training offers
Media linkages	Popularising of the Lake
Training developments	
Develop tours	

Competitive Advantages

The PBB has two distinct competitive advantages that differentiate it from the competition. The first is the commitment to excellence – our continued and continuous attention to detail and customer service. The owners recognise that our mission is to ensure that our customers have the finest experiences during their stay. We believe our selection of home made and locally sourced products will satisfy the most demanding appetites. We can offer the gourmet banquet and the medical dietary support unheard of in Hungary.

The second competitive advantage is the unique location and property. The PBB is so wonderful in part because of the historical buildings – which will become a magical place to behold and stay at. We will compliment the furnishings with an environment where the history comes alive, through the stories and the tastes presented to our visitors.

4 Historic analysis

This is a new venture and therefore there is no historical evidence to draw on. We believe that our market research and the performance of other businesses around Lake Balaton suggest that the PBB will be a success.

5 The organisational structure

5.1 Management summary

The PBB is owned and operated by the owners and their families. They bring with them formal and informal experiences that will inform and guide the philosophy of the business. With degrees in hospitality and many years experience of running bars, restaurants and working with guests, the business model is customer centred. As one of us has a background in accountancy, we will also manage and review the performance of the business on an ongoing basis, although we will employ accountants to file the official returns.

5.2 Personnel plan

The owners will share the responsibilities for running PBB between them.

They will oversee the Website and manage the bookings.

They will run the restaurant.

They will organise and run training events.

They will liaise with the media.

Initially the owners will continue working for their current employer, and will not take a salary from PBB until September, towards the end of the high tourist season.

They will handle the bulk of the day-to-day operations, front desk, and bookkeeping. One will begin taking a salary in month three to help to assure positive cash balances in the early stages of operation.

PBB will also employ part-time help to assist with housekeeping, landscaping, and maintenance chores. There is a wealth of talented and keen potential staff at the local University of Pannonia and other training colleges.

5.3 Contingency planning

We are totally committed to the vision of the PBB that we can see nothing but the success of the proposal.

We have calculated the financial plans on a cautious low estimate of occupancy and restaurant business.

If occupancy falls, reductions in price may be considered and offers such as three nights for the price of two introduced (a less obvious price cut).

Both owners are maintaining their current jobs and so there is a source of continued funding independent of the success of the PBB.

We believe that there are also alternative markets, in different countries, which we have not prioritised that could reinforce the growth of the business.

6 Hotel operations

6.1 Hotel identity

The PBB, located overlooking Lake Balaton on our beautiful peninsula, will offer a luxurious, quaint accommodation for people to enjoy. We will build on the existing reputation for quality and beauty that has already become associated with Tihany – (http://www.planetware.com/hungary/tihany-h-zl-tih.htm).

The PBB will have fourteen individual rooms all en-suite, a central sitting room which will serve as an area for socialising, a garden patio, outdoor BBQ area and the Highwaymen Centre (housed in a former out building) for its guests. Two of the guest rooms can be joined to form the Daniel Suite with a private kitchen, living room and outdoor sitting area and a separate entrance to offer a unique set of experiences within the framework of the PBB.

6.2 Hotel location

PBB is situated at the top of the peninsula, adjacent to the Abbey and with magnificent views across the Lake. We are located within casual walking distance from the town and for the more energetic, walking to the Lake is possible. This can be seen on the map at http://www.tihany.hu/en_terkep.htm.

We are on a quiet street with little traffic. The adjacent properties are of a matching elegant nature and charm up and down the street. The entire property next to us is owned by the church and therefore reasonably quiet.

We will benefit from the established festival programmes but these will not outshine or inconvenience our offer and our guests.

6.3 Hotel layout

The property unfolds behind the surrounding walls to reveal a central building and two outbuildings. In the central building you can find the reception area, the sitting room to the right and the dining area to the left. The main kitchens are situated on the ground floor to the right of the building. This will allow easy transfer to and from the Highwaymen Training Centre. The main building is also where the owners' accommodation is to be found, to the rear of the property. Below the building there are extensive cellars, which have been refurbished to provide excellent climate controlled food and wine storage facilities.

To the left of the main building is a two storey building which has been refurbished to provide fourteen en-suite rooms.

To the right of the main building, the old workshops have been converted into the Highwaymen Training Centre with demonstration kitchens, a small auditorium and a dining room.

7 The financial plan

7.1 Start-up summary

The PBB start-up expenses include:

- Home office equipment including: computer, copier, fax machine, extra telephone lines, and office furniture.
- Wireless Internet network access for guests.
- Website creation.
- Advertising/association dues for the several B&B associations.
- Furnishings and linens for individual guest rooms.
- Pest Control Program set up.
- Tableware (China, Silverware, and glassware).
- Signage.
- Safety Programs (Fire) (Anti-slip).

We have budgeted £32,000 for initial, functional yet tasteful furnishings.

Bed and Room Linen Expenses.

Comforters	£700
Sheets	£420
Blankets	£350
Pillows	£300
Towels	£1200
Dust ruffles	£140
Robes	£1680
Total	£4790

Equipment and Furnishings Expenses Breakdown.

Computers	£2800
Computer accessories	£300
Computer printers	£513
Poster printer	£800
Router	£148
Networking cables	£156
Furniture	£13,453
Lamps	£150
Artwork/decorations	£1846
Accessories	£1273
Highwaymen culinary collection	£1821
Kitchen equipment	£1400
Telephone upgrade	£180
Total	£24,840

The owners will directly invest £25,000 in starting up the business. We plan on acquiring additional direct funding via a bank and backed by an Economic Development loan package.

Start-up requirements	
Start-up expenses	
Legal	£1260
Insurance	£2903
Licenses and Permits	£320
B&B Associations & linking	£2400
Retrofit of premises	£3000
–	£0
Total Start-up Expenses	£9883

Continued

Start-up assets	
Cash required	£24,000
Start-up inventory	£2500
Other current assets	£13,667
Long-term assets	£56,000
Total assets	£96,167
Total requirements	£106,050

Start-up funding

Start-up expenses to fund	£9883
Start-up assets to fund	£96,167
Total funding required	£106,050

Assets

Non-cash Assets from Start-up	£72,167
Cash Requirements from Start-up	£24,000
Additional Cash Raised	£0
Cash Balance on Starting Date	£24,000
Total Assets	£96,167

Liabilities and Capital

Liabilities

Current borrowing	£0
Long-term liabilities	£81,210
Accounts payable (outstanding bills)	£0
Other current liabilities (interest-free)	£0
Total liabilities	£81,210

Capital

Planned investment	
Owner investment	£24,840
Other	£0
Additional investment requirement	£0
Total planned investment	£24,840
Loss at start-up (start-up expenses)	(£9883)
Total capital	£14,957
Total Capital and Liabilities	£96,167
Total Funding	£106,050

7 Financial plan

The following sections will detail important financial information.

Important assumptions

The following table highlights some of the important financial assumptions for the PBB.

General Assumptions			
	2010	2011	2012
Plan month	1	2	3
Current interest rate	6.00%	6.00%	6.00%
Long-term interest rate	6.00%	6.00%	6.00%
Tax rate	13.00%	13.00%	13.00%
Other	0	0	0

7.1 Projected profit and loss

The following table indicates projected, modest profits.

Pro-forma profit and loss			
	2010	2011	2012
Sales	£94,219	£1,03,184	£1,13,043
Direct cost of sales	£9,240	£9,698	£10,177
Other	£10,320	£12,320	£14,320
Total cost of sales	£19,560	£22,018	£24,497
Gross margin	£74,659	£81,166	£88,546
Gross margin %	79.24%	78.66%	78.33%
Expenses			
Payroll	£0	£0	£0
Sales & marketing & other expenses	£6,500	£10,000	£10,000
Depreciation	£1,200	£1,200	£1,200
Annual Web and Assoc. fees	£1,200	£1,600	£1,700
Utilities	£7,200	£7,600	£7,800
Payroll tax	£0	£0	£0
Insurance	£3,600	£4,800	£5,000
Total operating expenses	£19,700	£25,200	£25,700

Continued

Profit before interest and taxes	£54,959	£55,966	£62,846
EBITDA	£56,159	£57,166	£64,046
Interest expense	£4,639	£4,225	£3,793
Taxes incurred	£6,542	£6,726	£7,677
Net profit	£43,779	£45,015	£51,376
Net profit/sales	46.46%	43.63%	45.45%

Projected cash flow

The following indicates projected cash flow.

Pro-forma cash flow			
	2010	2011	2012
Cash received			
Cash from operations			
Cash sales	£94,219	£1,03,184	£1,13,043
Subtotal cash from operations	£94,219	£103,184	£113,043
Additional cash received			
Sales Tax, VAT, HST/GST received	£12,248	£13,414	£14,696
New current borrowing	£0	£0	£0
New other liabilities (interest-free)	£0	£0	£0
New long-term liabilities	£0	£0	£0
Sales of other current assets	£0	£0	£0
Sales of long-term assets	£0	£0	£0
New investment received	£0	£0	£0
Subtotal Cash Received	£106,468	£116,598	£127,739
Expenditures	2010	2011	2012
Expenditures from operations			
Cash spending	£0	£0	£0
Bill payments	£45,254	£56,845	£60,357
Subtotal spent on operations	£45,254	£56,845	£60,357
Additional cash spent			
Sales Tax, VAT, HST/GST paid out	£12,248	£13,414	£14,696
Principal repayment of current borrowing	£0	£0	£0
Other liabilities principal repayment	£0	£0	£0
Long-term liabilities principal repayment	£7,200	£7,200	£7,200
Purchase other current assets	£0	£0	£0

Continued

Purchase long-term assets	£0	£0	£0
Dividends	£0	£0	£0
Subtotal cash spent	£64,703	£77,459	£82,253
Net cash flow	£41,765	£39,139	£45,486
Cash balance	£65,765	£104,904	£150,390

Projected balance sheet

The projected balance sheet indicates that large amounts of funds are going to be raised initially. This will effectively be a contingency fund. We will look to place this money in a high interest bearing account that allows flexible access to the funds.

Pro forma balance sheet			
	2010	2011	2012
Assets			
Current assets			
Cash	£65,765	£104,904	£150,390
Inventory	£847	£889	£933
Other current assets	£13,667	£13,667	£13,667
Total current assets	£80,279	£119,460	£164,990
Long-term assets			
Long-term assets	£56,000	£56,000	£56,000
Accumulated depreciation	£1,200	£2,400	£3,600
Total long-term assets	£54,800	£53,600	£52,400
Total assets	£135,079	£173,060	£217,390
Liabilities and capital	2010	2011	2012
Current liabilities			
Accounts payable	£2,333	£2,499	£2,653
Current borrowing	£0	£0	£0
Other current liabilities	£0	£0	£0
Subtotal current liabilities	£2,333	£2,499	£2,653
Long-term liabilities	£74,010	£66,810	£59,610
Total liabilities	£76,343	£69,309	£62,263
Paid-in capital	£24,840	£24,840	£24,840
Retained earnings	(£9883)	£33,896	£78,911
Earnings	£43,779	£45,015	£51,376

Continued

Total Capital	£58,736	£103,751	£155,128
Total liabilities and capital	£135,079	£173,060	£217,390
Net worth	£58,736	£103,751	£155,128

7.2 Break-even analysis

The Break-even Analysis indicates the monthly revenue PBB must exceed to break even. This will fluctuate as the business plan is recalculated in the first twelve months of clearer estimates for usage of utilities and advertising costs.

Break-even Analysis	
Monthly revenue Break-even	£1,820
Assumptions:	
Average percent variable cost	10%
Estimated monthly fixed cost	£1642

8 Risk management

8.1 Risk reduction

We have sought to reduce risks in two ways.

Firstly, we have been actively developing links with suppliers and travel agencies over a number of months and believe that these relationships are based on friendships as well as sound business contracts.

Secondly, we have conducted extensive market research in the area of Lake Balaton and in some of the target markets and can ground our offer on the findings of this research. We believe our preparation will mean that there are fewer surprises in the first years of operation than new ventures might expect to face.

We believe that the hands-on approach of the owners will allow us to react quickly and positively to any emergent risks. Professionalism can help to contain the risk and move towards a rapid implementation of a positive solution.

8.2 Exit strategy

The PBB cannot be envisaged with an exit strategy. It is the realisation of a dream and will succeed. However in the worst case scenarios, we have designed the following responses:

Accommodation occupancy fails – switch emphasis to restaurants and training. If the accommodation fails completely, the space can be converted to extend the art gallery space and become a gallery for local artists, supported by a high quality café.

Restaurant fails – the restaurant can be scaled back to providing breakfast for guests and the space reused for the gallery. The breakfast space would then serve as the café for the gallery.

Training Centre fails – the business could be closed down and the facility converted to offer more accommodation. If the accommodation is also failing, the buildings can be converted into ateliers to promote the work of local artists with dedicated workshops and studios.

If everything fails, we will continue to live there as our homes and seek to re-position and re-launch the venture. If this does not prove possible, the high property prices in Tihany will mean that the buildings and the refurbishing of the outbuildings will provide a high residual value in the properties themselves.

9 Appendices

The outline suggests that here we reveal our personal income statements, which for the purposes of this exercise we will not do! Trust us – we have a reasonable guaranteed income stream but we are not rich, otherwise we would not be seeking external finance for this project!

Activity

Consult the notes you have taken about this proposal and consider your thoughts. What is your first reaction? Are you sympathetic to the proposal – or hostile? How would you justify your reaction?

Compare your reactions with the requirements outlined below for the Feasibility Study.

THE FEASIBILITY STUDY: CONCEPT AND IMPORTANCE

The concept of feasibility studies is very important in business development. This is where the good ideas of potential entrepreneurs are given harsh tests in order to establish whether the idea is worth funding or likely to produce a solid return on the investment. As Ransley and Ingram (2000: 58) state, the purpose of feasibility studies is "...to provide an objective, independent appraisal of a development opportunity (or an acquisition opportunity, in the case of an existing opportunity) and sufficient information for the client (and others involved in the project) to make a decision as to whether the project should proceed and, if so, in what form."

Feasibility studies – objectives

This means that it is possible (Ransley and Ingram, 2004: 60) to see that the feasibility study should attempt:

- To evaluate the proposed business environment
- To assess the existing supply and demand and hence the market requirements
- To inform the potential lenders or investors
- To provide evidence in support of planning applications
- To assist in prior negotiations with management companies and other relevant agencies

The feasibility study process

It is possible to break the feasibility study process into a series of stages and these are presented in Figure 6.5.

One of the key issues confronting businesses is how to conduct the feasibility study, as either an internal or an external process. There are pros and cons for both options, mostly focussed around the issues of whether or not the business has the capacity to undertake the study. There may be significant limitations on the business's own capabilities in terms of available expertise of staff, the time of staff and the involvement of the staff with the specific proposal. These arguments can be summarised as follows in Figure 6.6.

KEY FEASIBILITY CONSIDERATIONS

We can now take you through the constituent components of the feasibility study and would urge you to bear these thoughts in mind as you appraise the proposal you have already read. You should consider:

- The proposed design concept – can you see the potential in the proposal?
- Proposed site – are there sufficient arguments to justify the choice of site?

Preliminary Concept
|
Rough Costings
|
Feasibility Study
|
Revise Concept
|
Identify Location and Site
|
Revise Costings
|
Customer Numbers and Expenditure Projections
|
Financial Evaluation
|
Identify Funding Sources
|
Detailed Design and development plan

Source: adopted from Swarbrooke, 2002, p. 124

FIGURE 6.5 *The Feasibility Study Process.*

	Advantages	Disadvantages
In-house	• Understand the organisation's aims and objectives • Low financial costs	• Lack objectivity • High time cost • Can be restricted by attitudes and prejudices • Can be slow as not the only job staff have to do
Consultants	• Objective • Expertise of specialist staff • Can use experience gained from other projects • Can be quick in that dedicated staff time can be given to the project	• Lack understanding of the organisation's aims and objectives • High financial cost • Can simply put forward

Source: Swarbrooke, 2002, p. 125

FIGURE 6.6 *Advantages and disadvantages of carrying out feasibility studies in-house or through consultants.*

- Transportation/access – can you see the logistical aspects of the proposal making the development successful?
- Existing supply – is the proposal sufficiently different to create a new pattern of demand or does it meet a well-documented gap in the provision?
- Competition – what are the local competitors and where does the proposal sit in a wider view of the market?
- Planned additions – how does the augmented product add up? Is it internally coherent?
- Economic/social climate – are the economic and social conditions supportive of the proposal?
- Sources/characteristics of existing demand – do you have enough information to assess the current situation in the market?
- Future demand and likely market share – do you know how this will change in the future?
- Projected operating statements – do you have sufficient information in an appropriate form for you to trust the claims made by the proposal?
- Cash flow projections and investment appraisal – are the financial projections realistic and realisable?

There are also a number of common methods that are used to assess the capital investment (Swarbrooke, 2002: 157). These include:

- Accounting rate of return (ARR)
  - Profit returns compared to capital
- Payback period
  - Based on cash inflows generated
- Discounted cash flow (DCF)
  - Predicting timing/size of future cash flows
- Net present value (NPV)
  - Of predicted future cash flows
- Internal rate of return (IRR)
  - Required to balance cash inflows & outflows

Activity

Compare the two models we have introduced in this chapter and look at the similarities in the two approaches.

Also note the differences, both in terms of the content and the approach between the business plan and the feasibility study. Be careful because sometimes even where the same words are used, they have a different intention.

For example where the feasibility study reviews the project, the criteria are the hard objective criteria of profitability and market share, where for the owner and the entrepreneur they also capture the dreams and aspirations of the development.

Prepare your thoughts and then read through the rest of this chapter where we test the Petralan proposal more thoroughly.

The key considerations of a feasibility study require that the project proposal is researched and the assumptions of the business plan are grounded through objective empirical tests. We will now take you through the basic concerns that should be addressed when undertaking the feasibility study:

- Concept Development – the PBB sounds ideal, a romantic dream. However, in the feasibility study questions must be asked about the assumption that a luxury B&B offer would be popular in this setting. Moreover the easy dismissal of the competition from traditional hotels would also need to be substantiated and if possible performance figures from those hotels examined – what is the occupancy level? What are the unmet demands for accommodation? How many covers are local restaurants seeing? How much unmet demand is thought to exist by other local restaurant owners?

- Design brief – how do the elements stack up? Will the price that customers are willing to pay cover the expense of the luxury fixtures and fittings?

- Proposed site – again the business plan makes a great deal of the special location but peninsula locations can be inconvenient and visitors often find them small, under resourced and with poor levels of infrastructure.

- Transportation/access – how can you reach Tihany? How can transfers be organised?

- Existing supply – patterns of supply and demand in Tihany and around the Lake Balaton must be more closely examined and also comparisons drawn from other neighbouring destinations.

- Competition – is it safe to dismiss all the other offers. A more systematic competition analysis will be required.

- Legislative considerations – the legal and political contexts of ownership and development must be clarified. The simple statement that the company will be a LLC is not sufficient – are the proposed owners allowed to undertake such developments? Who would be responsible for any losses incurred.

- Economic/social climate – how will the economic trends support the luxury market? How will local people respond to affluent visitors occupying this special place?

Continued

- Sources/characteristics of existing demand – the three target markets are clearly defined but there is no attempt to specify the scale of these markets. Market research would have to be undertaken of the sources of those visitors in order to make the plan convincing.

- Future demand and likely market share – how will the markets change in the future? Are the markets sustainable?

- Projected operating statements – these statements would need to be assessed in terms of their comprehensive ability to account for the development of the business. One concern here is that the owners would work full time in the PBB but would also continue to work elsewhere – how is that possible and how long can it continue?

- Cash flow projections and investment appraisal.

- People (e.g. management and workforce) – a classic small business design with almost total reliance on the family, but is this practical? What labour exists around the Lake and in easy travel to work areas?

- Marketing strategy – how realistic are the targets? Can they be achieved? Is the media attention likely to be sustained as the PBB becomes established and stops being a news story?

- Physical resources, e.g. Premises, Furniture and Equipment – there are no concrete statements about the facilities or the state of the buildings. A feasibility study would have to examine the fabric of the building and the appropriateness of the fixtures and fittings (especially in the kitchens given the emphasis on food in the plan).

- Financing and assets – how likely is the level of financing to be achieved and what are the scenarios if there is a shortage?

- Financial projections – are the assumptions realistic? What happens if the targets are not attained?

BUSINESS RATIOS

A key aspect of the feasibility study would be the critical examination of the business ratios that would allow for the examiner to make a judgement about the relative health and likely success of the business. The range of ratios varies but we present some of the most common ones below. The business ratios reflect both a cross-sectional analysis and time-series analysis of the company's risk and profitability. The cross-sectional analysis consists of a comparison of the firm's ratios and those of the hotel and motel industry averages.

You can see that there are some significant differences in the ratios, especially in regards to the way the company is leveraged. This is due to the fact that industry averages also include very large hotel chains that usually have much higher capital costs and investments in long-term assets. Furthermore, the PBB has lower fixed overhead costs than other hotels and motels since B&Bs usually provide fewer services than larger competitors.

We present these figures here for two reasons. The first is that we could have (and should have) included them in Section 7 but then they would have represented the proposer's views of the likely success of the business venture. Here we present them as the objective conclusions of the feasibility study and this means that you do not have to try to recalculate them!

The second reason is that we would ask you to think about what these figures mean in the context of the business proposal and the evaluation of that proposal. We have prepared a wide range of calculations but – as a potential investor – you have to decide which ones are the most relevant and therefore most important for you in making your decisions.

Ratio analysis

	2010	2011	2012	Industry profile
Sales growth	0.00%	9.52%	9.55%	7.24%
Percent of total assets				
Inventory	0.63%	0.51%	0.43%	1.35%
Other current assets	10.12%	7.90%	6.29%	24.20%
Total current assets	59.43%	69.03%	75.90%	29.12%
Long-term assets	40.57%	30.97%	24.10%	70.88%
Total assets	100.00%	100.00%	100.00%	100.00%
Current liabilities	1.73%	1.44%	1.22%	16.94%
Long-term liabilities	54.79%	38.61%	27.42%	26.60%
Total liabilities	56.52%	40.05%	28.64%	43.54%
Net Worth	43.48%	59.95%	71.36%	56.46%
Percent of sales				
Sales	100.00%	100.00%	100.00%	100.00%
Gross margin	79.24%	78.66%	78.33%	100.00%
Selling, general and administrative expenses	138.22%	42.64%	43.67%	75.85%
Advertising expenses	5.03%	1.22%	1.09%	2.17%
Profit before interest and taxes	58.33%	54.24%	55.59%	0.35%
Main ratios				
Current	34.41	47.80	62.20	0.98
Quick	34.05	47.45	61.85	0.75

Continued

Total debt to total assets	56.52%	40.05%	28.64%	58.28%
Pre-tax return on net worth	85.67%	49.87%	38.07%	0.29%
Pre-tax return on assets	37.25%	29.90%	27.16%	0.70%
Additional ratios	2010	2011	2012	
Net profit margin	46.46%	43.63%	45.45%	n.a
Return on equity	74.54%	43.39%	33.12%	n.a
Activity ratios				
Inventory turnover	9.94	11.17	11.17	n.a
Accounts payable turnover	20.40	22.81	22.81	n.a
Payment days	14	15	16	n.a
Total asset turnover	0.70	0.60	0.52	n.a
Debt ratios				
Debt to net worth	1.30	0.67	0.40	n.a
Current liabilities to liabilities	0.03	0.04	0.04	n.a
Liquidity ratios				
Net working capital	£77,946	£116,961	£162,338	n.a
Interest coverage	11.85	13.25	16.57	n.a
Additional ratios				
Assets to sales	1.43	1.68	1.92	n.a
Current debt/total assets	2%	1%	1%	n.a
Acid test	34.05	47.45	61.85	n.a
Sales/net worth	1.60	0.99	0.73	n.a
Dividend payout	0.00	0.00	0.00	n.a

SUMMARY AND CONCLUSIONS

This chapter has taken you through a hypothetical example of a business plan and then demonstrated how this could be questioned further through a feasibility study. The purpose of the business plan is to outline and elaborate the possibilities of the proposal. The primary audience can be seen as those who are internal – in some ways connected to the proposal and wanting to see the proposal taken forward (and successful). This allows for the business plan to be constructed in such a way that captures the imagination of those involved and expresses the dream. This is still a business document but it is being written by those who are committed to the idea and therefore may not be entirely objective. It will develop a business case for the project but it will do this from the perspective of the proposer.

The feasibility study is a counterbalance to this – it is a pragmatic and objective exercise and it should never be personal. It seeks to explore the business logics of the proposal and to test the assumptions built into that scenario in objective ways. Many of the individual steps and the techniques are very similar to those that the entrepreneurs and developers will have used to build the business plan, but they will be utilised in a different way as the emphasis is placed on the testing of the claims rather than making the claims.

Both processes are important for the development of hospitality businesses, as there is a need for a balance between the enthusiasm and even exaggerated claims of the developers and the natural reservations of the investors.

REVIEW QUESTIONS

1. Explain the difference between a business plan and a feasibility study.
2. Are financial considerations the most important ones in the business plan?
3. Are financial considerations the most important ones in a feasibility study?
4. How can market information be used to support a business plan?

Case Study: Disneyland Paris (Euro Disney) – A Challenge?

The French site has proved more difficult than most operations that the Disney empire has taken on. Its early problems have been well documented (Tribe, 2001; Clarke and Chen, 2007). Following its changes in management and the security of new investment, its progress was again disrupted by the after effects of the terrorist attacks in America on September 11, 2001 – since then the company has not made a profit.

It is a complex business and if we look closely we can see the contribution of the different elements to the overall business performance. In 2008, the company, which is 40% owned by Walt Disney and 10% by Prince Alwaleed Bin Talal of Saudi Arabia, were confident that its painstaking journey to financial health was becoming a reality with a 20% jump in first-quarter revenues to €341 million (£255 million) and reported strong growth in visitor numbers, guest spending and hotel occupancy. Theme park revenues rose by 14% to €175.1 million and sales from its hotels and the Disney Village retail and entertainment park were up to 17% at €126.7 million. Turnover from the resort rose by 14% to €316 million, while revenues from property increased by €18.4 million to €24.4 million, mainly due to the sale of a property in Val d'Europe.

The performance was helped by a 10% increase in theme park attendances and a 3% rise in average spending per head as admissions and food and beverage sales both grew. Hotel occupancy increased by 6.8 percentage points and average spending per head was 11% better. Most of the improvement was from Spanish and British guests.

The opening of new attractions, such as Crush's Coaster and Car Race Rally, to mark the theme park's 15th anniversary had created another level of emotional connections with the guests. Further attractions, such as the Twilight Zone Tower of Terror and Stitch Live, an interactive experience were in development for 2009. It was also noted that attendances had increased the park was chosen by President Sarkozy as the place to go public on his love for the model-turned-singer Carla Bruni!

A spokesman said that the company had now reported seven consecutive quarters of strong growth and had yet to see any impact on consumer confidence from the global economic crisis. However, by the time the half year report for 2009 was published, it was noted that the Spanish and English markets had declined significantly, but this had been partially offset by a strong performance from the French market. The number of visitors increased by 111,000 year on year, reaching a record 7.1 million, but despite this increase in visitors, revenues fell by 7.3% to £496.5 million. First half costs were reduced by 0.4% to £533 million, resulting in an operating loss of £35.5 million, compared to a £1.1 million profit last year.

It should be noted that Disney-Paris's business conditions are subject to seasonality effects, with revenue typically lower in the first half of the year compared to the second. However, this year's results were also affected by the fact that the Easter holidays occurred in April rather than March. The most important factor in the decline in the revenues can be attributed to the £1.47 reduction in average spending per guest is £38.28. The fall in spending reflects a greater number of promotional offers deployed by the company. This demonstrates one of the problems with promotional offers as a long-term business strategy, as it reduces the spending per head. It should also be remembered that half of the 2000-acre site has yet to be developed and therefore there are considerable opportunities to develop the business further.

Sources

http://news.directline-holidays.co.uk/Euro-Disney-Revenues-Fall-By-7-General-Travel-Tourism-599

Walsh, D. Euro Disney performance no longer Mickey Mouse. Times Online January 24, 2008.

Tribe, J., 2001. Corporate Strategies, Thomson, London.

Clarke, A., Chen, W., 2007. International Hospitality Management. Butterworth-Heinemann.

Questions

1. What lessons about customer profiling can Disney learn from the change in behaviour within a one-year period?

2. How could Disney-Paris justify expansion using the parts of the site that remain vacant?

3. Should Disney-Paris consider diversification into other markets and/or other sectors to address the downturn in business?

4. How do changes in currency exchange rates impact on the markets and the customer perception of Disney-Paris?

GLOSSARY

Break-even point   The calculation of where income meets expenses. Not reaching the BEP means the business will operate at a loss – but passing the BEP will result in a profit as income exceeds expenses.

Business plan   The document that outlines the way the idea can be taken forward, written and produced by the entrepreneur and the developers.

Concept development The process which allows an idea to be expressed and defined as it takes the shape that will be used to build the business plan.

Feasibility study The process of objectively testing the assumptions and assertions found in the business plan.

Financial ratios These are the complicated financial calculations that allow you to test the performance of a business. For more help please visit the following Website which includes helpful explanations and worked examples: http://www.va-interactive.com/inbusiness/editorial/finance/ibt/ratio_analysis.html.

Market segmentation The process of identifying aspects of the total market that are potential customers for your business. Segmentation should include a viability analysis to ensure that the defined segment will contribute to the profitable operation of the business.

Project brief The terms of reference for the development. The most concise version of the concept that can be readily understood by an outsider of the project.

CHAPTER 7

Hospitality Business Development Routes and Directions

Learning Objectives

Having completed this chapter you should be able to:

- Understand how hospitality businesses can utilise strategies when attempting to gain a competitive advantage.
- Evaluate different hospitality business development routes and directions.
- Determine the criteria that can be used for making decisions about the different routes and directions.

CONTENTS

INTRODUCTION

There are many routes and directions that are available to the hospitality business. An understanding of these will offer the hospitality business opportunities to gain a competitive advantage. This chapter will initially outline what is understood by competitive advantage before reviewing frameworks that can be used to explore the different directions and routes that a hospitality business can pursue. Criteria that can be used when considering different strategic directions and routes will then be discussed.

COMPETITIVE ADVANTAGE

Hospitality businesses need to understand how they can gain a competitive advantage in an external environment that is characterised by complexity and uncertainty. Once particular hospitality products grow in popularity and generate increased demand from customers, it is not uncommon for the sector that offers those goods and services to become saturated with competitors. This has already been illustrated in Chapter 3 when discussing the concept of the sector life cycle. Hospitality businesses therefore have to explore ways in which their goods and services are positioned foremost in the minds of consumers and thereby attempt to achieve a competitive advantage over other organisations operating in that sector. It is important to initially define what is understood by competitive advantage and a number of definitions are outlined in Figure 7.1.

Is the way in which a company makes its products or services better or cheaper than those offered by it competitors (Capon 2008)

When two or more firms compete within the same market, one firm possesses a competitive advantage over its rivals when it earns (or has the potential to earn) a persistently higher profit (Grant 2008)

The ability of an organisation to add more value for its customers than its rivals, and thus attain a position of relative advantage. The challenge is to sustain any advantage once achieved (Thompson 2001)

FIGURE 7.1 *Definitions of competitive advantage.*

Activity

1. Review the definitions that are outlined in Figure 7.1.
2. What common themes emerge from these definitions?
3. Produce your own definition of what you understand by competitive advantage.
4. Thompson's definition refers to sustaining a competitive advantage. What do you understand by this and to what extent is it possible for a hospitality business to sustain an advantage? Suggest ways in which a hospitality business could possibly achieve a sustainable competitive advantage?

Once the hospitality business has a competitive advantage competitors can quickly copy this. The challenge for hospitality businesses, therefore, is to sustain the competitive advantage in the long term. Definitions of competitive advantage can tend to take the view that organisations should position themselves relative to their competitors. However, this neglects to consider the internal resources and competences that a business might have and how these can be best utilised to gain an advantage. In this respect, therefore, the basis upon which an organisation can gain a competitive advantage can be analysed from two different perspectives; the competitive positioning school of thought and the resource-based view of strategy. Theories such as Porter's generic strategies, Faulkner and Bowman's (1995) strategy clock and Ansoff's (1988) directional matrix are often associated with the competitive positioning school of thought. These theories present a number of different strategies that an organisation can pursue in an attempt to position the business in a superior position to its competitors.

BUSINESS DEVELOPMENT ROUTES

The hospitality business needs to consider the different business development routes that it could pursue in achieving a competitive advantage. These alternative routes will offer the hospitality business opportunities for gaining a positional advantage over competitors in the marketplace. According to Porter (1985) competitive advantage is based upon three generic strategies: cost, differentiation and focus. As illustrated in Figure 7.2. Porter argues that these strategies can take either a broad or narrow focus in scope.

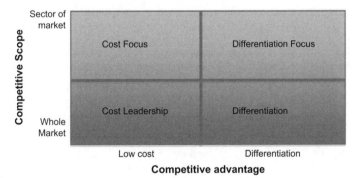

FIGURE 7.2   *Generic competitive strategies (adapted from Porter, 1985)*

Cost leadership

Cost leadership is where the hospitality business becomes the lowest cost producer in the industry or sector and can thus gain higher profits. A cost leadership strategy is one that targets the whole market. By reducing costs, the hospitality business is then able to pass the benefits of this to customers in the form of lower prices compared to competitors. Therefore, if pursuing this strategy, the hospitality business needs to explore how it can reduce the costs of its business without impairing the perceived value, by the customer, of the product offer. It should be noted that even though there may be a number of competitors who will attempt to achieve an advantage through cost leadership, there can only be one true cost leader in an industry or sector. Evans et al. (2003) identify a number of ways in which cost leadership can be achieved and these observations are applied to hospitality businesses as illustrated in Table 7.1.

Table 7.1 Cost Leadership Strategies

Cost Leadership Strategies	Example
Gaining economies of scale	Purchasing resource inputs such as food, beverage and linen supplies in bulk
More efficient distribution systems	Internet only sales strategy for reservations and room bookings in hotels
Low-cost resource inputs	Introducing energy efficient technologies that, though costly at first, enable the hospitality business to reduce costs over the long term
Copying product design features of competitors	Fast food outlets have been able to replicate and copy the systems and processes of competitors thereby reducing costs
Outsourcing of key product areas	Locating customer support call centres in locations where wage and running costs may be cheaper
Standardising the product	Branded budget hotels are similar in design, furnishings and operational processes and are therefore relatively straightforward to set up in different locations at minimal cost
Gaining 'experience curve' economies	Relative to potential new entrants into the industry, established hospitality businesses have systems in place to manage and operate their businesses, thereby gaining cost advantages

It is not uncommon for hospitality firms who follow a strategy of cost leadership to explore ways in which the business can generate revenue to further increase income generation. Hospitality businesses can do this by charging for the services that may have been freely available to customers prior to the low cost strategy being implemented. For example, charging for an earlier check in or late check out time, the charging of a fee for payment by credit card and the sale of 'take away' breakfasts where this service is not being offered in hotels.

Activity

1. Examine how businesses in the branded budget hotel sector, such as Travelodge and Premier Travel Inn, have followed a strategy of cost leadership. How have organisations in this sector attempted to reduce their costs?

2. How have businesses in this sector attempted to generate additional revenue from the goods and services that they offer?

3. Make further suggestions on how these businesses could cut costs and generate sources of revenue.

Differentiation

Differentiation strategy is when the hospitality business offers something unique and sells it at a premium price. The reason for the premium price is the additional costs that will be incurred by differentiating the product. To ensure differentiation can be achieved, the hospitality business has to add value to its product and/or service range. If this added value is perceived by customers of being superior to competitor offerings, then the hospitality business can then command a premium price. Capon (2008) notes the importance of distinguishing between real and perceived differentiations. Real differentiation is when the hospitality business produces goods and services that are actually distinguishable from competitor offerings. Perceived differentiation is based around the development of a hospitality businesses image via effective marketing and promotional strategies. The hospitality business can differentiate the product by using a number of different strategies as outlined by Evans et al. (2003) in Table 7.2.

Table 7.2	Differentiation Strategies
Differentiation Strategies	**Example**
Creating superior products to competitors via enhanced design, technology and/or performance	The design of the Burj Al Arab Hotel in Dubai has given the hotel iconic status comparable to other uniquely designed buildings such as the Sydney Opera House
Offering a superior level of service	Hotel companies such as the Ritz Carlton offer personalised butler services to their guests
Access to enhanced distribution channels	Hotels may offer a multi-channel approach to purchasing their goods and services. This may be through travel agents, directly via the Internet or hotel reservation centre or through digital television services.
Development of brand reputation through design, innovation, advertising and so on	The Savoy Hotel and the renovation of its property with superior product and service features
Superior product promotion	The ability to advertise through multiple channels (e.g. digital and online channels)
Adjustments in the price to the goods and services	Fast food outlets offering low value alternatives to its main menu range

Activity

1. Distinguish between those factors in Table 7.2 that can develop real differentiation and those that can develop perceived differentiation.

2. Consider other examples of hospitality businesses that have pursued strategies of real and perceived differentiations.

3. In addition to those strategies outlined in Table 7.2, how else a hospitality business may develop differentiation.

Focus

Focus is when the hospitality business targets a narrow segment of the market. The hospitality business may wish to focus on a particular niche sector of the market based upon, for example, demographic or need variables. In this respect the hospitality business can pursue a strategy of cost focus or focus differentiation. Differentiation focus is when the business differentiates the product to meet the needs of a niche market.

Example: Differentiation Focus

The ICEHOTEL in Jukkasjärvi, Lapland, Sweden was first created in the early 1990s and describes itself as the original 'Ice Hotel'. It has over 80 rooms and has to be rebuilt annually. Offering two alternative types of accommodation: bedrooms or suites, the beds themselves are made of ice but covered with an insulating sheet and reindeer skins. Guests sleep in sleeping bags and temperatures in the rooms can drop to about −5 °C. The ice hotel concept has since been replicated in other parts of the world including Canada and Switzerland. The ICEHOTEL has also extended its brand and licenses ICE-BARS around the world.

Source: www.unusualhotelsoftheworld.com.

Cost focus is when the business focuses on a sector of the market, which may be particularly price sensitive. The major hospitality businesses such as the Accor group have a diversified portfolio of hotel establishments that meet the needs of different markets. This is often based upon a cost focus where their budget brands such as Hotel Formule 1 and Etap cater for those with limited expenditure whilst their premium brands such as Sofitel are targeted at those with higher disposable incomes and have better perceived product options such as, for example, spa facilities and room furnishings such as the 'SoBed'. These additional features are then reflected in the premium prices of the hotel. Evans et al. (2003) identifies focus strategies that an organisation can pursue and these are illustrated in Table 7.3.

When considering the various generic strategies, Porter contends that a business needs to be clear about which strategy it is following otherwise it will become 'stuck in the middle' and have no clear bases upon which to gain competitive advantage. However, further to Porter's generic strategy

Table 7.3   Focus Strategies

Focus Strategies	Example
Focusing on a particular group of buyers	Luthan Hotel & Spa in Saudi Arabia which caters for women only
Specialising in particular geographic regions	London Town Hotels group which offers luxury hotels in London.
Catering for the benefits sought by a particular group of buyers	Blau Hotels and Resorts offer child friendly facilities including nanny and babysitting services

framework, Faulkner and Bowman (1995) present the 'strategy clock' and note how organisations can take a 'hybrid' strategy combining both low cost and differentiation, and a 'no-frills' strategy which targets price sensitive customers with the limited provision of any additional extras.

Example

The easyHotel is part of the Easy Group portfolio of businesses. The first easyHotel opened in London on 1 August 2005 and other easyHotel have since been built in Cyprus, Hungary and Switzerland. The hotels offer 'no-frills' facilities with rooms measuring approximately 6–9 square metres and are equipped with en-suite shower facilities. Additional charges are made on room cleaning, TV, towel changes, Internet access and luggage storage facilities.

Source: easyHotel.com.

Activity

1. Use the classification provided in Chapter 2 to choose a sector in the hospitality industry.
2. Evaluate the different competitive strategies of hospitality businesses operating in that sector. What are the benefits of following this strategy for the business? How is this strategy being achieved?
3. To what extent are any of the hospitality businesses 'stuck in the middle'? What advice would you offer in giving further coherency to their overall strategic direction?

BUSINESS DEVELOPMENT DIRECTIONS

Once the bases of competitive advantage have been considered, the hospitality business will then need to determine its strategic direction. A framework for considering the different directions is Ansoff's (1988) directional matrix, which was initially introduced in Chapter 1 and will be discussed in further detail in the following. Ansoff's (1988) directional matrix (see Figure 7.3) offers four different strategic directions which the hospitality business can pursue. These directions are based upon its markets and product range. The model has been extended by Johnson et al. (2008) to include a fifth alternative, consolidation.

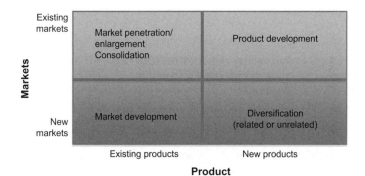

	Existing products	New products
Existing markets	Market penetration/ enlargement Consolidation	Product development
New markets	Market development	Diversification (related or unrelated)

Markets (vertical axis) — Product (horizontal axis)

FIGURE 7.3 *Directional matrix (adapted from Ansoff, 1988).*

Market penetration/enlargement

Market penetration is where the hospitality business attempts to grow its market share by focusing on its existing markets and product range. Capon (2008) refers alternatively to this as market enlargement where the business attempts to grow its market by selling its existing products. The hospitality business therefore has to implement strategies that encourage its target markets to buy more of its current products. Market penetration is often pursued when there is room for further growth in the marketplace and there is an upward trajectory in the sector or industry's life cycle. The hospitality business can pursue this strategy by exploiting its existing resources. This may take the form of revising the marketing of the service offering so as to increase sales.

Consolidation

A strategy of consolidation is when the hospitality business will focus on maintaining its current markets with its existing products (Johnson et al., 2008). According to Johnson et al. (2008) this is a defensive strategy that, in contrast to market penetration and enlargement, is not focused on growth. It is particularly necessary when competitive conditions become fierce with the emergence of new competitors and entrants into the industry, which then eats into the businesses, market share. This may lead to a period of consolidation activity in the industry sector when hospitality businesses decide to merge or acquire one another. Consolidation can also be necessary when factors in the external environment and changes to the spending of discretionary income can influence consumer behaviour to purchase your products.

Example

Nando's is a fast food chain which uses chicken as the focus of its meal products. The chicken products are marinated in a special sauce called 'PERi-PERi' which gives the food a distinct flavour. The chain uses this as the focus for its marketing activities and to differentiate itself from its competitors. In November 2008, Nando's embarked upon a three-month mass-marketing campaign that was based upon the distribution of over 2 million sachets of the PERi-PERi sauce to UK households. The sachets included voucher tokens and directions on how to best use the sauce. During a period when many hospitality businesses were facing the impact of the economic downturn, the campaign was orchestrated to generate brand awareness and reinforcement amongst its key target markets.

Source: www.Mintel.com

Market development

Market development is when the hospitality business decides to enter into new markets using its existing products. This can be based upon identifying and targeting new market segments or entering into new geographical regions where markets can be exploited. Hospitality businesses that have expanded globally, such as McDonalds, have pursued a strategy of market development. In this respect, the existing product is replicated in the new market. When national markets stagnate and there are too may competitors selling similar or substitute products, hospitality businesses will often seek out new international markets if they have the resources to do so. For example, in August 2008, Hilton Hotel Corporation announced that it was to launch a new boutique hotel brand in the UK. This was in response to the growing boutique hotel market and to ensure less over reliance on the business market. Consumer tastes can become increasingly fickle and hospitality businesses therefore have to be receptive to the demands of new and emerging markets as and when they arise. However, it cannot be assumed that the existing product can be easily transferred to a new market and a number of risks may prevail. These risks are outlined as part of the discussion of the decision-making criteria.

Product development

Product development is when the hospitality business develops new products for existing markets. This can be as a consequence of changing consumer tastes and the hospitality business therefore has to tailor and update its products to meet the needs of its existing markets. The development of alternative meals such as salads by McDonalds was due to changing consumer tastes towards health-related products. If competitors have produced new alternative products then this can also act as a catalyst for the hospitality business to embark on product development. Marriot Hotels have been renovating many of their properties (see end of chapter case study). Part of this renovation project is the development of 'multi-use' lobbies which can be used for eating and business networking. This innovation enables Marriot to maximise its existing product resources whilst generating new innovations so as to stay ahead of competitors in the industry. In pursuing a strategy of product development, the hospitality business has to ensure that it has the resources to be able to sufficiently invest in research and development.

Diversification

Diversification is when the hospitality business enters new markets with new products. This can take the form of related or unrelated diversification. Related diversification is when the hospitality business enters into a new market with a new product which is related to its core business activity. For example, if a hotel firm were to purchase a restaurant chain this would be related diversification, as the hotel provider would be entering into a new market but with a related area of business.

Unrelated diversification is when the hospitality business enters a new market with a new product that is unrelated to the core business. For example, a contract caterer may decide to acquire a train operator. The logic behind this direction would be so that the organisation could supply its catering products on board the trains. This would be unrelated diversification as the core business activity of the contract caterer is completely different from that of the acquired train operating business. Firms that have hospitality-related interests, such as the Easy Group and Virgin, are examples of organisations that are highly diversified and have extended their brands across a range of different businesses.

To some extent there can be a blurring between related and unrelated diversifications. As has been addressed in Chapter 2, the hospitality industry is made up of many direct and indirect sectors, many of which can be perceived as being related to some degree or another. This can make it difficult to fully distinguish to what degree the direction may be related or unrelated. However, what is important is to understand the extent to which the hospitality business has the required resources to be able to manage and incorporate the related or unrelated business into its activities. Indeed, the hospitality business needs to be aware that a number of risks can be associated with pursuing a strategy of either related or unrelated diversification. The business may have to implement new organisational systems and structures to successfully embed the new business. The hospitality business, therefore, has to consider the extent to which it has the expertise, resources and know how to effectively incorporate the unrelated business into its day-to-day activities.

Example: Diversification at Whitbread

Whitbread began as a brewer in 1742 introducing brands into the market such as Stella Artois and Heineken. In 1991 Whitbread withdrew completely from the brewing sector to focus on its hotel and restaurant chains. This includes the budget hotel chain Premier Inn, restaurant chains, Beefeater, Table Table and Brewers Fayre, and also the coffee shop chain Costa Coffee.

Sources: www.Whitbread.co.uk.com.

Example: Diversification at McDonalds

In light of declining sales in the fast food market in the late 1990s, the chief executives of McDonalds explored new directions for the business. Therefore, in 2001, McDonalds opened its first hotel, The Golden Arch, in Zurich Switzerland. The 211 room hotel is classified as a four star establishment and is primarily targeted at business travellers during the week and families at the weekend. The furnishings replicate the hygiene and cleanliness principles that McDonalds adheres to, such as hardwood flooring. Golden Arches headboards also adorn the bedroom fittings.

Source: www.McDonalds.com.

Activity

1. To what extent do both of these examples illustrate related and unrelated diversifications?
2. Why have both companies decided to diversify their businesses in the way that they have?
3. What factors would Whitbread and McDonalds both have to consider when pursuing these development routes?

RESOURCE-BASED VIEW

An alternative approach to understanding the alternative routes and directions that a hospitality business can pursue is what is widely known as the resource-based view (RBV). The Hospitality Business Positioning Analysis Framework presented in Chapter 4 identified the importance of internal analysis to the organisation. This internal analysis is crucial to understanding how the organisation can utilise its resources to gain an advantage over competitors.

The resource-based view is based upon analysing the hospitality business from a systems perspective. This perspective acknowledges that the organisation consists of a series of resource inputs, which it converts via a transformation process to outputs. The value creation that is generated via this process results in the hospitality business being able to position itself favourably relative to its competitors. The hospitality business is made up of a number of both tangible and intangible resources and the business needs to understand how to successfully configure these resources to gain an advantage over competitors. Tangible resources include human, financial, and physical resources whereas intangible resources include brand reputation and image. The resources can be further classified into threshold and strategic or unique resources.

■ Threshold Resources

Threshold resources are those which the hospitality business must have if it is to operate in a given sector. For example, a family restaurant will need a physical premises with which to sell its goods and services to customers. The restaurant will also require human resources in the form of managers to run the premises, chefs and kitchen staff to produce the food, waiting staff to serve the customers and cleaners and maintenance staff to ensure the day-to-day health, safety and hygiene of the restaurant. Technological resources will be needed to process orders and to take payment from customers. Therefore at a minimum the restaurant will need these resources, otherwise it will be unable to compete with others targeting the same market.

■ Strategic or Unique Resources

Strategic or unique resources are those resources which are over and above the industry standard and enable the hospitality business to gain an advantage over competitors. A number of criteria can be used to classify whether a resource has strategic value to the hospitality business. Strategic resources can be classified upon the basis of whether they meet the VIRUS (Valuable, Inimitable, Rare, UnSubstitutable) criteria (Haberberg and Rieple, 2008) that is whether the resource is 'Valuable' or becomes valuable over time; the extent to which the resource is able to be copied and can become 'Inimitable'; the extent to which the resource is 'Rare' and difficult to obtain; and the extent to which the resource becomes 'UnSubstitutable' by competitors.

TGI Fridays has a unique culture which differentiates it from competitors. This culture is developed through the careful recruitment of its human resources, who must have specific skills and abilities to work for the business. These human resources become a strategic resource that adds value to the business and develops the distinctiveness of the organisation's culture and working practices. This distinctive culture is very difficult for competitors to copy and replicate and enables TGI Fridays to therefore sustain an advantage over competitors through service delivery.

According to Haberberg and Rieple (2001) those organisations that are able to develop strategic resources that meet the VIRUS criteria are more likely to be more profitable than competitors in the medium term; stay profitable as competition intensifies; and be more resilient as the environment changes.

Competences

In addition to resources, the hospitality business has to understand its competences. Competences are the attributes that the hospitality business requires if it is to compete effectively in the marketplace. Competences emerge from the organisations, bundle of resources and can encompass skills, knowledge and technology. In the same way as threshold resource can be understood, the hospitality business will also require a standard set of competences to be able to compete effectively. For example, a hotel will require competences in coordinating a means of distributing, marketing and selling its goods and services; the maintenance of the hotel and related front and back office facilities including rooms, restaurants and kitchens; and the development and training of human resources. However, like strategic resources, the hospitality business can also develop core competences. Core competences are over and above the industry standard and can act as a basis for gaining added value and competitive advantage.

Prahalad and Hamel (1990) note that core competences should satisfy the following criteria:

- The core competence should provide the company with access to a wide range of markets. The Intercontinental Hotels Group has global coverage in a host of geographical markets due to their competencies in arranging the distribution and marketing of their goods and services.

- The core competence should make a major contribution to the perceived customer benefits of the end product. Hyatt International has core competences in arranging premium services for its guests. It can therefore charge a price that reflects the services that are being offered.

- The core competence should be difficult for competitors to copy. McDonalds has core competences in arranging the training and development of its human resources, ensuring the standardisation of its goods and services in its international network of restaurants.

Based upon the VIRUS criteria (Haberberg and Rieple, 2001), Table 7.4 offers a framework for classifying an organisation's strategic resources and core competences.

Table 7.4	Strategic Resources and Core Competences	
Criteria	**Strategic Resources**	**Core Competences**
Valuable		
Inimitable		
Rare		
UnSubstitutable		

Activity

1. Choose a hospitality sector and identify the threshold resources and competences that are required to operate a business in that sector.

2. Using the same sector, identify hospitality businesses that have strategic resources and core competences. Using the criteria that are outlined in Table 7.4, state what these strategic resources and core competences are.

3. To what extent do these strategic resources and core competences enable the hospitality business to gain a sustainable competitive advantage?

ROUTES AND DIRECTIONS: DECISION-MAKING CRITERIA

Hospitality businesses have to be aware of those factors that may influence their decisions on the chosen development route or direction. Therefore, when determining the various development routes and directions for the hospitality business a number of criteria should be considered, as illustrated in Figure 7.4. The criteria can be used as a means for understanding the level of risk that can be associated with pursuing a particular development direction or route.

First, the hospitality business needs to ascertain the degree of demand for its goods and services. The rate of growth in the sectors, life cycle will ascertain the number of sales that are currently being generated and the extent to which this is anticipated to grow. If sales are growing within the sector then the hospitality business may continue to pursue strategies of market penetration in an attempt to enlarge its market share. If demand is beginning to plateau or decline, the hospitality business will need to consider strategies of market and product development so as to generate further growth for the business.

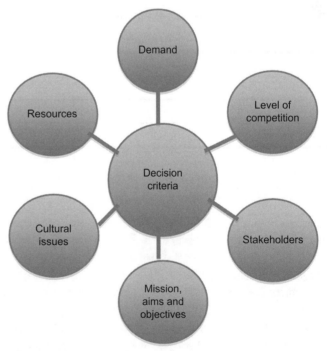

FIGURE 7.4 *Decision-making criteria for routes and directions.*

Second, the level of competition in the sector in terms of number, size and type will influence the hospitality business's future direction. As mentioned previously, the stage in the sector's life cycle will influence the number of new entrants and the directions that the hospitality business may pursue to generate barriers to these new entrants. Furthermore, if the sector is maturing there may be a shakeout of competitors, resulting in opportunities for acquisition or merger activity to take place.

Third, the hospitality business needs to have a clear vision and mission about what it aspires to be and what the central purpose of the organisation is. Any route or direction that the business decides to pursue needs to be compatible with its overall aims and objectives and where the organisation intends to position itself relative to its competitors. This is important as the business could very easily suffer from strategic drift where it has no clear direction and is drifting away from factors that are emerging in the external environmental.

Fourth, the hospitality business has to consider cultural issues. If the business decides to enter into a new geographical market, what are the cultural implications of doing this? The hospitality business has to consider whether it will need to adapt its goods and services to meet the needs of the local culture. As illustrated in the example in Chapter 1, McDonalds changes its standard menu to meet the needs of the local population. If changes are to be made, the hospitality business has to consider to what extent it has the financial, human and intellectual resources for it to make the necessary adaptations to its goods and services. The hospitality business should also consider the extent to which the route and direction might have an impact upon the organisation's culture. If the hospitality business decides to pursue a strategy of unrelated diversification into a completely new area, the business has to consider the extent to which it will be able to incorporate this into the cultural philosophy of the firm.

Fifth, the hospitality business should determine the extent to which it has the necessary resources to pursue a particular direction. Furthermore, to ensure the sustainability of the development direction, the business should attempt to develop resources that meet the VIRUS criteria as outlined earlier. Particular routes and directions will have an increased bearing on the business's resources and in many respects a greater level of risk. For example, when embarking on a strategy of new product development, the financial risk in terms of the level of investment required needs to be considered. The hospitality business will have to invest a large amount of capital resources into developing the new product, which if unsuccessful once on sale to the target market, may be costly to the business.

Finally, the stakeholders of the hospitality business will have an influence over its strategic direction and will be impacted upon by the direction that the business takes. The stakeholders of the business including banks, shareholders, governments, employees, customers, suppliers and community groups will all have different needs and expectations that should be identified. It will not be possible for the hospitality business to meet all these different needs and expectations by pursuing a particular group so it therefore has to ascertain who has the most influence over the direction of the business. Mendelow (1991) classifies different stakeholder groups by their different levels of power and interest. This includes key players (high level of power and interest); keep informed (high level of interest but low level of power); keep satisfied (high level of power but low level of interest; and minimal effort (low level of power and interest). The key players are the stakeholders that the hospitality business has to pay closest attention to as they have the greatest level of influence over the direction of the organisation.

Activity

1. Which of the criteria do you believe is the most important for hospitality businesses to consider? Use examples of hospitality businesses to justify your answer.
2. To what extent are there other decision-making criteria that a hospitality business should consider? Why should the hospitality business address these in its business decision-making?

SUMMARY AND CONCLUSIONS

There are many routes and directions that a hospitality business may pursue in an attempt to gain an advantage over competitors. This chapter has discussed strategies, including the generic strategies of cost leadership, cost focus, differentiation and differentiation focus, whilst also acknowledging additional routes including hybrid and no-frills strategies. This chapter then went on to discuss alternative development directions, including market penetration, market development, new product development and related and unrelated diversifications, before reviewing the resource-based view of business development. The importance of addressing the decision-making criteria when evaluating different routes and directions was finally addressed. Hospitality businesses should consider their future development routes and directions carefully. A business that rushes into making rash decisions will ultimately face the consequences of its actions and its future direction is likely to be destined to fail. Hospitality businesses should therefore use the decision-making criteria as a basis for understanding the feasibility of any future route or direction.

REVIEW QUESTIONS

1. Choose a hospitality business and answer the following questions.
2. To what extent does the business have an advantage over competitors in its sector? Make suggestions on how the business can either obtain or sustain an advantage over competitors.
3. Evaluate what the future development direction of the firm should be. Justify why the business should pursue this development direction. What are the potential risks of pursuing this direction for the hospitality business?
4. Review the hospitality business' resources. To what extent do they meet the VIRUS criteria?
5. Offer advice to the hospitality business on its future development routes and directions based upon the decision-making criteria outlined in Figure 7.4.

Case Study: Business Development at Little Chef

Little Chef is a chain of roadside restaurants based in the United Kingdom. Sam Alper, a caravan manufacturer, opened the first Little Chef in 1958 with only 11 seats in Reading. His concept of Little Chef was based upon the roadside diner model in America and over the next three decades the business has grown to over 400 sites. The restaurants are predominantly based on A roads and positioned such that they are easily accessible to the passing traveller. In recent years Little Chef has encountered a number of difficulties and even went into administration in 2007.

Little Chef has had a number of owners since the mid-1990s including Forte, Granada (took over the Little Chef chain in 1996 as part of the acquisition of Forte), Compass Group (in 2001), private equity group Permira (in 2002) and The People Restaurant Ltd (in 2005). Under the ownership of The People Restaurant Ltd, Little Chef went into administration in early 2007. Private equity firm R Capital then acquired the business for £9 million. At this point the business had been reported to be losing £3 million a year. The chain now has 180 sites.

In recent years Little Chef has had to compete with the massive influx of fast food establishments and the growing number of petrol station forecourts that have diversified into selling takeaway drinks and snacks. This is in addition to the greater range of eating options available to travellers through, for example, branded pub chains. Coupled with this have been the social trends towards healthy eating and eating on the move. Business travellers also often want to get to their end destination quickly and are therefore more likely to want to take the motorway instead of A roads which can add further time to their journey. Fluctuations in

Continued

demand can also be impacted upon by roadworks, the weather and the time of the year.

The chain under subsequent ownerships had suffered from poor investment and a lack of clear direction. The Little Chef brand is closely associated with its 'Fat Charlie' logo which adorns its restaurants. Famously, a previous owner of Little Chef (Permira) embarked on a rebranding exercise of the logo. This entailed a slimmed down version of Fat Charlie and was intended to negate the image that Little Chef was synonymous with unhealthy foods. However, the rebranding exercise encountered a negative public reaction and was subsequently never rolled out across the chain.

Under R Capital, Ian Pegler, a former boss of Little Chef during its ownership by Forte from 1990 to 1994, was recruited as Chief Executive of the firm and was tasked with revitalising the brand. Dishes such as bangers and mash and Caesar salad were replaced with meals such as fish pie, pasta salads, curries, and liver and bacon. Lighter breakfast options with granary bread, fruit juices and muesli breakfasts were also introduced. The chain has also developed a take away option which includes breakfast rolls, jacket potatoes, toasties and burger options. Free Wi-Fi connections have also been installed. However, the chain has been reticent to cut costs as this may impact upon margins and has the potential to be poorly perceived by customers. In 2008 the chain commissioned celebrity chef Heston Blumenthal (the owner of the triple Michelin starred Fat Duck restaurant in Bray, Berkshire) to offer advice on the way forward for Little Chef. This has resulted in a new-style Little Chef being trialled at the Popham restaurant near Basingstoke. If the Popham branch is successful then the intention is to roll this out across the Little Chef chain.

Source: The Observer.

Question

1. To what extent have environmental and competitive factors impacted upon Little Chef as a business? To what extent has Little Chef been suffering from strategic drift?

2. Evaluate to what extent Little Chef has been 'stuck in the middle' with no clear development route or direction. What have been the implications of this for the chain?

3. Search the Internet for further information about Little Chef's future development routes and directions and evaluate the effectiveness of these. What suggestions would you make on Little Chef's future business development? Analyse how Little Chef can use the decision-making criteria outlined in Figure 7.4 when deciding upon future routes and directions.

4. What factors may continue to act as a threat to Little Chef pursuing its future business development routes and directions?

GLOSSARY

Competences   Competences are the attributes that the hospitality business requires if it is to compete effectively in the marketplace. Competences emerge from the organisations bundle of resources and can encompass skills, knowledge and technology.

Consolidation   When the hospitality business will focus on maintaining its current markets with its existing products. This may also lead to a period of consolidation activity in the sector, when hospitality businesses decide to merge with or acquire one another.

Core competences   Core competences are over and above the industry standard and can act as a basis for gaining added value and competitive advantage.

Cost leadership   Cost leadership is where the hospitality business becomes the lowest cost producer in the industry or sector and can thus gain higher profits.

Differentiation   Differentiation strategy is when the hospitality business offers something unique and sells it at a premium price.

Focus   Focus is when the hospitality business targets a narrow segment of the market.

Market development   Finding new markets for the existing products.

Market penetration   Increasing the market share of the existing product in the existing market.

Product development   Developing new products for the existing markets.

Related diversification   Related diversification occurs when the hospitality business decides to enter into product areas that are related to its core business activity.

Strategic resources   Strategic or unique resources are those resources which are over and above the industry standard and enable the hospitality business to gain an advantage over competitors.

Threshold resources   Threshold resources are those which the hospitality business must have if it is to operate in a given sector.

Unrelated diversification   Hospitality business decides to enter a product area that is unrelated to its core business activity.

Withdrawal   If sales are declining to the extent where it has become unfeasible both in terms of time and resources to attempt to rejuvenate the brand, it may be necessary for the hospitality business to ultimately withdraw the product from the market.

CHAPTER 8

Hospitality Business Development Methods

Learning Objectives

Having completed this chapter you should be able to:

- Understand the alternative development methods available to hospitality businesses.
- Evaluate the costs and benefits of embarking on different development methods for hospitality businesses.
- Consider the risks involved in pursuing different development methods for hospitality businesses.

CONTENTS

INTRODUCTION

Once the hospitality business has considered the alternative routes and directions that it can pursue, it will need to adopt a development method. This chapter will present the different strategic methods which the hospitality business may adopt whilst also appraising their advantages and disadvantages. The rationale for pursuing these different development methods will also be considered.

The hospitality business needs to decide which development method is the most appropriate for it to pursue its desired strategic direction. The selection of strategic methods will offer the opportunity for the hospitality business to expand its portfolio of activities and further strengthen its resource base. The different types of strategic methods in the hospitality industry are normally outlined as follows:

- Organic development
- Mergers and acquisitions
- Strategic alliances
- Franchising (including consortia)
- Management contracting.

Each of these development methods has its advantages and disadvantages. The hospitality business needs to decide which is the most appropriate development method to use. Its decisions on this will be based upon the type of development route and direction the business is pursuing, the resources the business has at its disposal and the level of risk the business is willing to incur.

INTERNAL OR ORGANIC DEVELOPMENT

Organic or internal development is where the hospitality business utilises its existing resources and competences to pursue a particular direction. The hospitality business therefore makes the strategic decision to pursue a strategic direction on its own and incur all the risks that may be associated with that decision. There are a number of reasons why a hospitality business may make this decision. The business may have particular resource strengths that it can capitalise upon. This may include large amounts of financial capital that it is able to draw upon and enable the business to develop new products or enter new markets. The reputational resources of the hospitality business in terms of its brand and associated image may enable it to extend this into new product and market areas. This has been to the advantage of many leading hotel companies and fast food chains that have leveraged their brands as part of a globalisation strategy.

There are certain advantages for the hospitality business pursuing a development method of organic growth. The hospitality business is able to retain total control over the development route and direction. By doing so it can plan more effectively by making the most appropriate allocation of resources and more closely monitor the rate in which it wants the development to progress. The business is also able to retain all the gains that may derive from the outcome of the development route and direction. In particular, the financial and reputational gains that may be derived from the success of the growth route.

On the counter side, the hospitality business will need to assess the extent to which it has strategic resources to pursue a strategy of organic growth. The hospitality business has to be cautious about overextending its resource base to the extent that the development route impacts upon the business's other activities. The hospitality business has to assess the extent to which it has the knowledge and expertise to pursue a particular direction on its own. For example, if an Italian restaurant business decided to diversify into opening a chain of Greek restaurants, would it have the necessary expertise and knowledge resources to pursue this development route? The hospitality business will also have to incur the financial and reputational costs for any development route that does not successfully materialise. Furthermore, when compared to the other strategic methods, organic growth can be a slower process for achieving the business development route and direction. When the external environment is dynamic and fast moving, which is the case within the hospitality industry, this can present difficulties as the business needs to move and quickly capitalise upon opportunities.

Example: Organic Growth at KFC and Domino's Pizza

In February 2009, and after both reporting an increase in sales, KFC and Domino's Pizza announced the development of new sites. KFC stated that it was to expand its portfolio of restaurants from 200 to 300 over the next three to five years, whilst Domino's Pizza has plans to have over 1000 outlets opened within 2010. KFC stated that the majority of its new store openings would be in the North of England and South Wales and some of the openings will be through franchise arrangements. The rise in sales was accounted for changing consumer preferences towards cheaper takeaway alternatives and away from more expensive restaurant meals. This is in light of the external economic conditions and the credit crunch, which had impacted upon discretionary income and consumer spending power.

Activity

1. Discuss to what extent external environmental conditions promote further opportunities for fast food businesses.

2. Why would KFC envisage most of its expansion in restaurants coming in the North of England and South Wales?

3. Read the section later in the chapter on franchising. Why might KFC use franchise arrangements to expand its business?

MERGERS AND ACQUISITIONS

Mergers and acquisitions occur when hospitality businesses combine with one another to exploit resources and competences. There are differences between mergers and acquisitions. A merger is when two or more organisations agree to become one organisation, whereas an acquisition occurs when one organisation purchases another. The acquisition may be consensual and enable the acquired business to utilise strategic resources that otherwise would not occur. However, this development method can be hostile in nature and it should not be assumed that the hospitality business wants to be acquired. A number of reasons have been highlighted for a business considering an acquisition or merger (Evans et al., 2003; Capon, 2008; Haberberg and Rieple, 2008; Johnson et al., 2008) and these are listed as follows:

■ **Speed of entry**

The speed in which the business can gain entry into a product or market area. The hospitality business can gain a foothold into a product or market area by utilising the expertise and knowledge base of a business it has acquired or it has merged with. Capon (2008) notes how this can be a key development method when businesses wish to expand internationally and markets have matured in the businesses'domestic marketplace.

■ **Increase market share and power**

The merger and acquisition can enable the business to increase its market share within the competitive environment. If the hospitality business seeks to acquire or merge with a related competitor this reduces the level of competition in the industry sector. Furthermore, the combined business can generate a greater power base for the firm, enabling it to influence conditions and forces that prevail amongst competitors.

■ **Cost base reductions and economies of scale**

The acquisition or merger can enable the business to exploit reductions to its cost base and gain economies of scale. Indeed, following a merger or acquisition, it is not uncommon for the combined businesses to embark on reduction in its resource base where duplication in expertise, knowledge and methods of operation may occur. This can lead to the restructuring of the combined businesses resulting in a reduction in human resources or the sale of parts of the business that no longer are relevant to the activities of the core business.

■ Raising capital

When a hospitality business decides to acquire another firm, it can also use it as a way of asset stripping. This occurs when the businesses' key assets are sold to other firms as a method of generating further financial capital for the business. This occurred in the 1990s when Granada acquired the hospitality business Forte and went about selling parts of the business that were no part of its overall business plan.

■ Synergy

There is potential for synergies to occur between the merged or acquired businesses. Synergy is when the resultant effect of the combined businesses is greater than what can be achieved alone. Synergistic effects are realised when increased added value is generated from the business combining together (Evans et al., 2003).

In contrast to the benefits of mergers and acquisitions, the hospitality business also has to be aware of the possible drawbacks. The potential problems of mergers and acquisitions may include the failure of successfully integrating the combined companies so the synergistic effects do not occur. This can be for a number of reasons as illustrated in the following:

■ Cultural issues

There may be cultural incompatibility between the merged or acquired hospitality businesses, leading to conflict between managers and employees within the organisation. This can particularly be the case when the business acquires or merges with a firm that is from another country of origin and factors including language, norms of behaviour and so on can impact upon the integration of the businesses.

■ Organisational systems and structures

The organisational structures and systems of operation may not naturally fit together and this can result in costly adjustments to operating procedures within the business. In relation to these two previous points, if the hospitality business realises that it may have difficulty in integrating the acquired firm, it may have to operate it as a separate subsidiary (Capon, 2008).

■ **Trust**

Trust between merged organisations needs to prevail. It can sometimes be the case that one firm will act as the dominant partner in the combined relationship so as to ease the integration of the businesses. However, disagreements between who should act as the dominant partner can have the potential to derail the success of the merger.

■ **Overstretching of resources**

The hospitality business may overstretch itself through the acquisition of another firm. This is in terms of the financial resources that have been used to purchase the business as well as the management resources that are required to ensure that the businesses are successfully integrated.

■ **Changing environmental conditions**

If the hospitality business decides to acquire another firm, it needs to consider how future environmental conditions can result in the acquired or merged firm not being as appealing as originally intended (Capon, 2008).

■ **Overvaluation of the acquisition**

The price paid for the business needs to be accurate so that realised value is generated following acquisition (Evans et al., 2003).

ASSET SWAPPING

An asset swapping arrangement may act as an alternative to the direct acquisition of part of a business from another firm. Asset swapping is when two businesses decide to swap assets that are of, or as near to, equivalent value. If there is a difference in value between the assets to be swapped then any shortfall can be made up by the respective hospitality business. Asset swapping occurs when the businesses are able to mutually gain from the transaction. This may be because the swapped assets are able to add additional value to the business. This could be in the form of cost reductions, market or product development or diversification. The asset swap may also allow the hospitality business to remove parts of the business that are a drain on resources and impacting upon its future development.

Example: Mitchells and Butlers and Whitbread

In July 2006, Mitchells and Butlers paid Whitbread £497 million for 239 Beefeater and Brewers Fayre pub-restaurant sites. The justification for the acquisition was based upon Mitchells and Butler further asserting itself in the high growth residential dining market particularly in the South West and South East of England. The acquisition also enabled Mitchells and Butler to continue to reposition the business towards the eating out market. The intention of Mitchells and Butler was to rebrand the pubs within two years to Harvester, Premium Country Dining, Toby and Vintage Inns brands. For Whitbread, the deal enabled them to focus on those Beefeater and Brewers Fayre sites that were next to Premier Travel Inns or could be developed into a combined operation. However, in July 2008, both firms engaged in an asset swap. Whitbread acquired 21 Express by Holiday Inn hotels from Mitchells and Butlers (M&B) in exchange for 44 stand-alone Brewers Fayre and Beefeater pub restaurants both equally valued at £78 million. Whitbread stated that the 44 pub restaurants sold were on sites where development of a Premier Inn had not been possible due to planning constraints.

Source: Caterersearch.com.

Activity

1. From the above example evaluate the rationale for the development methods adopted by Mitchells and Butlers and Whitbread? What may be the costs and benefits of these development methods for both firms?

2. Identify other examples in the hospitality industry of mergers and acquisitions. What has been the rationale for this development method for the hospitality businesses concerned?

STRATEGIC ALLIANCES

Strategic alliances and joint ventures are formal arrangements between two or more organisations where they work together to fulfil a mutually beneficial development route or direction. The alliance partners can benefit from one another through shared resources and access to untapped markets. By joining forces with another partner, alliances can enable hospitality businesses to build upon areas of strength or to compensate for weaknesses. Alliances can enable partners to share resources and competences that each may be lacking and utilise these to gain entry more quickly into new markets and product areas. Alliances can also reduce the level of risk on embarking on a development route independently.

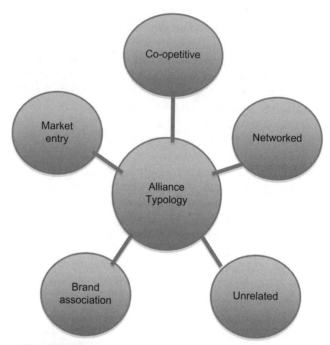

FIGURE 8.1 *Alliance typology in the hospitality industry.*

In the hospitality industry alliances can take many forms and these are illustrated as a typology of alliances in Figure 8.1. The typology enables an understanding of the relationships that can be formed between different hospitality businesses. These different alliances are formed to enable the hospitality business to pursue a particular strategic development route or direction that it would find difficult to pursue alone.

■ Co-opetitive alliance

Co-opetitive alliances are based upon the premise of competitors from the same sector forming an alliance. Though they may view themselves as direct competitors, via a process of 'co-opetition' (Brandenburger and Nalebuff, 1997) they can combine forces to become much more powerful in the marketplace. An example of this is the Global Hotel Alliance which is made up of 11 independent hotel brands. The alliance is able to collectively distribute their goods and services through their online site as well as enabling the further generation of revenue across the network of hotel groups. A co-opetitive alliance is related in nature and will be formed between organisations that operate in the same sector of hospitality industry.

Consortia are another example of co-opetitive alliances. Consortia are groups of independent hospitality businesses that are marketed under a single brand. Though being able to retain their independence and individual character, each hospitality business has to conform to a consistent set of standards that is expected by the customer from the brand. Best Western International is an example of a hotel consortium and is made up of over 4000 hotels from across the globe.

■ Networked alliance

A networked alliance is where hospitality businesses forge an alliance to facilitate the distribution of their goods and services. This is via online and/ or digital platforms and may come in the form of a hospitality business forging an alliance to more easily distribute their goods or services. This occurred in 2001, when the large-scale hotel groups Meridien, Accor and Hilton International formed an alliance to create Andbook.com which was an online booking platform for their hotels. Networked alliances can also be between ancillary service partners that can facilitate the promotion of their goods and services. For example, the hotel company, Intercontinental Group, have a number of their hotel brands promoted through social networking sites such as YouTube, Facebook and Second Life. They also use technologies such as Google Earth to more easily facilitate the booking of their hotels.

■ Market entry alliances

A market entry alliance is when the hospitality business forges an alliance with a firm that enables it to gain entry into a new market. This type of alliance is used to gain entry into the market quickly and to utilise the expertise of the alliance partner in doing so. This development method is particularly useful when the hospitality business accesses a growing market. For example, Whitbread, owner of Premier Travel Inn, entered into alliances with the Indian real estate developer, Emaar-MGF, and Emirates Group to develop the Premier Travel Inn brand in India and Dubai, respectively.

■ Brand association alliance

A brand association alliance is formed to reciprocally enhance the promotion of two or more brands. The intention is to mutually benefit each other from the brand association that is made and the values that the brand communicates to the target audience. For example, the motorway service operator, RoadChef, has agreements with a number of high street brands including McDonalds, Pizza Hut and Costa Coffee. With the latter it operates under the signage of 'RoadChef Costa Coffee' enabling customers to associate a key brand that acts as a draw for further sales growth between the two companies.

A further example of brand association is between Marriott International and the children's entertainment brand Nickelodeon which intends to develop 20 lodging developments by 2020 called Nickelodeon Resort by Marriott. The partnership enables Marriott to target the growing business market that also travel with their families. It also enables Nickelodeon to further extend its brand to a generation of users that have grown up and are familiar with the entertainment channel.

■ Unrelated alliance

An unrelated alliance is where the hospitality business forms an alliance with an organisation from an unrelated industry. The purpose of this may be to generate synergies between the organisations that would be difficult to achieve alone. For example, in October 2008 the budget supermarket chain Aldi and Travelodge forged an alliance to develop joint sites in Middlesbrough and Newquay. As a consequence of the economic conditions and the move by customers towards budget brands, both organisations embarked on growth strategies. Though, Aldi operates in an unrelated field to hospitality, both organisations operate a business model that is based upon cost reduction and this relationship enabled cost synergies to be gained from the joint development as well as enabling both businesses to continue with their expansion plans.

It should be acknowledged that there is a degree of overlap between the different alliance typologies. For example, a networked alliance is likely to be made up of a number of related competitors leading to a co-opetitive alliance structure. There can also be brand association alliances between unrelated hospitality businesses as the Nickelodeon Resort by Marriott example has illustrated. Nevertheless, the typology enables the hospitality business to consider the different alliances that are available to them when considering a business development route and direction.

Similar to acquisition and mergers, the hospitality business needs to consider how the alliance partner can be successfully integrated into the operational aspects of the firm. In this respect it is important that there is a good 'strategic fit' between the respective businesses and that they meet the four C's operational functioning criteria as forwarded by Medcof (1997). That is, capability and whether the partners are capable of effectively engaging in the alliance; compatibility and the ability of the partners to operate reciprocally in an alliance relationship; commitment, in terms of the alliance partners having the staying power to achieve the potential benefits of the alliance; and finally, control of the alliance in determining its strategic direction and growth potential.

In addition, the alliance should be aware of a number of factors that could lead to its potential failure. This includes an over-dependence of one partner on another, leading to the reliance on the partner forms resources. Resentment by partner organisation could also prevail due to a loss of independent control and the possible domination of one partner over another. Trust between the partners is therefore crucial, otherwise there is the potential for one organisation to exploit the resources and capabilities of the other partners, before leaving the alliance. The alliance structure should be carefully planned and a rigorous feasibility plan should be developed to ensure that synergies could be generated as a consequence of partners forming an alliance.

Activity

1. Using Figure 8.1 identify examples of hospitality businesses that have formed alliances in the hospitality industry.

2. Why have these alliances been formed? What potential benefits do they bring to the partner hospitality businesses?

3. What could be the potential drawbacks to the hospitality businesses joining the alliance?

FRANCHISING

Franchising occurs when there is a contractual arrangement between two parties, that is the franchisee and the franchisor. The franchisee trades under the franchisor's brand name and operating procedures in return for an initial fee and percentage of return once trading. Franchising has become a popular strategy amongst many hospitality-related businesses that have sought to expand their businesses rapidly across the globe. This includes fast food companies, for example, McDonalds and Subway and coffee retailers, such as Costa Coffee, who have used franchising as a development method to grow their businesses quickly.

There are a number of benefits to operating a franchise network. Franchising enables hospitality businesses to exploit alternative markets at a relatively low cost. They can gain economies of scale by the growth in the business and have minimal involvement in the operating costs of the franchise. They will also gain from the devolvement of legal obligations to the franchisee. This may include planning or licensing applications which can be time consuming to process and could actually be quicker for the franchisee to obtain at the local level. It will also largely be the case that the franchisee management will be highly motivated as they are making a significant investment and will want the franchise to succeed.

For the franchisee, they have access to the brand image of the firm which will automatically be positioned in the mind of the consumer. This entails minimal effort and costs associated with marketing the product and business. The franchisee also gains from having access to the expertise of the franchisor. This is in the form of expertise, training, methods of operation and so on. This enables the franchisees to set up and operate their businesses relatively quickly, allowing them speed of entry into the marketplace.

A number of costs need to be considered when considering a franchise arrangement. The franchisor has to ensure that brand standards are maintained across the businesses' portfolio of franchise operations. If a franchise operation gains a poor reputation or negative publicity, this has the potential to impact upon the rest of the franchise network. Enforcing a process of change can also be a slower process than for a business that is owned and operated solely by the hospitality business. The franchisee may also be driven by short-term gain as opposed to the longer term viability of the business. This can lead to a conflict in goals in the franchise arrangement.

For the franchisee, they have to ensure that they have an initial start, up fee and are committed to the payment of royalties to the franchisor once in operation. There is also a loss of control to a certain degree and the franchisee is beholden to the operating and business practices of the franchisor. The franchisee is unlikely to be able to develop its own product and service variations as these need to adhere to a brand standard that is stipulated by the franchisor. This includes the suppliers that are used by the business, restricting the potential for the franchisor to use cheaper alternatives. The franchisee is therefore restricted to the business development of the franchisor and the directions which they wish to pursue. In this respect, the franchisee is dependent upon the continued viability of the franchisor. The costs and benefits are summarised in Table 8.1.

Table 8.1	Franchising: Costs and Benefits	
	Costs	**Benefits**
Franchisor	■ Need to ensure brand standards are maintained across the network ■ Process of imbuing change across the franchise network ■ Conflicts with the possible short termisim of franchisees	■ Rapid market expansion ■ Minimal capital required for expansion ■ Gain economies of scale ■ Minimal operating costs ■ Motivated franchisee management ■ Reduced legal obligations
Franchisee	■ Initial stat up fee required and the commitment to the payment of royalties ■ Loss of control ■ Lack of autonomy in choosing alternative suppliers ■ Business development is restricted by the franchisor	■ Access to key resources including knowledge, training and expertise and marketing reputational and brand resources ■ Enables speed of entry into the marketplace ■ Access to standardised and proven systems of operation

Example: easyHotel and Franchising

The easyHotel brand uses franchising as a model for business expansion and market development. From opening its first easyHotel franchise in Basel in 2005, it has expanded to have franchise arrangements with Eclipse Hotels for the easyHotel in Luton, Splendid Hotel Group for easyHotels throughout London, Portuguese firm Best Ecran to operate easyHotel in Portugal, P Orange GmbH for easyHotel in Austria and with i.gen hotels for easyHotel in Germany. It also signed a master franchise agreement with Istithmar, a Dubai-based company, to expand the easyHotel chain across the Middle East, North Africa and India.

Source: www.easyHotel.com.

MANAGEMENT CONTRACTING

A management contract is an arrangement where a company (owner) contracts another firm (operator) to manage and run the business. Management contracts, therefore, enable the owner to devolve the responsibility of running the business to the operator. The operator will often have the necessary expertise and knowledge on how to run the business and in return, will receive a management fee based upon profits and revenues generated. Management contracts enable the owners to gain entry to markets where they may lack expertise and require local knowledge to operate and manage the business. The risks in using management contracts are therefore less than if the owner was to manage the operation itself in an unknown market. Management contracts are not uncommon in the hotel sector of the hospitality industry with examples including InterContinental Hotels Group, Marriott and the Accor group. Nevertheless, both the owner and the operator should acknowledge the business routes and directions that they intend to pursue when considering management contracting as a development method.

Bader and Lababedi (2007) highlight a number of terms that hospitality businesses have to consider when embarking on a management contract as follows:

■ **Term of the contract**

This refers to the length of time the contract will be in existence. This usually is anything from 10 to 20 years but it depends upon the brand profile and positioning of the operator.

■ **Operating fees**

This is the operating fee that will be paid by the owner to the operator. This may include a base fee that is calculated on the basis of revenues, in addition to a fee based upon a percentage of profits. The profitability fee acts as an incentive for the operator to maximise the running potential of the business.

■ **Operator guarantees**

Operator guarantees is the level of profit that the operator will generate for the owner. If there is a shortfall in profits, a guarantee may be set in place that ensures that the operator makes up the remaining deficit. Fourth, are performance measures and the basis upon which revenues and profitability will be calculated.

■ **Performance measures**

Performance measures can be based upon the revenue per available room (RevPAR) and the percentage of gross operating profit (GOP) generated by the operator.

■ **Owner approval**

Owner approval is the level of autonomy that the operator has in making adaptations to the operation of the business. This may includes budgeting, the recruitment of management staff and the outsourcing of operational aspects of the business.

■ Capital expenditure

This is the percentage of income that needs to be set aside or the replacement of furnishing and fittings. This is to ensure that the business is able to maintain the brand standards of the firm.

■ Non-compete clause

This is a clause that ensures the owner is guaranteed that the operator will not open up a competing or same brand within a specified vicinity of the business. This is to ensure that the business is not directly impacted upon through the loss of custom and revenues to the competing business.

■ Dispute resolution

Dispute resolutions are the measures that are put in place if a dispute was to occur between the owner and operator. This may include payment for expenses incurred as a consequence of the dispute, bodies that will arbitrate in any dispute and the legal implications that may reside in a dispute.

■ Termination

These are the terms that need to be negotiated if an agreement was to be terminated. This may be for reasons of insolvency, criminal fraud or failing to continually meet the performance measures.

Example

In December 2008, the Jumeirah Group signed a management agreement with Shun Tak Holdings for a new five star deluxe hotel in the Cotai area of Macau, China. The Jumeirah Macau Hotel, scheduled for completion in 2013, will have views of the Macau Dome, where many of the city's major sports and cultural entertainment events are hosted. Shun Tak has a strong presence in Macau with substantial direct and indirect investments in the transportation, gaming and hospitality industries. In the press release, Gerald Lawless, Executive Chairman of Jumeirah, stated that 'Macau has a rich and unique heritage of Asian and European influences, and the Jumeirah Macau Hotel will certainly be a perfect addition to our international portfolio of hotels and resorts, in line with our promise to STAY DIFFERENT.... this is the third management agreement that we have signed in China, with the first Jumeirah HanTang Xintiandi scheduled to open in Shanghai in 2009 and Jumeirah Guangzhou Hotel in 2011'.

Source: www.hospitality.net.

Activity

1. In the example above, evaluate what the business development route and direction has been for the Jumeirah Group pursuing a strategy of management contracting?

2. Search the Internet for other examples of management contracts in the hospitality industry.

3. Why have these management contracts occurred? What has been the rationale for the business development routes and directions?

4. What are the potential costs and benefits of these management contracts to both the owner and the operator?

SUMMARY AND CONCLUSIONS

This chapter has discussed the different development methods of organic development, mergers and acquisitions, strategic alliances, franchising and management contracting. This has included an evaluation of the costs and benefits of each of the development methods as well as an appraisal of some of the risks involved in pursuit of this method. The hospitality business has to consider all the available options before embarking on any particular method. To a large extent, the method will be influenced by the business development route and direction that the hospitality firm is seeking to pursue. For example, the desire of the business to enter quickly into a new market may require a development method of acquisition, alliance or franchising. On the other hand, if the hospitality business has the necessary resources and competences to pursue the development method alone then organic growth may be a better option. As part of its feasibility plan, it is important that the hospitality business reviews all the available options before embarking on any particular method. It should consider the long-term implications of the development method as well as the short- to medium-term operational and cost implications that it may incur for the business.

REVIEW QUESTIONS

1. Briefly explain what you understand by the following business development methods:
   - Organic development
   - Mergers and acquisitions
   - Strategic alliances

- Franchising
- Management contracting.

2. Choose a hospitality business and decide what should be the most appropriate development route for the business. What advice would you give on how the business should embark on this method?

3. What is your justification for this method and what may be the costs and benefits of this development method for the firm?

Case Study – Development Methods in the UK Restaurant Sector

Context

The restaurant sector in the UK is predominantly made up of medium-sized operators comprising 5 to 20 operations. However, there are a number of major players that have over 40 sites. According to PricewaterhouseCoopers (PwC) the recession impacted significantly on the restaurant sector with the closure of over 500 restaurants in 2008. The impact had been felt right across the sector, with a number of celebrity chef restaurants closing during 2009. This includes Brasserie Blanc in Manchester owned by Raymond Blanc, and the closure of four of Antony Worrall Thompson's restaurants. He also had to place his company, AWT, into administration following the Lloyds Banking Group refusing to extend an overdraft facility. PwC noted that across the sector it was the mid-range restaurants that had failed to offer value for money or a distinctive experience that was most affected by closure. The impact on overall profitability of restaurant chains has also been challenged by a decline in mid-week restaurant outings and increased competition from pub restaurants. Nevertheless, in terms of expenditure, eating out is second to spending on holidays.

Prior to the recession the sector experienced a series of strategic manoeuvres by the restaurant companies. This had consolidated the position of the major players in pursuit of sector growth.

The Restaurant Group

The Restaurant Group (TRG), which owns Frankie and Benny's, Chiquito's, Garfunkel's, Blubeckers and Edwinns Brasseries, is the largest restaurant operator in the marketplace. It has over 300 restaurants and serves up to 30 million meals per year. The group targets the value end of the market with the majority of outlets based in airports or leisure and retail parks. These sites have higher barriers to entry and are difficult for other restaurant operators to access. Frankie and Benny's focuses on Italian–American cuisine and Chiquito's on Mexican cuisine. The company often uses a strategy of locating the restaurants that are either adjacent or within the same vicinity of each other.

In June 2005, TRG acquired Blubeckers for £27.05 million from CI Traders. The chain was made up of predominantly rural or semi-rural properties located in the south and south-east regions of the UK and targeted families and mature consumers. The deal enabled TRG to target the 'grey market' which it had largely under-represented at the time. The deal also came with five Edwinns Brasseries. In October 2007, the group also purchased the Brunning & Price chain of restaurants for £32 million. The chain had 14 rural or semi-rural outlets based mainly in the Northwest of England.

Tragus Holdings

Tragus Holdings (which own Café Rouge, Bella Italia, Strada and the Brasseries Abbaye, Oriel, Ortega, Potters, Belgo and Huxleys) is the second largest independent restaurant group in the UK. It has over 270 sites across the country and serves over 20 million meals every year. In December 2006, Tragus was acquired by the private equity arm of The Blackstone Group for £267 million. The focus of the Tragus group is

Continued

'casual dining' and its strategy has been to pursue organic growth with acquisitions where it can exploit growth potential.

In February 2007, Tragus acquired 16 MA Potters sites for just over £14 million. These have now been rebranded as Potters as part of the brasserie arm of the business. This was quickly followed with the purchase of premium Italian restaurant chain Strada in May 2007 for £140 million. Tragus already had a presence in the Italian market via its branded Bella Italia chain. This acquisition enabled Tragus to enter the premium end of the Italian market. The deal also included the acquisition of five brasserie style Belgo and Bierodrome restaurants. The Strada chain had been purchased two years previously from the Signature Restaurant Group by Richard Caring for £60 million.

In April 2007 a bidding war for the tapas chain La Tasca occurred between Tragus and Iranian investor Robert Tchenguiz who owns the Bay Restaurant Group, comprising the Ha Ha Bar and Slug and Lettuce bars. Tragus already owned a 6.88% share of La Tasca and the La Tasca chain would have enabled a strategic fit with its existing restaurant portfolio. Tragus already had an upmarket tapas-based restaurant in the form of Ortega. However, Tchenguiz outbid Tragus and purchased La Tasca's for £104 million.

Paramount Holdings Ltd

Paramount is a private company whose brands include the Parisian themed Brasserie Chez Gérard and the Italian themed Bertorelli chain. In 2005 Paramount made a failed bid for Little Chef but later that same year purchased 53 Caffé Uno outlets from TRG for £33 million. The deal effectively doubled the size of the group and it used the acquisition to partially convert a number of the Café Uno's to Brasserie Chez Gérard. The deal enabled TRG to pull out of the high street where a number of the Caffé Uno's were based.

Carluccio's

Carluccio's is an Italian themed caffé, restaurant and food shop founded in 1991 by Antonio and Priscilla Carluccio. The company has predominantly followed a strategy of organic growth and has 41 outlets based across the UK.

The chain which was floated on the Alternative Investment Market (AIM) in December 2005 is unique as it incorporates food shops into its restaurants. The company also opened its first Carluccio's franchise in Dublin in 2008. The franchise was opened on acknowledgment that local market expertise was required for the operation of the business.

TGI Friday's

TGI Friday's is an American themed restaurant experience. In March 2007, Whitbread completed the sale of 45 TGI Friday restaurants to a joint venture between Carlson and private equity group ABN Capital for £70.4 million. Under the terms of the deal, ABN owns 60% while Carlson owns 40% of the business. Though the TGI Friday's operates a franchise arrangement in the US, the joint venture partners have not pursued this business in the UK.

Sources: www.ft.com, www.caterersearch.com, www.pwc.co.uk, www.mintel.com.

Questions

1. Analyse the external environment of the restaurant sector using a LoNGPEST analysis (see Chapter 3)? What are the key opportunities and threats for the sector?

2. Reflecting on the content of Chapter 7 and the different development routes, what has been the rationale of the restaurant companies for pursuing particular methods?

3. Identify and evaluate the development methods of the different restaurant companies discussed in the case study. Why were these methods chosen? To what extent could the companies have used alternative development methods?

4. Search for further information on the Internet about each company's overall financial performance, growth, market share and brand reputation. Evaluate to what extent these development methods have been beneficial to the firm's competitive position in the marketplace.

GLOSSARY

Asset swapping   Asset swapping is when two businesses decide to swap assets that are of, or as near to, equivalent value.

Franchising   Franchising occurs when there is a contractual arrangement between two parties, that is the franchisee and the franchisor.

Management contracting   A management contract is an arrangement where a company (owner) contracts another firm (operator) to manage and run the business.

Mergers and acquisitions   A merger is when two or more organisations agree to become one organisation whereas an acquisition occurs when one organisation purchases another.

Organic growth   Organic or internal development is where the hospitality business utilises its existing resources and competences to pursue a particular direction.

Strategic alliances   Strategic alliances and joint ventures are formal arrangements between two or more organisations where they work together to fulfil a mutually beneficial development route or direction.

CHAPTER 9

New Product Development (NPD)

Learning Objectives

Having completed this chapter, readers should be able to:

- Introduce the concept and importance of NPD in the hospitality industry.
- Explore the relationship between NPD and innovation in the hospitality industry.
- Understand the scope of hospitality innovation and NPD.
- Discuss the key success factors of NPD in the hospitality industry.

CONTENTS

Introduction

Definitions

Critical Success
Factors of NPD

Conclusion

Review Questions

Glossary

INTRODUCTION

New product development is continuing to be an area that is receiving increased awareness, both in theory and practice (Shani et al., 2003). It is regarded as an essential activity for firms that desire to face competition on the basis of quality and suitability of purpose (Ciappei and Simoni, 2005; Cooper, 1999; John and Snelson, 1990). Cooper (1999) argues that developing new products or fail, as a company, are the only two options available for any service organisation in today's competitive business environment. Along the same lines, Booz et al. (1982) argue that the success in launching new products is increasingly responsible for the growth and profitability of firms. Kotler and Armstrong (2004) also suggest that NPD is of utmost importance to enable a company to meet customer wants and needs effectively. Finally, Shepherd and Ahmed (2000) argue that new products are fundamental to the development and sustainable success of the contemporary corporation.

In addition, there is a strong relationship between product innovation and success in the hospitality industry. Laugen et al. (2005), Lewis and Chambers (2000) and Morrison (2001) suggest a strong correlation between market performance and attention to product innovation. Bowie and Buttle (2004) argue that new products offer the opportunity to open up new markets and maintain significant market shares in those segments. As the life cycle matures, product innovations unrelated to price, such as design, customisation and quality are linked to competitive sales growth.

Previous research on NPD in the tourism and hospitality industry is limited. Bradford (1994) discussed innovation through acquisition, within the restaurant industry, which involves the purchase of small growing companies by large corporations as an alternative to developing new concepts internally. Jones (1996) developed a generic 15-step process that companies use to manage NPD/innovation in the hospitality industry. The author had earlier, in 1995, applied Scheuing and Johnson's model for new service development (NSD) to flight catering. His research found that airlines lack many of the systematic procedures suggested by Scheuing and Johnson. Shoemaker (1996) monitored how customers develop a series of actions considered as significant, compulsory or appropriate for a service transaction. Variations from the script can be a source of dissatisfaction. Thus, when developing new service delivery systems, companies must assist customers in developing a new script. Miner (1996) created a customer based and detailed approach to developing new products in a restaurant. The six-stage process includes product ideas, initial evaluation, customer reaction, sensory testing, field-testing and product introduction.

The changing market environment has forced marketing experts to reconsider the way in which they approach their tasks. Indeed, consumer tastes, wants and needs are changing from time to time and new competitive patterns are emerging. Therefore, it has become essential for an organisation to adapt, develop and innovate to achieve a competitive advantage and become successful (Kotler et al., 2002).

DEFINITIONS

Product innovation is regarded as an essential activity for firms that desire to face competition on the basis of quality and suitability of purpose (John and Snelson, 1990). In simple terms, innovation refers to any good, service or idea that is perceived by someone as novel or new (Kotler et al., 2002).

Capitalising on the proposed six categories of product innovation suggested by Heany (1983), Lovelock has adopted them for use in the service context. Lovelock (1996) presents six categories of new products. These are major innovations; start-up business; new product for currently served markets; product line extensions or additions; improvements to existing products; and style changes. Generally, the higher the level, the greater the risks and expenses entailed and the more difficult the management tasks (Lovelock, 1996). All of these provide a variety of ways to examine what innovation actually means to the company or to the market. Each category of innovation has strategic implications in terms of associated risk to the organisation and the significance that innovation plays in the overall marketing plan of an organisation. Generally, the higher the level, the greater the risks and expenses entailed and the more difficult the management tasks (Lovelock, 1996).

Example: Yotel

The first Yotels were opened in London Gatwick and Heathrow in 2007 and Schipol, Amsterdam in 2008. They are an extension of the YO brand (see Yo! Sushi example – Chapter 1) which is owned by Simon Woodroffe. The Yotel concept was inspired by the capsule hotels in Japan and BA First Class cabins. The guest rooms, known as 'cabins', are compact in size and incorporate multi-functional sofa beds and fold out study desks. The cabins have a design feature that means the windows are internal rather than external and through effective reflective lighting look out into corridors.

Source: www.yotel.com.

Student Activity

1. In terms of Lovelocks categories of new products, how would you classify the Yotel example?

2. What degree of risk would you associate with this NPD?

3. Identify other examples of new hospitality product development as per Lovelock's categories and evaluate the degree of risk for each of them.

Crawford (1994: 472) defines innovation as 'the act of creating a new product or process. This includes invention as well as the work required to bring an idea or concept into final form. An innovation may have various degrees of newness, from very little to highly discontinuous, but that must include at least some degree of newness to the market not just to the firm.' In this book, NPD and innovation are entwined, as it is difficult to separate one from the other.

On the other hand, product development definitions in the popular marketing textbooks generally focus on the word new. A new product is 'A good, service or idea that is perceived by some potential customers as new' (Kotler et al., 2004: 215). There are eight stages in NPD including the development of original products, product improvements, product modifications and new brands developed through the firms own R&D efforts (Kotler et al., 2004). Keegan et al. (1995: 418) define a new product as being 'a product being introduced to the market for the first time as a result of invention, innovation or improvement'. These authors offer a nine-step development process which includes idea generation, screening, business analysis, concept testing, product and strategy development, marketing mix planning, test marketing and product launch.

Cooper (1993) provides a more thorough approach in his definition of a new product and what newness essentially means. He suggests that new can be new to the company or it can be new to the market or customer and presents six classes of new products. These are new to the world products (new products that create an entirely new market); new product lines (new products that allow a company to enter an established market for the first time); additions to existing product lines (new products that supplement a company's established product lines); improvements to existing products (new products that provide increased performance or greater perceived value and replaced existing products); repositioning products (existing products that are targeted to new markets or market segments); and reducing costs (new products that provide similar performance at lower cost). All of these classes provide a variety of ways to examine what new products can mean to the company or to the market. However, Johne (1996) argues that cost reductions and repositioning are not distinct types of product developments in their own right. In addition, truly innovative new products and those in the 'new to the world' category have a higher failure rate than those products, which are being continuously improved (Cooper, 1993). All these new product classes are common in the hotel industry.

When exploring the process or activities which assist in the successful introduction of a new product, it is important to define new product development, which is a process consisting of specific activities and decision points. However, it has been argued by service marketing academics that the development of a service product differs from the development of a tangible product due to the characteristics of services comprising intangibility, inseparability, perishability, heterogeneity and lack of ownership. Literature provides a wide range of approach to understanding the NPD process and factors contributing to the success of new products. Important contributors, which have been identified as crucial to the success of NPD include customers, competitors and employees (Johne and Storey, 1998).

For the purpose of this book, the focus is on innnovation and NPD within the hospitality industry. New product in this context will be those that are new product lines; additions to existing product lines; or improvements to existing products.

Student Activity

1. Review the above definitions. What are the defining features of these definitions? What common themes emerge from each of them?

2. Provide your own definitions of NPD and innovation.

3. Explore the similarities and differences between NPD and innovation in the hospitality industry.

Although basic NPD models consist of six, seven, eight or nine steps (Lancaster and Massingham, 1999; Baker, 2000; Kotler et al., 2004; Keegan et al., 1995), there are a number of different variations of the new development process (Cooper, 1993; Crawford, 1994). The most well-known NPD model originates from Booz et al. (1968, 1982) and consists of seven steps as shown in Table 9.1. Despite different approaches to NPD and NSD in the literature (Scheuing and Johnson, 1989), this book followed Booz et al. (1982) simple model of the new development process (see Table 9.1).

However, this book considers the model developed by Booz et al. (1982) to be appropriate for the following reasons. First, it provides a clearly simple and

---

Table 9.1   NPD Model

New product strategy	Identify the strategic business requirements that the new product should satisfy.
Idea generation	Search for product ideas to meet strategic objectives.
Screening and evaluation	A quick analysis of ideas made against criteria that reflect the objectives of the organisation.
Business analysis	A detailed analysis of the attractiveness of an idea in business terms.
Development	Transition of the idea into an actual product for the market.
Testing	the commercial experiments necessary to verify earlier business judgements.
Commercialisation	The when, where, to whom and how decisions of the launch.

Source: Booz et al. (1982).

concise structured model of NPD based on research over many years into US-based companies. Second, Lovelock (1996) argues that the basic steps in NSD are broadly similar to those in manufacturing, beginning with objective setting and then proceeding through idea generation, concept screening, concept development, generation/evaluation of the final service product and its associated marketing strategy, design of a system for continuous performance evaluation, and product introduction. Third, it is one of the most recognised NPD models (Hart, 2000). Fourth, most of the NSD models are intuitively based rather than empirically based. Finally, this model is accepted by hospitality marketing scholars (e.g. Buttle, 1996; Kotler et al., 2003).

This book considers the model developed by Booz et al. (1982) to be appropriate for the following reasons. First, it provides a clearly simple structured model of NPD based on research over many years into US-based companies. Second, Lovelock (1996) argues that the basic steps in NSD are broadly similar to those in manufacturing, beginning with objective setting and then proceeding through idea generation, concept screening, concept development, generation/evaluation of the final service product and its associated marketing strategy, design of a system for continuous performance evaluation and product introduction. Third, renovation deals with the tangible, hard or physical part of the hotel product/service mix.

Example: Denny's

Denny's is a family dining chain with approximately 1500 outlets based in the United States, Canada, Costa Rica, Guam, Mexico, New Zealand and Puerto Rico. When developing new products, the chain tests these out on its customers four to six weeks before general release across the chain. The test often involves focusing on a concentrated area to assess demand for the product. It did this when it tested its Sizzlin' Breakfast Skillets which were initially tested by a Denny's franchisee in Boise, Idaho. The success of the test resulted in rolling out the product across the entire chain.

Source: www.nrn.com/.

Student Activity

1. Using the scenario of a hospitality business of your choice, you have been asked to develop a new product for the business.

2. Develop the new product based upon the different stages of the NPD model (see Table 9.1).

CRITICAL SUCCESS FACTORS OF NPD

Though there is a body of literature on NPD, it has previously focused on industries other than hospitality. However, this is not to say that the principles and processes previously discussed are not relevant. As a result of the literature being spread across various industries, the terminology used varies, though there are often very close similarities (Craig and Hart, 1992), such as New Services Development (Jiménez-Zarco et al., 2006) or innovation (Hüsig and Kohn, 2003). This chapter uses the six influencing factors identified by Craig and Hart (1992) as a foundation to understand the most important factors that affect the success of NPD:

- NPD process
- Management (also described as NPD Management (Jensen and Harmsen, 2001)
- Information
- Strategy
- People
- Company characteristics.

Once they had identified the six factors, the authors recognised that there was a high level of overlap between them, particularly the groupings of *NPD process*, *People* and *Information*, and those of *Management*, *Strategy* and *Company characteristics* (Craig and Hart, 1992).

Craig and Hart (1992) are not the only authors to suggest key influencing factors. The reason that they are still relevant, however, is because subsequent suggestions have not been significantly different. Although Hüsig and Kohn (2003) view the 'Fuzzy Front End' or FFE (i.e. the initial stages that they argue come before the actual process of NPD) of NPD as an individual process in its own right, the key influencing factors that they identify are very similar to the ones set out above: strategy, culture, organisation, senior management and process. Hüsig and Kohn (2003) also recognise that FFE research is more conceptual than that on NPD. This is partially to do with the relative infancy of the subject. This relates to the problem of businesses not absorbing NPD research outcomes due to their conceptual and not operational nature (Jensen and Harmsen, 2001).

Cooper and Kleinschmidt (1995) examined influencing factors on the performance of new products at a company level and also produced a list of five: NPD process and the specific activities within it; NPD program organisation; NPD strategy of the company; company culture and climate for innovation; and commitment to NPD by senior management. As with

Hüsig and Kohn (2003), these factors all appear in the influences suggested by Craig and Hart (1992).

A key issue with NPD is success. Jensen and Harmsen (2001) state that the main drivers for success are internal company factors. However, success is not universally defined as it is multifaceted (sometimes referred to as multidimensional) and difficult to measure (Griffin and Page, 1996; Huang et al., 2003). Griffin and Page (1993) grouped 75 measures into five overall factors and 16 core measures. Their five factors were: measures of firm benefits; program-level measures; product-level measures; measures of financial performance; measures of customer acceptance. Based on this, and using Australian SMEs as a sample, Huang et al. (2003) found four factors that form the basis of commonly used measurements of success: financial performance, objective market acceptance, subjective market acceptance, and product-level measures. Within their sample, the most common specific measures used for success were customer acceptance, customer satisfaction, product performance and quality (Huang et al., 2003).

Griffin and Page (1996) state that success can be measured at two levels: the NPD program level and at the individual product level. This determines the measures of success used, which is another factor in why universal measures of success are elusive. They group previous research together to identify three dimensions of project success: consumer-based, technical or process-based and financial success (Griffin and Page, 1996). However, they state that there is another challenge in that the 'perfect product development project does not exist' (Griffin and Page, 1996: 479), whereby although one measure of success may be achieved, it is often done so at the expense of another dimension.

Student Activity

1. Identify examples of hospitality product successes and evaluate why they have been successful?

2. Consider examples where hospitality products have failed and evaluate why this occurred.

NPD process

This is defined as the whole process of development, from the initial idea generation through to product launch into the market (Craig and Hart, 1992). This process is closely linked to the other factors. The correct strategy needs to be in place to lead the NPD process. This is to ensure that all the development elements are in place and occur at the right point. However, as mentioned elsewhere, the strategy that defines the process must not be too rigid so as to negatively affect the creative process (Jiménez-Zarco et al., 2006). The NPD process is also heavily interlinked with other factors, in particular the people involved (Craig and Hart, 1992).

Craig and Hart (1992) identified several models of the NPD process which contained numerous stages or activities, though they concluded that the models were too idealised. They also showed that Cooper and Kleinschmidt (1986) had identified 13 stages from initial screening to market launch that, if completed, increased the probability of commercial success but that companies rarely carried out. Craig and Hart (1992) state that the essence of the models relates to making decisions based on commercial and technical information, with the underlying objective of reducing uncertainty. However, they also note that every activity identified within the process has the potential to increase development time, which can have a long-term detrimental effect on commercial success (Craig and Hart, 1992).

Cooper and Kleinschmidt (1995) identified a high quality new product process as the main influencing factor on identified NPD success. Tracey (2004) states that, 'an exceptional new product development process should certainly be considered a valuable intangible resource' (p. 50). Cooper and Kleinschmidt (1995) found that successful firms had ensured that the process included elements such as early product definition as well as being both flexible and market-orientated, with quality customer involvement. Flexibility can be used to accelerate projects, or negate additional time accrued by undergoing multiple stages, for example by allowing stages to overlap each other (Jiménez-Zarco et al., 2006; Craig and Hart, 1992).

Management

Management, or NPD management, refers to top-level management support, with the more specific project management role considered as being a *People* factor (Craig and Hart, 1992). However, there are some factors that crossover between the two levels of management and apply equally to both. Teams, especially if they are made up of people from different departments and backgrounds, need strong leadership and clear goals to perform effectively (Jiménez-Zarco et al., 2006). This leadership needs not only to be present within the specific project group, but also at company level. Equally, Hüsig and Kohn (2003) argue that although the commitment of senior management is an influential factor in the success of NPD, its significance is limited without suitable resources such as support of skilled people and appropriate budget.

Jiménez-Zarco et al. (2006) state that managerial decisions are critical because of the significant resources that are required for such a complex process. Griffin and Page (1996) conclude that the most suitable measures for success depend on the strategy, at both project and company levels. Strategy and top-level management are, by their very nature, intertwined (Craig and Hart, 1992). Tracey (2004) argues that managers who encourage an integrated NPD process create an intangible resource that can provide a competitive advantage that is sustainable. He emphasises the importance of senior management support by arguing that not only is integration during the NPD process a key factor, but that it is the responsibility of the management to ensure that it happens at a sufficient level (Tracey, 2004). Jensen and Harmsen (2001) refer to the fact that despite research on NPD success, the outcomes are not often heeded by managers, although they also go on to state that this could be as a result of the research being more academic than practical.

Cooper and Kleinschmidt (1995) identify not only senior management support as a key performance driver but also senior management accountability. They argue that though management-related factors such as clear messages and availability of funds and resources are crucial, they also need to be readily available for decisions and advice and technically literate. Huang et al. (2003) suggested that management needed to recognise that multiple criteria should be used when measuring the performance of new products, and be aware that the criteria are correlated.

Information

Of the six factors, *Information* is the one that runs through all the others and underlies the whole process of NPD. As such, it is difficult to separate it from the others, but it is important to understand the role and importance of information within the overall process (Craig and Hart, 1992). It should be noted that Leonard-Barton (1992) defined a framework for a company based on knowledge, consisting of four different knowledge dimensions:

- Knowledge and skills embodied in employees.
- Employee knowledge and skills embedded in technical process.
- The managerial system being the creation and control of knowledge.
- Values and norms, infused through the other three dimensions.

Leonard-Barton (1992) states that the four dimensions are all interrelated and interdependent, and Jensen and Harmsen (2001) therefore suggest that they can all be applied in varying degrees to each influencing factor as defined by Craig and Hart (1992).

Although there is crossover between Leonard-Barton's (1992) *Knowledge* and what Craig and Hart (1992) termed *Information*, the terms are referring to different elements, much as there is similarity and difference between innovation and NPD (see Introduction).

When Tracey (2004) argues for a wider participation of departments and stakeholders in the NPD process, the benefits are as a result of the information that these parties bring to the product development. Information is also crucial in reducing uncertainty, as this can help reduce conflict during integration and co-ordination (Craig and Hart, 1992).

Information is a key factor from the very start of the NPD process. Hüsig and Kohn (2003) identify it as being critical in the pre-development stages, both in terms of technical knowledge but also as knowledge transfers between persons/departments. Jensen and Harmsen (2001) suggest that a key to improving successful product development is by making identified factors more practically operational in nature, thereby increasing companies understanding of how to implement them. Regarding *Information*, they therefore describe a critical factor as an increased understanding of the knowledge and skills of individual employees in NPD (Jensen and Harmsen, 2001).

According to Craig and Hart (1992), information is influential in two key ways: its role in what they term functional co-ordination, i.e. knowledge transfer between people and departments; and its role in the NPD process.

Student Activity

1. Evaluate the different information needs that a hospitality business might require for successful product development?
2. Discuss how information can be an important factor throughout the NPD process.

Strategy

The 'strategy of a company dictates how it will operate internally, and how it will approach the outside world' (Craig and Hart, 1992: 18). The strategy of a company in regard to NPD is influenced by the success of said NPD. Equally, the measures of success of project level NPD are determined by the project strategy (Griffin and Page, 1996). Hüsig and Kohn (2003) state that NPD projects are more successful when the project strategy is closely aligned with the overall strategy of the company. Similarly, Craig and Hart (1992) identify the strategic orientation of NPD within the company as a key influence on the outcome.

Griffin and Page (1996) identify the following relationships between strategy and success: the factors that produce project success differ according to the project strategy; different strategies result in different types of success; the project strategy mix used differs across more and less successful firms. They also recognise that from a company-wide perspective, the level of dependence on NPD is directly affected by the strategy adopted.

Craig and Hart (1992) make the case that NPD should be integrated within the overall corporate strategy, making the process more formalised. This allows for proper planning, support and structure for the process. Within the development of the strategy itself, however, they identify five areas that need to be addressed:

- Product differentiation – emphasising the need for products to be sufficiently different to the current market in areas such as quality or technical superiority.
- Technology and marketing – the importance of integrating two key elements of NPD.
- Pro-activity – the strategy should be proactive rather than reactive to the market.
- Synergy – the successful melding of the company's existing activities with NPD.
- Risk acceptance – the awareness that although it has a high risk of failure, NPD should not be stifled (though as discussed elsewhere, it should be noted that some products can be viewed both as a failure and a success).

People

People are, of course, essential to any NPD. However, in this case the term is referring to the specific functions that individuals can represent and how they factor into NPD, for example co-ordination of different specialisms (such as marketing or R&D) or project management (Craig and Hart, 1992). Hüsig and Kohn (2003) state that although the commitment of senior management

Example

Craig and Hart (1992) suggest that key areas where *People* are influencing factors include: (a) Co-ordination of different functions, for example marketing and R&D; (b) The communication of information; (c) Project management; and (d) Skills needed for successful development.

is influential in the success of NPD, it is little more than symbolic without suitable resources such as the support of appropriately skilled people.

Tracey (2004) suggests that to gain competitive advantage, wider integration and co-operation with internal departments and external stakeholders (such as suppliers and customers) is essential. It is more effective and efficient to have expertise, such as marketing, involved throughout the process rather than advising on the end product. However, this is easier in theory than in practice (Craig and Hart, 1992).

Integration and co-ordination also raises issues in terms of involvement and influence. As mentioned under *Company Characteristics*, Hüsig and Kohn (2003) show that if customer input on NPD is over-emphasised, then it can have a negative influence. They also suggest that too much external collaboration too early in the process can lead to delays, implying that ideas need to be more developed and focused before being taken to a wider audience. It has also been suggested that some differentiation needs to exist to allow optimisation on certain tasks (Moenaert and Souder, 1990). The provision and sharing of information, at all stages throughout the process, has a key role to play in integration and co-ordination (Craig and Hart, 1992).

Jensen and Harmsen (2001) state that the skills and knowledge of individual employees should enjoy greater recognition by companies, as an increased understanding of their influence could lead to increased success of NPD.

Student Activity

1. What skills do a hospitality business's people need in the development of new products?

2. Identify the external stakeholders for a hospitality business when developing new products. Evaluate the influence these stakeholders should have over the development of new products for the hospitality business.

Company characteristics

This refers to how elements within the actual set-up of the company can have a positive or negative impact on NPD, such as organisational structure or mechanisms for integration (Craig and Hart, 1992). This factor has strong ties with Leonard-Barton's (1992) knowledge dimension of *Values and norms* which, for example, refers to the value that the company places on different types of knowledge. This has a direct influence on integration.

Tracey (2004) indicates that a lack of integration, both between internal departments and with external stakeholders, remains a key issue for many companies and NPD. This is despite the topic not being particularly new or unknown. He suggests that companies that focus on NPD with short-term cost-based policies may view wider integration with other departments and stakeholders as overly complex and inefficient, thus increasing development cost (Tracey, 2004). He suggests that an approach called concurrent engineering (CE) should be advocated. Originally designed to encourage integration between design and process engineering, it has developed into 'a concept that promotes building competitive advantage through the inclusion of members from every function area; as well as supplies and customers; on a formal development team with a documented process and an established leader' (Tracey, 2004: 38). The results of his study show that wider participation in general does have long-term benefits, but also that theory and practice often differ (Tracey, 2004). Griffin and Page (1996) also note the discrepancy between theory and practice, showing that although 44% of surveyed firms would like to use customer satisfaction as a measure of success, only 10% actually do.

Organisational structure is also identified as a key category of factors that influence the success of NPD (Jiménez-Zarco et al., 2006). However, in this instance the term has a wider definition as it also includes what Craig and Hart (1992) identify as *strategy* and *management* (Jiménez-Zarco et al., 2006). Both sets of authors agree on the importance of an innovative culture, where guidance does not restrict creativeness (Jiménez-Zarco et al., 2006; Craig and Hart, 1992). Jensen and Harmsen (2001) suggest that *Values and norms* is a critical factor, but one that has not yet been fully grasped by either research or companies themselves.

Student Activity

1. Choose a hospitality business and evaluate its company characteristics. To what extent does the business have the appropriate characteristics to be able to embark upon NPD?

2. What suggestions would you make to the hospitality business in developing it characteristics for NPD?

CONCLUSION

This chapter has contained a comprehensive discussion of the concept of NPD in the general marketing literature and in hospitality marketing in particular. This chapter has also dealt with various aspects of NPD and innovation in the hospitality industry. It includes discussion of the definition, types, process, and importance of NPD. It starts with clarifying the significance of NPD and identifying the relationship between NPD and innovation in the hospitality industry. Finally, this chapter has concluded with an analysis of the critical success factors of NPD in the hospitality industry. In doing so, this chapter has used the six influencing factors identified by Craig and Hart (1992) as a foundation: (a) NPD process; (b) Management (also described as NPD Management) (Jensen and Harmsen, 2001); (c) Information; (d) Strategy; (e) People; and (f) Company characteristics. Having clarified that, the book now turns to explore and discuss another concept that is considered to be of great importance to the development of any hospitality operation, which is property renovation.

REVIEW QUESTIONS

1. Define the concept of NPD and explore its significance within the context of the hospitality industry.
2. 'Product innovation is regarded as an essential activity for firms that desire to face competition on the basis of quality and suitability of purpose.' Explore.
3. Discuss the impact of each of the following factors on the success of NPD in the hospitality industry:
   - NPD process
   - Management
   - Information
   - Strategy
   - People
   - Company characteristics
4. 'The most well known NPD model originates from Booz et al. (1968, 1982) and consists of seven steps as shown in Table 9.1.' Identify examples from hospitality organisations that explain the role of each of these steps in the NPD process.
5. Evaluate how a hospitality management organisation might gather customer information that would inform the development of new food and beverage products and services.

Case Study: Developing New Products in the Egyptian Hospitality Industry

Drawing on empirical research, this case study makes a contribution towards the engagement and expertise of hotels in the new product development (NPD) process. The study provides an investigation into the development and practices of new products within the hospitality industry in Egypt. The methodology used in this study was a quantitative survey that was conducted in 2005. A total of 91 hotels were selected as the samples of the survey. A total of 63 valid returns were received by the closing date of the survey, representing a 69% response rate.

Most of the respondents (75%) considered NPD as very important and important (46.4% very important, 28.6% important) for their hotels. It is worth mentioning that none of the respondents answered 'not important' at the other end of the scale. This finding suggests that innovation or NPD is not exclusive to hotels of a particular size. Moreover, most respondents agreed (62.3% strongly agreed and 34.4% agreed) that hoteliers should give further recognition to the importance of NPD, which means that the Egyptian hotels can gain better value and benefits from it. Along the same line, all hoteliers stated that NPD has an essential marketing role.

Although the majority of hoteliers (88.3%) agree that there are clearly defined stages that make up the NPD process in their hotels, they do not use formal and detailed guidelines to carry out their innovation. The majority (68%) of all hotels do not have formal guidelines in place to guide NPD process from idea to launch and instead they use informal ones.

Respondents were asked to identify the main reasons for developing new products for their hotels. Information relating to the importance of NPD in hotels, in Table 9.2, indicates that 'to keep up with the competition' is the most important reason to develop new products, followed by 'to satisfy current customers'. These findings confirm what have been mentioned above in relation to the importance and benefits of NPD. On the other hand, to upgrade the hotel to a higher category is the least important reason to develop new products.

The top sources of new product ideas for most hotels were competition (88%), customer feedback (82%), suppliers (59%), staff (7%) and head office (8%). Interestingly, none of the three or four star hotels mentioned their 'staff' as a source of new ideas whilst about 15% of the five star hotels

Table 9.2   Importance of NPD

	1*	2	3	4	5*	Mean
to keep up with the competition	0.0%	1.6%	11.1%	52.4%	34.9%	4.20
to satisfy current customers	1.6%	4.8%	17.5%	55.6%	20.6%	3.88
to decrease operational expenses	0.0%	11.1%	42.9%	33.3%	12.7%	3.47
to attract new customers	3.2%	15.9%	25.4%	46.0%	9.5%	3.42
to improve the operational efficiency of the hotel	0.0%	17.5%	41.3%	27.0%	14.3%	3.38
to maintain corporate image and standards	1.6%	22.2%	39.7%	33.3%	3.2%	3.03
to comply with the new trends and technology in the market	6.3%	34.9%	31.7%	27.0%	0.0%	2.78
to cope with the governmental requirements	12.7%	41.3%	33.3%	11.1%	1.6%	2.58
to upgrade the hotel to a higher category	14.3%	57.2%	22.2%	3.2%	3.2%	178

1 = Strongly Disagree; 5* = Strongly Agree.*

Table 9.3   Approach to NPD

Approach	5* Hotels	4* Hotels	3* Hotels
No new products	–	7.7%	12%
Such as competition	68.4%	77.6%	88%
Develop new products	31.6%	14.7%	–

encourage staff to put forward innovative ideas. Similarly, 43% of the three or four star hotels mentioned their 'head offices' as a source of new ideas whilst about 75% of the five star hotels receive new ideas from their head offices. Respondents were asked to rank in order of importance the main factors which influence their hotels' decision to introduce a new product or service to their customers. As Table 9.3 suggests that most hotels adopt the 'Such as Competitor' type of product innovation and only five hotels (three five star hotels; one four star hotel and one three star hotel) are trying to develop products that will lead the market. Therefore, most Egyptian hotels have the reactive strategy of 'Such as Competitor' product development. The other five hotels that have a proactive NPD strategy are the market leaders of the three hotel categories in Cairo.

Respondents were asked to underline the significance of various stages of the NPD process. The findings revealed that Egyptian hotels do not entirely follow the seven stages of the model proposed by Booz et al. (1982). Accordingly, this disregard of some NPD activities in Egyptian hotels might be attributed to the following reasons: (a) the nature of NPD in most of these hotels, which is mainly product modifications and (b) the involvement of the head office in chain hotels.

Moreover, the results show that hotel management appears to draw more attention to the idea generation and screening stages of the development process of hotel services.

Respondents were also asked to highlight the importance of different product/market development strategies for their hotels. Table 9.4 indicates the importance placed on each strategy.

It shows that the majority of Egyptian hotel marketers consider 'market penetration' and 'market development' as the most important growth strategies. However, these two strategies provide limited opportunities for innovation as

Table 9.4   Importance of Each Product/Market Development Strategy

Strategy	Very important	Important	Moderate	Unimportant	Very unimportant	Mean
Increasing sales of present products in existing markets	83.1%	16.9%	–	–	–	1.17
Developing new markets for existing products	45.8%	54.2%	–	–	–	1.54
Developing new products for existing markets	32.2%	15.3%	44.1%	6.8%	1.7%	2.31
Developing new products for new markets	3.4%	6.8%	39%	37.3%	3.51%	3.51

Table 9.5   NPD Forces

| Rank | Five star | | Four Star | | Three star | |
	Force	Percentage	Force	Percentage	Force	Percentage
First	Head office	71.4%	EHA	53.8%	EHA	55.6%
Second	Customer	61.9%	Customer	46.1%	Competition	42.3%
Third	Competition	38.1%	Competition	38.5%	Customer	38.5%
Fourth	Technology	28.6%	Technology	30.8%	Technology	26.9%
Fifth	*EHA	4.8%				

they depend on using existing products to increase market share or sales. Strategies that offer larger opportunities for product development are given low importance. This might be attributed to the lack of both finance and experience.

When asked whether their hotels had developed any new products or facilities in the past 10 years, very few were able to identify examples of such product development or innovation. For instance, only 34% of the three star hotels have introduced a new service to their customers in the last 10 years. It needs to be noted that, however, the majority of the three star hotels have been in operation for more than 20 years. Similarly, 48% of the four star hotels have introduced new services to their customers in the last 10 years. On the other hand, 85.7% of the five star hotels have introduced at least one new service to their customers in the last 10 years.

Respondents were asked to rank the main forces driving the NPD programs in their hotels. Surprisingly, Egyptian Hotel Association's inspection was found to be the main force to product development in most hotels, competition came as the second force, while technology and head office were the third and the fourth forces, respectively. To obtain more detailed information, the data were cross-tabulated within the three hotel categories. A cross-tabulation analysis indicates category differences in the main forces driving NPD in hotels (Table 9.5). However, this reflects again the fact that NPD in Egyptian hotels is market driven.

From the preceding discussion, it can be argued that product development decisions are exercised more from a marketing dimension in the case of five star operations than in the case of three and four star ones. This is evident in the extent that the five star operations revised their products and services, their integration of research into reaching decisions pertaining to what services should be introduced and, accordingly, their development and introduction of new services to suit their customers. This was also indicated in the product/market development strategy.

Source: Adapted from: Hassanien, A., Eid, R., 2006. An investigation of NPD in hotels. Journal of Hospitality and Leisure Marketing 15 (2), 33–53.

Questions

1. Why do Egyptian hotel marketers consider 'market penetration' and 'market development' as the most important growth strategies?

2. Identify and discuss the main forces driving the NPD programs in Egyptian hotels. To what extent do you agree that NPD in Egyptian hotels is market driven? Why?

3. The main conclusion of this case study is that NPD decisions are exercised more from a marketing dimension in the case of five star operations than in the case of three and four star ones. Discuss.

GLOSSARY

Critical success factors of NPD   The essential factors and issues that affect the success and development of new products.

Innovation   Crawford (1994: 472) defines innovation as 'the act of creating a new product or process. This includes invention as well as the work required to bring an idea or concept into final form. An innovation may have various degrees of newness, from very little to highly discontinuous, but that must include at least some degree of newness to the market not just to the firm.'

New product development (NPD)   A new product is 'A good, service or idea that is perceived by some potential customers as new' (Kotler et al., 2004: 215).

NPD categories   These are major innovations; start-up business; new product for currently served markets; product line extensions or additions; improvements to existing products; and style changes (Lovelock, 1996).

NPD Classes   These are new to the world products (new products that create an entirely new market); new product lines (new products that allow a company to enter into an established market for the first time); additions to existing product lines (new products that supplement a company's established product lines); improvements to existing products (new products that provide increased performance or greater perceived value and replaced existing products)' repositioning products (existing products that are targeted to new markets or market segments) and reducing costs (new products that provide similar performance at lower cost) (Cooper, 1993).

NPD process   The different stages and activities which assist in the successful introduction of a new product.

Hospitality Property Renovation

Learning Objectives

Having completed this chapter, readers should be able to:

- Introduce the concept and importance of renovation in the hospitality industry.
- Explore the relationship between innovation and hospitality property renovation.
- Understand the scope of hospitality property renovation.
- Explore the different types of hospitality renovation.
- Discuss the different elements and process of renovation in the hospitality industry.

CONTENTS

INTRODUCTION

This chapter examines and concentrates on the role of product modification in the hospitality industry as a tool for business development. Nowadays many hospitality operations are facing the challenge of supply that is in excess of demand in some market areas. Consequently, many hospitality organisations are not adequately meeting their financial obligations because of the supply/demand imbalance. As a result, the industry has to focus on maximising returns from existing products rather than on developing new facilities. Sullivan (1994) notes that hotel renovation is an ongoing process of continuous improvement and forward thinking. Owners realise that, while a renovation is an investment in time and money, it drives business to a hotel and contributes to a property's long-term success.

Along the same lines, hospitality operations emphasise totally new product less than other services operations. For example, once the hotel building is built, the changes that are possible are limited. On the other hand, renovation often creates upgraded products as rooms are refurbished to meet emerging market needs. Therefore, property renovation is considered the main tool for product modification or improvement in the hospitality industry for the following reasons:

- to extend the useful life of the property to stay competitive;
- to reposition the property within its marketplace; and
- to improve the operational efficiency of the property.

MacDonald (1995) argues that renovation is certainly not a new concept to the hospitality industry, nor will it fade away as a trend or fad like some of its marketing counterparts have. But the hospitality industry is on the verge of completing a cycle that has brought renovating at least into the forefront of development. Over the past number of years, finding money to renovate a property has probably been an easier and more profitable task than finding funds to build a new hotel.

Moreover, according to Paneri and Wolff (1994) a survey conducted by the American Hotel & Motel Association revealed that 97% of its members are more likely to renovate their properties than to build new hotels. Also, Lynn and Seldon (1993) refer to Forbes magazine research that found the ratio of new construction to property renovation in the hospitality industry had moved from/60:40/in the 1980s to/40:60/in the 1990s with a further shift to/ 20:80/predicted by the end of this decade. According to the 1996 American Hotel & Motel Association Membership Survey, 64.4% of member properties had been renovated over the past 12 months, while 58.8% plan had to be renovated over the following 12 months (Chipkin, 1997). Levels of investment in hotel renovation programmes are very high. For example, Baum and Wolchuck (1992) stated that ITT Sheraton Corporation spent $47 million to transform the Sheraton Manhattan City Square in New York from a hotel whose main clientele was leisure and tour groups to a hotel attracting corporate business travellers.

Renovation, when well planned, can elegantly rejuvenate a hospitality business, offers the chance to reposition the property and might attract both more and loyal customers in the long run. It is the intention of this chapter to investigate the role played by property renovation in hospitality business development and to determine how the objectives of a renovation programme can be achieved. This chapter includes discussion of the definition, types, process and importance of renovation. This extends into illustrating the relationship between business repositioning and property renovation in the hospitality industry. Prior to the examination of the issues concerned, however, it is important for the purposes of the study to discuss new product development because product modification (renovation) is classified under this concept.

INNOVATION/RENOVATION

As mentioned before (Chapter 9) product innovation is regarded as an essential activity for firms that desire to face competition on the basis of quality and suitability of purpose. Lovelock (1996) presents six categories of new products as follows:

- major innovations;
- start-up business;
- new product for currently served markets;
- product line extensions or additions;
- improvements to existing products; and
- style changes.

All of these provide a variety of ways to examine what innovation actually means to the company or to the market. Each category of innovation has strategic implications in terms of associated risk to the organisation and the significance that innovation plays in the overall marketing plan of an organisation. Generally, the higher the level, the greater the risks and expenses entailed and the more difficult the management tasks (Lovelock, 1996). However, it is clear that all of these categories, except the first one, are common in the hospitality industry and all of them require renovation to achieve their objectives. Accordingly, product innovation and property renovation are inseparable in the hospitality industry. That is why property renovation can be seen as those activities associated with the development and/or modification of the hotel's tangible assets used to produce services in order to extend the useful life of the property to stay competitive, improve the operational efficiency of the property, and/or to build up a better image for the property within its marketplace.

Hassanien and Baum (2002) argue that property renovation is considered an essential, if not the most important, tool for product innovation in the hotel business. In other words, renovation, if it is well planned and implemented, can achieve product innovation, which leads to enhanced profitability, guest satisfaction and possibly market leadership.

For the purpose of this book, the focus is on renovation as a tool for innovation or new product development within the hospitality industry. New product in this context will be those that are new product lines; additions to existing product lines; or improvements to existing products. Accordingly, hotel property renovation can be seen as those activities associated with the creation and development of (tangible) assets used to produce services.

Student Activity

1. What do you understand by the term renovation?

2. Why would a hospitality business need to embark on a process of renovation?

3. Identify different types of renovation that a hospitality business might pursue.

TOWARDS A RENOVATION CONCEPT

Related concepts

Renovation is a key issue used throughout the literature but at the same time there is no generally accepted definition of renovation, and different authors use different terms to define the same concept. In addition, the term, renovation, is replete with terminology that is often redundant and imprecise. As a result, in the literature of hotel marketing and design, there is often a semantic confusion over terminology in discussing renovation, refurbishment, rejuvenation, maintenance, redevelopment, restoration, upgrading, rehabilitation, renewing and redesign. While all of these terms refer to the process of maintaining, modifying or improving the tangible hotel product, there are important differences between them. In practice, in the hospitality industry, these terms are all used interchangeably.

An examination of the literature reveals that there is often confusion over terminology with respect to these terms but the problem is not more than semantic. However, to avoid some of the problems of semantics, it is worthwhile to identify these terms in this section in order to differentiate between them. In order to achieve this, some of the definitions will be examined.

Moss (1996: 288) identifies renovation and refurbishment as follows:

Refurbishment. Cleaning painting and related tasks performed for the purpose of restoring surfaces degraded by abrasive or corrosive agents in the atmosphere, or by scratches, nicks or gouges received during in-service handling. Refurbishment can be thought of as addressing 'cosmetic blemishes' rather than conditions that lead to degradation of functional capabilities or useful life.

Renovation is the restoration of some or all of an item's operating life after it has been expended by prior usage. Renovation is distinguished from corrective maintenance to the extent that the renovation task generally entails restoration of worn or abraded elements of the item's basic structure, in addition to corrective maintenance comprising replacement of worn, damaged or degraded removable parts.

Lewis and Brush (1998) state that unfortunately, renovation, refurbishment and redevelopment are used or misused interchangeably in hospitality. They have tried to reduce this confusion and overlapping by defining them as follows:

Renovation means to renew or bring back to original form. This can be a tall order and is seldom appropriate, either in terms of properly targeting the hotel's markets or because of inherent operational shortcomings. Renovating cosmetically rather than functionally can work to a limited extent in historical facilities, as long as the upgrade is confined to the guest areas and an appropriate budget is developed to bring the hotel up to code. In short term, it may not be apparent, but danger may lurk either in higher operating costs, guest satisfaction or both.

Refurbishment means cleaning, or repainting new or refinished furniture, fixtures or carpeting; and often, repainting or pointing exteriors. This works best for relatively new structures that effectively serve their target markets and are likely to continue for the next half-decade.

Redevelopment, as a term, is often mistakenly used instead of renovation, refurbishment or rehabilitation. But it implies a different approach. For one, it almost always represents a major investment and implies major changes in the property. It is not a short-term fix for a poorly performing (or recently acquired) property. Its justification is essentially the same as for a newly built facility.

However, Lewis and Brush's definitions are vague for the following reasons. First, to define the term 'renovation', they use the word 'renew' that is a synonymous to the same term and others as mentioned before. Second, the definition of 'renovation' is confused with 'conservation', which should not be the case. Although renovation does conserve hotel buildings, conservation is considered one type of renovation not the common-sense definition. Third, the term 'redevelopment' has been defined earlier as 'the act or process of redeveloping; *esp.*: renovation of a blighted area'. That means it implies renovation, the definition of redevelopment is not clear what 'major changes' imply.

Another view is stated by Boykin (1991), who claims that hotel operators have four, which she calls four Rs, options or design alternatives for rejuvenating their properties. These are renovation, restoration, replacement and reinstatement. She differentiates among them according to the following criteria:

Renovation: This is to complete or partial renewing or repair of a guest room or public space. It may involve structural changes that transform the room or area into a totally new look, or it may be limited to the modification of materials such as wall coverings, tile, carpet, fixtures or furniture.

A complete renovation may be divided into phases for capital-budget purposes and operational practicality, whereas a partial renovation could be completed on a short, but strict schedule.

Restoration: This process is no less involved than renovation. Restoration of a guest room, public area or entire property is a process by which the spaces are reconstructed to their original character, condition or structure without marring the grandeur of the building's original architectural design. If the structure has been designated a historic landmark, restoration guidelines may impose certain constraints on what can be changed or added. A significant amount of research by the design team will be required to ensure authentication of moldings, fabrics, furniture and window treatments.

Replacement: The replacement of materials and Furniture, Fixtures & Equipment (FF&E) specifications is often used by hotel operators to increase the longevity of a room or area, particularly when capital dollars are not available for immediate renovation. When the replacement method is used in a guest room or public area, the practical – and, often, most needed change – involves soft goods. This includes the replacement of such items as bedspreads, draperies, carpet and upholstery. Though not limited too soft goods, any specified FF&E item should be replaced when necessary.

Used mainly as a temporary solution, the replacement method infuses new life into a worn and outdated design.

Reinstatement: Often, a classic and traditional design in the past proved successful both for operators and guests. As opposed to changing a successful concept, the operator and designer may choose to repeat – that is, reinstate – the worthy design.

In a guest room, for example, all case goods may be reinstated, or just a few may qualify after serious evaluation.

According to Boykin (1991), 'renovation' is the biggest 'R' that implies the other three 'Rs'. In other words, they could be classified as types of renovation. Although this view does not consider the other terms; especially refurbishment and rehabilitation; it can be considered in determining the scope of the term 'renovation'.

However, this thorough review of the definitions brings out a number of general conclusions. First, although there seems to be general disagreement on the meaning of these terms, there has been a tendency for opinions to converge on scope and definition (see for example, Anonymous, 1994; Lewis and Brush, 1998). Second, there may often be confusion over terminology with respect to most of the terms but the researcher views that as a semantic problem. One of the main reasons for this semantic confusion is that the dictionaries and the design and architecture literature themselves are not always clear on the difference between the above terms. For example (Lawson, 1995: 315–333), a leading hotel design and architecture scholar, uses maintenance, refurbishment, renovation, replacement, renewals, as synonyms. Third, it is difficult to distinguish between the above terms. Fourth, although the problem is not more than semantic, we argue that the term 'renovation' is the most suitable and appropriate term because:

(a) it is the most commonly used term in the hotel literature [e.g. an examination of the ABI Inform database (1986–2000) reveals that renovation has been mentioned in 871 articles on hotels; while the others receive less than that: 54 articles for refurbishment, 117 articles for replacement];

(b) the dictionary definition of the term renovation can be considered one of the most suitable definitions;

(c) to renovation is referred to as the most common term in practice in hotels; and

(d) after consulting architecture and interior design academics, 'renovation' has been suggested to be the clearest and the most appropriate one of the previous terms that entails all of the soft and hard changes in the tangible product of hotels.

Student Activity

1. Review the above definitions. What are the defining features of these definitions? What common themes emerge from each of them?

2. Provide your own definition of renovation.

DEFINING RENOVATION

Semantic confusion has led to another ambiguity regarding the exact definition of the renovation concept. Examination of most authors' writing on this topic does not reveal a coherent set of characteristics as they seem to be very open even where definitions are provided. However, some of these definitions are limited to just one type of renovation (e.g. Boykin, 1991) while the others are too vague to outline the scope of renovation (e.g. Lewis and Brush, 1998). Another limitation of these definitions is the confusion with other terms as mentioned before.

In determining the scope of the term renovation in this research and based upon these previous considerations, renovation is defined as being:

'The process of retaining or improving the "hospitality" business's image by modifying the tangible product, due to a variety of reasons, through any changes in the "business" layout (e.g. property structure-new extension) and/or any additions or replacement of materials and Furniture, Fixture & Equipment.' (Hassanien and Baum, 2001)

Several aspects of this definition may be highlighted as follows:

1. It identifies renovation as a process that incorporates different levels of activities.
2. It has a broad scope that comprises most of the other terms (e.g. replacement, restoration, redesign, redecorate, reinstatement, etc.) mentioned previously.
3. It explains the close relationship between new product development and renovation in the hospitality industry.
4. Renovation is restricted to the tangible part of the hotel product/ service mix.
5. There are many reasons, which will be discussed below, to renovate a hotel.
6. Renovation should be classified as a marketing tool since it is concerned with hotel image.
7. The definition is not restricted to just one type of renovation but includes or subsumes all types.
8. The definition does not limit renovation within the existing hotel building but encompass any changes in the hotel layout. For instance, if the hotel were going to build a totally new extension (or addition) separate from the current building, this would be considered as renovation within the terms of the definition.

THE SIGNIFICANCE OF RENOVATION

There are many different reasons that explain the role played by renovation in the success of hotels. These reasons might be classified as strategic, operational or functional needs or objectives to be met by renovation.

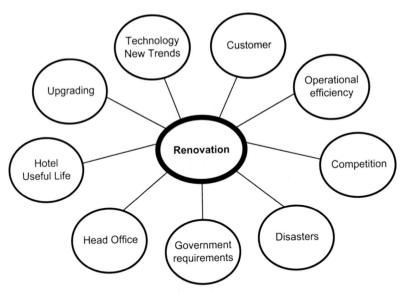

FIGURE 10.1 *Renovation reasons.*

Key authors (Baum and Wolchuk, 1992; Baum, 1993; Lynn and Seldon, 1993; Watkins, 1995; Bruns, 1996; Chipkin, 1997) list many different reasons (as shown in Figure 10.1), which make renovation essential for hotel operations. These reasons include:

(a) to keep up with the competition;

(b) to maintain or increase your market share by satisfying the current or potential customers. For example, in their research study on guest comment cards, Losekoot et al. (2001) found that the majority of complaints and customer dissatisfaction were related to the hard, physical or building facilities issues;

(c) to improve the operational efficiency of the hotel that will lead to an increase in both productivity and long-term savings in operational expenses;

(d) to maintain corporate image and standards;

(e) to upgrade the hotel to a higher category (e.g. from four star to five star);

(f) to comply with new trends and technology in the market (e.g. the green movement);

(g) to cope with the governmental requirements (e.g. The American Disability Act in USA); and

(h) to recover from natural or human-made disasters such as hurricanes, earthquakes and terrorism.

Student Activity

1. Identify examples where hospitality organisations have pursued renovation for the reasons outlined in Figure 10.1.

2. What factors have led the hospitality organisations to pursue this renovation?

3. To what extent is the renovation strategic, operational or functional in its need or objective?

BARRIERS TO RENOVATION

The main barriers to renovation in the studied hotel firms identified in the hospitality industry are shown in Table 10.1. These barriers are based on the findings of an empirical multiple case study research on six international five star hotels (Hassanien, 2007). This research confirmed that there are significant barriers to renovation in all cases. However, the significance of the barriers and resistance to renovation varied according to the nature of the renovation; the extent to which it was master or major, and the hotel's financial situation. Overall, financial difficulties and the cost of renovation were found to be the most important constraints to renovation in all cases. In most cases, limited budget was a significant constraint to renovation in hotels. All managers indicated that they are trying to overcome such challenges through prioritising and phasing their renovation plans. This was reflected in the following statement by the general manager of hotel A: 'Since budgets for renovation are typically limited, hoteliers usually need to decide what changes are priorities and what they can live without. You start with

Table 10.1   Barriers to Renovation in International Hotels (Hassanien, 2006)

Renovation Barrier	Hotel A	Hotel B	Hotel C	Hotel D	Hotel E	Hotel F
Financial difficulties	Yes	No	Yes	Yes	Yes	Yes
Cost of renovation	Yes	Yes	Yes	Yes	Yes	Yes
Owners	Yes	No	Yes	Yes	No	Yes
Fear of losing customers	Yes	Yes	No	Yes	Yes	Yes
Time limitations	Yes	Yes	Yes	Yes	Yes	Yes
Priority of other businesses	Yes	No	Yes	Yes	No	No
Bureaucracy	Yes	No	No	No	No	Yes
Head office	No	No	Yes	Yes	No	No
Privatisation	Yes	Yes	No	No	No	Yes

things you must do and try to get to the things you can do and come up with a package that works with (the client's) overall objectives – occupancy, room rates and so on.'

The owner was an important barrier to renovation in cases A, D and F. This was expected since Hotels A and F are owned by the government. On the other hand, one hotel under study did not identify owners as a barrier for renovation. In the case of Hotel E, the General Manager stated: 'Our owners have experience as developers and operators. They shared their expertise and input and they gave us another set of eyes'.

It was noted that overcoming barriers to renovation in the six cases was not only the job of the hotel unit. This was because of the support of the headquarters, which invariably helped unit general managers and, when necessary, sent expert teams to the hotel. As an example, in the cases of Hotel A, it was stated by the manager that the headquarters had previously piloted and implemented this renovation in units elsewhere and that these earlier trials had provided important guidance in the implementation of the renovation in this hotel. It was also evident that in the cases D, E and F, the company head office had made available the necessary resources and had provided guidelines and support in developing their renovation strategies. This support clearly helped managers in overcoming barriers to renovation and in solving problems in a more efficient way.

A further interesting finding was that time limitation was found to be an important barrier to renovation in hotels. Hotel owners did emerge as a barrier to renovation in most hotels. It is also worth noting that in most of the cases investigated, all renovation programmes were altered and delayed because of resistance from hotel owners. Several managers stated that the owners in the hotel industry are now powerful enough to impede renovation. This can perhaps be explained in terms of the nature of the hospitality industry, where there is major competition between hotel chains on a limited number of five star hotels.

TYPES OF RENOVATION

There are few attempts in the literature to classify different types of renovations. Most of these use time intervals (to determine the frequency of renovation periodically) and the amount of work involved with each type as the main dimensions of their classifications (Anonymous, 1994; Aeberhard, 1995). Renovation types are classed as minor, major and master renovations. While there seems to be an agreement between them on the time dimension, there is some disagreement on the second dimension (the amount of work), which further complicates the situation. Stipanuk and Roffmann (1996) take a different approach by using the spatial change and/or the additions or replacement of materials as criteria in classifying renovation and minor, major and restoration. However, it is proposed here that time should be omitted from any definition or classification criteria because the frequency of renovation work depends on many other variables (such as changes in market conditions, hotel performance, legal and insurance standards, etc.), which do not always rely on time.

Thus, the Stipanuk and Roffmann's classification is utilised with a slight modification, which is the addition of hotel image as a third dimension and the renaming of the third type of renovation as 'master', instead of 'restoration'. Accordingly, the following three types of renovation can be identified:

Minor renovation refers to replacement or renewal of some non-durable furnishings (e.g. carpeting) and finishes within a space without changing the space's use or physical layout in order to maintain the hotel image.

Example

With the growing influence of the female market, hotel companies have had to adapt their products to cater specifically to their needs. This includes acknowledging tastes in décor and colour schemes, the provision of facilities such as powerful hairdryers and well-lit mirrors in bathrooms and the inclusion of an in-room minibar and coffee maker. For business women travelling with children, the Four Seasons Hotel in Mexico City, for example, provides in-room facilities including toys, play room space and baby equipment.

Source: www.4hoteliers.com.

Major renovation refers to replacement or renewal of all furnishings, equipment and finishes within a space; in order to improve partially the hotel image, which may include extensive modifications to the physical layout of the space and/or upgrading the former used systems (mechanical or electrical).

Example

The Excalibur in Las Vegas, United States, is a 4008 room medieval themed hotel that, in 2007, undertook a major renovation of its guest rooms. The Excalibur Hotel completely renovated 2000 of its rooms as 'widescreen rooms' that incorporated 42-inch widescreen plasma televisions screens and clock radios with iPod© docking stations. The rooms were furnished with pillow top beds and bathrooms included new granite countertops.

Source: www.excalibur.com.

Master renovation is more comprehensive than major renovation and involves the entire property in order to change partially or totally the hotel image, especially in the case of mature or tired hotels where the aim is to breathe new life into these hotels (i.e. new extension).

Example

The consequences of Hurricane Katrina in August 2005 had a major impact on many hotel properties in the New Orleans, Louisiana region of the United States. This led to the major multi-million dollar renovation of the Sheraton Metairie-New Orleans (previously known as the Wyndham Metairie Hotel). The renovation included both interior and exterior improvements and the development of new facilities including a business centre and a club lounge. The renovation enabled the hotel to exploit opportunities to take a leading position amongst its target market.

Source: Hotel and Motel Management.

Student Activity

1. Identify further examples of hospitality organisation that completed minor, major and master renovations.
2. What renovations have been made and what has been the reason for these renovations?

Renovation versus new construction

Renovation is always less sophisticated than new construction in terms of its resources, management and viability. Certainly construction entails more steps, more unknowns, more money and probably more time. But a renovation quite often must occur on the midst of an ongoing, active business. Finding money to finance a renovation is only part of the game. Hospitality operators and managers need to consider how to schedule the work to avoid alienating paying customers, how to get it done within that schedule, how to make sure the work does not exceed the budget and more (Rowe, 1995).

Lynn and Seldon (1993) argue that feasibility models for renovation typically are more accurate than those for new property developments because the renovator has generally better market information and historical income and operating data, which assists with estimates.

Similarly, Lawson (1995) points out that the costs of acquisition and renovation are normally less than new building, and renovation works may attract grant aid in addition to tax credits. The cost of added blocks of rooms is often 25% less than an equivalent new hotel and can give higher returns. Along the same lines, Academic scholars argue that renovating or repositioning an existing hospitality operation in an existing market is usually less risky than building a new one from scratch. That is because the challenges associated with a new development are more costly and complicated than positioning or repositioning an existing brand (Hassanien and Baum, 2002a,b; Verginis and Wood, 1999).

RENOVATION ELEMENTS

Figure 10.2 summarises the different elements required for hospitality renovation projects in terms of management, resources and involved participants. Of course, the scope and importance of each element may vary according to the nature and type of each project. However, all of these elements need to be clearly identified and considered in any renovation project. The deployment of these elements will be further explained in the renovation process section below.

THE RENOVATION PROCESS

An inclusive model is presented to show the different phases involved within the renovation process. This model consists of four fundamental interrelated

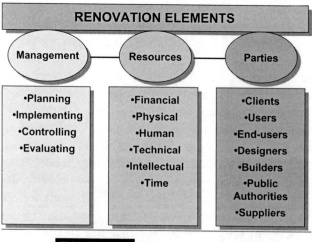

FIGURE 10.2 *Elements of renovation.*

phases, which are common to any type of renovation. It differs fundamentally from previous approaches in three respects:

(a) it considers the renovation process as a cycle since it is an ongoing process in hospitality organisations;

(b) it includes other forces or drivers of renovation in addition to the customer; and

(c) it gives particular consideration to the marketing element in the process.

It should be noted that the authors approach the subject from a hospitality management perspective, and therefore do not propose to address 'technical' or specialist areas. Consequently, a special attention will be drawn to the role of the client (hospitality owners/operators or mangers) throughout the renovation process.

DRIVER ANALYSES

First, the project should be justified by determining its objectives to decide whether the renovation has economic viability (Paneri and Wolff, 1994). Thus, management needs to determine and analyse the main driver(s) or force(s) to identify objectives. Much of the literature concentrates mainly, if not only, on the customer as the prime driver for renovation (e.g. Turner, 1968; Doswell, 1970; West and Hughes, 1991) and seems to ignore the other forces, such as governmental requirements and chain standards. Although the customer is a main driver, some other drivers exist and cannot be neglected.

PLANNING AND CONTROLLING

Planning is the process of defining goals and objectives for the project and determining the appropriate means for achieving them. Baltin and Cole (1995) state that carefully planned renovation enables the hospitality organisation to maintain or increase its market share while insufficient planning may not be significant enough to justify the renovation's costs. There are five main elements in the planning phase including aims and objective, team, budget, timing and marketing. These five elements will be further explained in the following sections below. Above all of them, it is very important to control the process properly. However, different types of techniques (i.e. computerized and manual) are available nowadays and they should be used for the control of time, costs, materials and performance on renovation projects (CIRIA, 1994). One of the most effective and efficient tool for the success of any renovation project is the project brief. According to Ransley and Ingram (2000: 49) a project brief is *the pivotal document that establishes the project objective and parameters for all parties concerned*. A clear and detailed project brief is regarded as one of the most important critical success factors of any renovation project. This will prove useful when management is looking at budgeting. The brief should give details regarding the main features and aspects of the project such as its aims and scope, budgeting spending limits, quality standards, timescale (e.g. start and completion dates), legislation [e.g. planning permission, building warrant, Health and Safety laws, the Disability Discrimination Act (DDA)] and so on.

However, the planning stage of the renovation process follows some logical interrelated steps as explained below.

Determine objectives

Based on external and internal analyses, management can determine objectives (Boykin, 1991). Whatever renovation type is most appropriate for a property's needs, the course of action will require one or all of the following elements.

The first and most important stage of any project is the creation of clear-cut, written objectives. If the property is a franchise hospitality organisation managed by a professional management group, it is essential that the management company's objectives be coupled with the owner's objectives to ensure corporate level. In addition, these objectives will be subject to change if circumstances change. These objectives should be justified as well. For example, because of the increased number of travellers to the market, the management has decided to expand at the rate of 25 rooms per year for the next four years, to a total of 100 new rooms.

ALTERNATIVE PLANS

Management must then look at alternative plans for achieving the objectives. For example, if the objective is to attract business travellers, one way might be to build a new wing onto the present structure. Another would be to allocate some of the existing rooms for business travellers. Costs, market segment, building design and other circumstances should be considered at this stage.

Assessing the impact of the various alternatives on the enterprise is also important. For example, accommodating an increased number of guests in the new units might create a need for additional kitchen facilities or increased dinning room space. There might be a need for additional parking facilities or even for a larger front office to check-in the additional guests.

TEAM

Once the renovation decision is taken, a team for the project must be selected. Most of the authors recommend that the assembling of the team should be an early priority in any renovation to create a plan that will enhance the marketability of the product (e.g. Fairhead, 1988; West and Hughes, 1991; Sullivan, 1994; Learner, 1996; Rowe, 1996). Along the same line, Paneri and Wolff (1994) take the view that the external parties (such as the interior designer, architect and contractors) should be involved in the planning phase to provide their collective expertise in accomplishing budgets, schedules, phasing and contingencies. The main parties involved in hospitality renovation projects are presented in Table 10.2.

The management should appoint experts in accomplishing its renovation to minimize risks (Fox, 1991; Rowe, 1995).

Table 10.2	Participants of Renovation
Participant	**Definition**
Clients	The client may be an individual (e.g. business owner/operator) or a private or public sector organisation (e.g. hotel chain or the ministry of tourism) that has the authority and resources to carry out the renovation project
Users	These are the people who must operate and maintain the renovated building or facilities. Although the same organisation my be both client and users but they are represented by different individuals (e.g. board of directors and staff respectively)
End users	Despite being the most ignored party in renovation projects, they are the most important participants. They are customers who will use the final product
Designers	These are the architects, structural engineers, electrical and civil engineers, quantity surveyors and so forth.
Builders	These are the people who undertake the physical construction work
Public authorities	These are the bodies responsible for ensuring that renovation work fulfils statutory requirements in relation to construction and building standards and safety. Examples include city or town councils, ministry of planning, ministry of tourism or tourist board, water authority, gas authority, power authority and so forth.
Suppliers	The bodies who provide furniture, equipment, appliances, fittings and fixtures.

Adapted from Austen and Neale (1984).

Renovation projects are usually complex and need to be specific in terms of their planning, implementation and evaluation. Communication is regarded as an essential tool for hospitality managers to carry out their renovation projects. Hospitality business managers have to act as facilitators between the different involved external and internal parties of the renovation team participants (Ransley and Ingram, 2004).

From a hospitality management perspective, possibly the most important team member of any renovation project is the client, who is usually the owner/operator and the representative designated manager in the case of small or large hospitality business renovation projects, respectively. The client plays an essential role from beginning to end of any renovation project. Their basic duties include (Ransley and Ingram, 2004; Swarbrooke, 2002; Alexander, 1996):

- Appointment of an appropriate team to carry out the renovation work.
- Appointment of a capable team leader for the smooth flow of works all the way through the project.
- Providing the team with clear and detailed information regarding the aims and specifications of the project.
- Effective communication with the team members.
- Ensuring communication links between the team members.
- Ensuring the effective execution of business throughout the renovation process with minimum interruption to customers or guests.
- Visiting the site regularly to monitor and control the quality of work done.
- Ensuring that the end products mirror their initial design concepts and aims.
- Ensuring that enough funding is available throughout the project.
- Ensuring a contingency plan and budget for unforeseen circumstances. (For example, a sudden rise in interest rates, subsurface soil conditions, inclement weather, shortages of essential materials and other similar events can affect significantly the cost of renovation).
- Ensuring the compliance of the project with any legislation such as planning permission and health and safety rules and regulations.
- Preparing a 'snagging' list of all deficiencies, unsatisfactory work or imperfections upon the completion of the project.
- Carrying out a 'post project review' to assess the viability of the finished project.

BUDGET

Funding the renovation programme is considered one of the most important and critical elements in the renovation process (Bruns, 1996). Hence, an honest and realistic budget should not be overlooked. Paneri and Wolff (1994) advise hospitality owners and managers to be aware of additional costs that cannot be seen and may occur in the near future. To encourage broader renovation programmes, some hotel chains, such as Ramada and Days Inn, help owners, in different ways, in undertaking renovation. According to an International Society of Hospitality Consultants (ISHC) (Berg and Skinner, 1995) survey, each limited service hotel should allocate about 4% of its gross revenue for renovation and about 7% for renovation in full service hotels to stay competitive. The most common sources of renovation finance are debt equity capital (e.g. bank loans) and/or equity capital (e.g. ownership or self-funded projects) (Ransley and Ingram, 2004).

TIMING (SCHEDULING AND PHASING)

Fox (1993) takes the view that it is important to plan around occupancy periods and to try to accomplish as much as possible during the slow times. Also, Sullivan (1994) states that recognising when to renovate is just as important as the renovation itself. Paneri and Wolff (1994) pose some questions that need to be answered in order to decide to stay open or to close during renovation. Similarly, Seacord (1997) discusses the virtues and drawbacks of the same decision. It is the responsibility of the renovation team to compile a clear written brief for the project that includes the budget, schedules and so on (West and Hughes, 1991). Another key to meeting schedules is getting all the proper materials on site before work starts (Rowe, 1995).

MARKETING

Whatever the renovation type, marketing has an important role to inform the public (e.g. customers, travel agents, meeting planners and corporate travel managers) about it. Experts suggest that renovation should be marketed ahead of time through publicity, promotion or special events (Koss-Feder, 1994a,b).

IMPLEMENTATION

Baltin and Cole (1995) note that once management has agreed to the objectives and strategies behind the renovation, the physical work can progress. What a good designer does best is create the embodiment of the targeted plan for reaching the desired market. Another critical aspect of this phase is the communication between all parties involved in the project and the cooperation to enhance the flow of events (West and Hughes, 1991). That is why some hotels employ a project manager to act as a supervisor during renovation (Sullivan, 1994).

EVALUATION

The project should be evaluated from time to time during the development process, as well as after finishing the programme, to see how the actual situation is when compared with the expected plans. This evaluation should be based on subjective criteria (e.g. feedback from all key user groups such as customers, staff and corporate management) (West and Hughes, 1991) and/or on objective criteria (e.g. revenues and occupancy rate) (Sullivan, 1994). In addition, the process of renovation is multi-stepped. At a practical level, its implementation will vary due to many external and internal factors.

CONCLUSION

This chapter has dealt with various aspects of renovation in the hospitality industry. It includes discussion of the definition, types, process and importance of renovation. Moreover, the literature on renovation is extended to illustrate the relationship between new product/innovation and property renovation in the hospitality industry.

It started with clarifying and identifying the relationship between renovation and innovation/new product development. Then it discussed the semantic problems with regards to renovation definitions, related concepts and types. Finally, this chapter concluded with an analysis of the renovation process. Building on the literature analysis, an inclusive framework is designed to show the different phases involved within the hospitality renovation process. This model consists of four fundamental interrelated phases, which are common to any type of renovation. As argued, it differs fundamentally from previous approaches in three respects: (a) it considers the renovation process as a cycle since it is an ongoing process in hotels; (b) it includes other forces or drivers of renovation in addition to the customer; and (c) it gives particular consideration to the marketing element in the process.

In short, hospitality renovation is a sophisticated linear process that comprises different stages. The viability of the project should be assessed by the team throughout each stage and the whole process. Similarly, the end users (i.e. current or potential customers) and users (e.g. employees, supervisors and managers) need to be considered during every stage of the process in order for the hospitality business to gain the maximum benefits of renovation in terms of profitability, customer and employee satisfaction.

REVIEW QUESTIONS

1. Define the concept of renovation and discuss the reasons for a hospitality business needing to embark on a renovation process.
2. Acting in the role as a renovation consultant to a hospitality business with which you are familiar, consider the following questions:

   A. What aspects of the business would you suggest require renovating? To what extent should this be classified as a minor, master or major renovation?

   B. Discuss how the business should proceed through the renovation process by offering advice to the business on the following:
   - driver analysis
   - planning and controlling (including goals and objectives)
   - alternative plans
   - the project team
   - the budget
   - timing
   - marketing
   - implementation
   - evaluation.

Case Study: Renovation at Marriott International

Marriott International is a global company with 3000 hospitality properties located in 67 countries. The company's portfolio of brands is separated into different tiers. This includes the luxury tier (incorporating The Ritz-Carlton, JW Marriott Hotels & Resorts and Bulgari Hotels & Resorts), the quality tier (incorporating Marriott Hotels & Resorts, Renaissance Hotels & Resorts, Renaissance ClubSport) the upper moderate tier (incorporating Courtyard by Marriott and SpringHill Suites by Marriott, the moderate tier (incorporating Fairfield Inn by Marriott), extended stay tier (incorporating Residence Inn by Marriott, TownePlace Suites by Marriott, Marriott Executive Apartments and Marriott ExecuStay) and timeshare properties (incorporating Marriott Vacation Club, The Ritz-Carlton Club, Grand Residences by Marriott, and Horizons by Marriott Vacation Club).

In 2007, Marriot International embarked on a £600 million restoration of its global hotel portfolio in the Middle East, the United Kingdom, Continental Europe, Asia Pacific and the Caribbean and Latin America. In Europe, the renovations included seventeen Renaissance and Courtyard branded hotels including The Shelbourne in Dublin and the Paris Marriott Rive Gauche Hotel & Conference Centre. The other renovated properties are based in Vienna, Zurich, Amsterdam, Paris, Budapest, Hamburg, Moscow, Leipzig, Heidelberg, Cologne and Prague. In London, The Grosvenor House underwent renovation to become a JW Marriott-branded luxury hotel and the London Marriott County Hall hotel has also undergone renovation.

In the Middle East, the Cairo Marriott Hotel in Egypt has been renovated including upgrades to guest rooms with flat screen TVs and high speed internet access. In the Caribbean, the San Juan Marriott Hotel & Stellaris Casino in Puerto Rico and Aruba Marriott Resort & Stellaris Casino have had major renovations of their casinos, guest and meeting rooms and restaurant and lounge areas.

In the Pacific, the Wailea Beach Marriott Resort & Spa had its guest rooms and restaurant and lounge areas redesigned with the addition of a spa and fitness centre. In Hawaii, the Waikoloa Beach Marriott Resort & Spa renovated all its guest rooms and included a spa, ballroom and infinity edged swimming pool as part of its restoration. In Asia, Marriot has embarked upon a renovation of its major hotels including JW Marriott Hotel Hong Kong, the JW Marriott Hotel Bangkok and the Brisbane Marriott in Australia.

Sources: www.businesstravelnet.com, www.marriott.com.

Questions

1. Using the internet, search for the properties highlighted in the case and find further information about the renovations that have been made.

2. Classify the types of renovations have been made to the properties by minor, major and master.

3. Identify and discuss the reasons for Marriott International embarking on such an extensive restoration programme of it global hospitality portfolio?

4. What aspects of the renovation process would Marriott have had to pay particular attention to when undertaking its global restoration programme?

GLOSSARY

Major renovation   Major renovation refers to replacement or renewal of all furnishings, equipment and finishes within a space in order to partially improve the hotel image, which may include extensive modifications to the physical layout of the space and/or upgrading the former used systems (mechanical or electrical).

Master renovation   Master renovation is more comprehensive than major renovation and involves the entire property in order to partially or totally change the hotel image, especially in the case of mature or tired hotels where the aim is to breathe new life into these hotels (i.e. new extension).

Minor renovation   Minor renovation refers to replacement or renewal of some non-durable furnishings (e.g. carpeting) and finishes within a space without changing the space's use or physical layout in order to maintain the hotel image.

Project brief   A project brief is the pivotal document that establishes the project objective and parameters for all parties concerned.

Renovation   The process of retaining or improving the 'hospitality' business's image by modifying the tangible product, due to a variety of reasons, through any changes in the 'business' layout (e.g. property structure-new extension) and/or any additions or replacement of materials and Furniture, Fixture & Equipment.

CHAPTER 11

Conclusions

Learning Objectives

Having completed this chapter you should be able to:

- Review the contribution of the book you have just worked through
- Explore the issues surrounding the development of hospitality businesses
- Evaluate the chances of success of new product developments in the hospitality industry

We began this book by saying that hospitality business development might be seen as a quite obvious, clear and straightforward process. We have been working with a very broad definition of the processes involved to try to capture the ways in which the businesses can use internal, external and joint resources to maintain or improve their positions in the markets. The businesses can move within the same markets or seek to enter new ones, by launching a modified offer or an extended offer. Certainly the process depends on identifying smart goals and objectives, allocating the required resources for its implementation and then getting it done. In reality, nevertheless, business development is not always an easy task for hospitality organisations because it involves several interacting controllable and uncontrollable factors such as the organisation, its stakeholders and the dynamic changing nature of its micro and macro environments. We think that this very broad definition is essential from a management point of view because it forces us to look at the possibilities of business development from many different perspectives that can then fully reflect both the content and context of hospitality business development. We have attempted to demonstrate the complexity of this with the examples and case studies that you have been working through. By adopting a processual model of business development we have been able to explore the constituent elements of business development. This means that this book has moved through a series of chapters that have addressed the various aspects of hospitality business development. What we want to do in this conclusion is not only remind you of the arguments that we have made but demonstrate how the elements come together. We have presented an analytical separation but the complexities of analysing the development of hospitality businesses demand a synthetic approach.

At the heart of our approach to hospitality business development has been the customer and the businesses' ability to know what their customers are thinking, feeling and expecting from them. This customer-centric approach means that the business model operated by the business must begin and end with the perceptions of the customers. We have seen that businesses can improve their performance through a variety of ways, including modifying or enhancing the features and attributes of the current offer through to developing new products and services for the existing market or moving into new ones. You have been shown how these moves can be done by the business acting on its own or in cooperation with other businesses through strategic alliances and partnerships. No matter which way you look at the business development processes, this book should have shown you why we think the customer is the most important element in business development, especially for the range of services offered in the hospitality industry.

The hospitality service offer cannot be seen as a simple offer. We have utilised a distinction between the core and augmented product to develop our analysis, but in practice a holistic view of the offer is necessary. We explored the fast food industry and described the ways in which the core offer is heavily prescribed and defined around the delivery and consumption of food to satisfy the basic needs of he consumer. Here we can look to a consumer perception of the tangible attributes of the offer – the location, price, quality and even brand. We have demonstrated that the similarities in the offers of the leading brands, the core offers, make differentiation difficult and the decision comes to rest on the intangible aspects of the augmented products. This will be constructed differently by different consumers, so elements such as speed of service may carry greater weight for some customers than others. Even where the augmented offer is similar, customers will still find ways of recognising and valuing the offer in their own ways. For instance, both Burger King and McDonalds provide children's menus and accompany the food with the offer of a toy. For one of our little boys (Daniel, aged 5) the choice is simple – he would go to Burger King every time. Remembering that he does eat the burger any way, you can see that his choice is determined entirely by the augmented product. In McDonalds the toys are packaged in the meal and you have to wait to see what is in your box – but with Burger King, all the toys available are displayed and you are encouraged to choose the one you want. This means the child does not get duplicates or disappointments – and often the choice can take longer than the delivery of the food. Here the augmentation is very simple but has meaning and therefore value to the targeted customer. This tells us a great deal about the placing of the customer at the heart of the business model and the importance of developing the augmented product within the market.

When approaching hospitality business development it is necessary to look for and recognise the significance of the differences as well as the similarities within the markets. Often the core hospitality product can be separated into various sectors, for instance few people would confuse the luxury five star hotel with a Backpackers Hostel although both are defined by the provision of accommodation. There are official categories, based on the tangible offer, that differentiate hotels through star rating systems. However, there are also elements that contribute to the perceived value of the offer, which means that customers develop loyalty to particular hotel chains and airlines. This again takes us into the creation of and reaction to the hospitality businesses' augmented products as it is the customers' perceptions that determine whether the offer is successful or not. The flexibility to react to and even anticipate the changes in customers' expectations will be what allows businesses to gain a competitive advantage, whether this means adapting the design, décor and furnishings of the tangible offer or repositioning the brand to create a better fit between the offer's values and those of the customers. We have to be aware of changing trends, fashions and consumer tastes in order to ensure that business development enhances the fit of the offer to the demands of the customers.

Hospitality businesses do not operate in splendid isolation. The managers of the hospitality businesses have to be fully aware of the influences that come from the businesses' operating environments, both in terms of the micro and macro environments. There are a variety of tools and techniques that can be used to help with the analysis and we reviewed the use of SWOT, LoNGPEST, the sector life cycle and competitive structural analysis. It is important to be aware of the limitations of these mechanisms as they are only as reliable as the data available from the market and the rigour of the use made of them, but they do provide a firm basis for mapping and understanding the dynamics of the competitive markets. We do not think that they offer the promise of easy answers, but they do offer a way of deepening the understanding of the complexities of the markets and should be the basis for better informed business decision-making.

Businesses have to make decisions not only about the product offer but also about where these offers should be presented and how they should be brought to those markets. We therefore considered the arguments around positioning and repositioning a hospitality business. We also presented a comprehensive discussion of the concept of repositioning in the general marketing literature and in hospitality marketing in particular. We drew on both the general marketing and the hospitality marketing literature to suggest that an inclusive model was necessary. Again the analysis cannot be perfect as it is very difficult to obtain accurate and reliable information about many of the key elements involved in the positioning of hospitality businesses. However, the model introduced here does identify the different phases involved. Our model differs fundamentally from previous approaches in three important respects. First, the positioning process model was extended to cover some of the forces of positioning (chain standards, technology and governmental requirements) that had often been ignored in the previous analyses. We would also draw your attention to one of these new factors for the analysis being the knowledge of, and relationship with, the business's existing and potential customers. Second, our model attempts to capture the dynamics of the positioning process as it highlights the different contributions of the full range of variables and sub-variables involved in the marketing mix and can help to demonstrate how they impact on the positioning and repositioning of the hospitality businesses. Third, our model stresses that the previous linear descriptions of the positioning process are inadequate, even at a simple descriptive level, as we demonstrated that positioning is an ongoing and continuous process within the hospitality industry.

Although we separated the two in our presentation, it should now be clear that the positioning process should therefore start with the external and internal analyses of the hospitality business environment. The internal corporate analysis necessitates the businesses identifying the scope and range of their resources, products and services. This internal analysis will bring together assessments of the human, financial, intellectual and physical assets in the business and highlight the limitations and/or constraints that the business needs to address to move forward. The conclusions drawn from these exercises should guide the business decision making processes and help in the identification of viable target markets which will respond positively to the existing offer or the proposed modifications or enhancements.

We believe that these analyses must include some attempts to analyse the market and competitive positions of the business and its offers. Statements of strengths and weaknesses should be tested against the state of the market, the performance of the competitors and the perceptions of the customers. Our model makes market analysis an integral part of the process, as this is where the businesses can make themselves aware of the value of attributes amongst the customer base. The decision-making process should evaluate the different opportunities for product and service development and differentiation. Market location, along with other factors, such as the overall categorisation of the offer, quality standards, trends in customer behaviour, demographic, psychological and other characteristics of sources of demand, can be seen as important attributes. These discussions will also necessarily examine any alternative approaches to the market and of segmenting the customers, with the decisions informed by a full critical analysis of the impact of adopting any new proposals – especially in terms of how they reshape the overall size and potential for maximising the markets that are most likely to be profitable for the business.

Our belief is that hospitality businesses should be able to design and implement efficient and well-organised positioning action plans based on the analysis and the development of their marketing mix elements. By integrating all the forms of analysis that we have discussed, the business can produce a definitive 'positioning statement', which identifies and specifies where the business sees itself wanting to be in the market. This combination of all the factors we have discussed means that the business can define its desired market position, develop a positioning plan that will link product and service improvements to the values of the market and establish a successful and differentiated offer in the market.

The testing of this positioning statement comes from researching whether there is an offer which is seen as distinctive from those of the competitors in the market and this again brings us back to the centrality of the customer. It is the customers' perceptions of the offer which will be the judge of whether the positioning statement has been effective.

The implications of our positioning process model are clear to us as the customer is first, last and always at the heart of the model. There is therefore a clear logical development as we put forward the view that the whole of the business model, covering its planning, operation and evaluation, should be revisited. We would argue that introducing a customer-centred business model is a pre-requirement for success in the globalised and highly competitive hospitality business. By drawing on the literature, we have shown that there has been a long trend away from product-centred models towards a market-based business model which culminates in the customer-centred model discussed in this book. The customer is where the business successes and/or failures lie. It is therefore essential that the relationships between the businesses and their customers are strengthened and fully utilised in all aspects of the business. Earlier versions of the business model saw customers as the end point in the business, or as a part in the product/service delivery exchange, but we are proposing that the whole of the business, including the traditional business functions of human resources and operations, are driven by consumer-centred approaches. Customer-centred approaches cannot be adopted as an add-on to other models as the assumptions of other models do not allow the central role for the customer. What we see is that every action of every one in the hospitality business is linked to the awareness of the perceptions of the customers and this will increase the likelihood of customer satisfaction and eventuality business profitability.

We have demonstrated how hospitality businesses have shifted towards strategies that maintain and retain customers, initially seen as important because of the cost savings generated by retaining customers. However, we also showed how businesses have tested product and service developments with their customers and matched the level of development to customers' perceptions of value. Changes that are not perceived as relevant will not be valued by the markets and will in effect drive down profitability rather than increase it. Market leadership will come from and be maintained by those businesses that best relate to their customers and develop the mechanisms for ensuring that the awareness of what the customers' value is transferred throughout the business and informs all business decisions made by the organisation.

We then considered how hospitality businesses could move forward through the production of a business plan. The role of design and project definition was elaborated, before we explored a hypothetical example of a business plan, and then demonstrated how this could be questioned further through a feasibility study. We outlined the main factors that would impact on the business plan and how sources of finance could be linked to the development. The purpose of the business plan is to outline and elaborate the possibilities envisaged for the successful development of the proposal. The audience should be seen as those who are in some ways connected to the proposal and wanting to see the proposal taken forward (and become successful). This allows for the business plan to be constructed in such a way that captures the imagination of those involved and expresses their dreams. This is still a business document and should be produced as such but it is being written by those who are committed to the idea and therefore may not be entirely objective. The feasibility study can be seen as a counterbalance to this as it offers an external and less subjective assessment of the proposal. It is a pragmatic and objective exercise and should never become personal. It is therefore an external document. It seeks to explore the business logics of the proposal and to test the assumptions built into that scenario. We also looked at whether the feasibility study should be carried out internally or by someone external to the business and more distanced from the proposal. The feasibility study will utilise many of the techniques and explore the concerns we have highlighted throughout this book and will challenge the perceptions and interpretations placed on the market and profitability estimates provided by the proposer. We hope we have shown how the factors discussed in the first part of this book come together to first build and then test the business case put forward. It is important that both the proposer and the evaluator of the project have a clear understanding of these factors and it is important that both constructions of the realities of the market are presented and debated. Where we start from can impact on how we construct what we see and how we believe the future will shape up. Commitment to a project is admirable – and some would say necessary – to drive it forward. However, over-commitment can also lead to blindness and overlooking critical factors that can undermine the likelihood of success. Therefore, although the two processes to develop the business plan and to undertake a feasibility study may appear very similar when they are modelled, it is important to recognise the essential difference of perspective in recognising the different roles they perform.

What we hope this book has demonstrated is that the very complexity which is seen as one of the defining aspects of the hospitality industry means that there are a great many possibilities for new directions and developments. Throughout this book we have demonstrated through the case studies that there are many routes and directions that hospitality businesses can develop to enhance or change their offers and establish some form of competitive advantage over their rivals. For this very reason, we want to reinforce the importance of businesses having a clear sense of purpose – a vision and a mission that underpins and guides their sense of priorities. The mission demonstrates clearly what the core business is and where the company sees it as being ideally positioned. We would also add that it should contain a summary of the business values, ideally the customer-centredness that we have been advocating. Without a clear vision or mission, it is possible for businesses to develop in an unplanned, almost ad hoc way, and it is very important to avoid this strategic drift and remain focussed on responding to issues that emerge from the operating environment of the business.

At the strategic level we reviewed the well-recognised strategic options facing decision makers, including Porter's (1985) notion of the generic strategies of cost leadership, cost focus, differentiation and differentiation focus whilst also acknowledging that there are some additional routes that can be developed by introducing hybrid and no-frills strategies. Our discussions demonstrated that the process has to be evaluated according to how the strategies promise to deliver market penetration, market development, new product development and related and unrelated diversifications. These considerations sit alongside and may sometimes challenge a case built on the more traditional resource-based view of business development. We made the case for the benefits of the investment of time and effort in this strategic evaluation as we believe that successful business development only comes from a sure understanding of the basis and rationale for the proposed development. The careful examination of the options is important as a failure to detect problems at this stage can have dramatic effects on the business later when the decisions are implemented. Therefore hospitality businesses should make the fullest possible use of the decision-making criteria in exploring the feasibility of the proposals and the future route or direction.

We suggested that the strategic evaluation could be underpinned by a series of criteria based on the elements of the business plan and the factors that can shape the directions of the business. These were summarised and are represented here in Figure 11.1. Hospitality businesses have to be aware of those factors that may influence their decisions on the chosen development route or direction. By questioning these factors, the businesses can deepen their perceptions of the risk factors and develop their understanding of the consequences that follow on from specific strategic choices

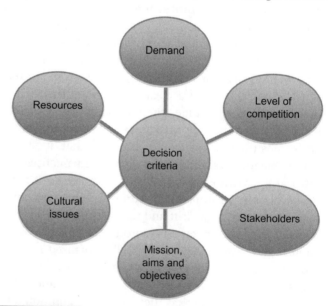

FIGURE 11.1 *Decision-making criteria for routes and directions.*

The strategic review will be informed by the perception of the levels of customer demand and the expectations about rates of growth for the offers. This can be mapped in terms of a lifecycle analysis for the sector and the decisions informed by a calculation of the future rate of growth – positive or negative – in the market overall and for the business in particular. In markets where there is evidence of continuous growth, then market penetration strategies may be justified as this could lead to achieving a larger market share. On the other hand if the market information shows any signs that the market demand has reached a plateau or indeed is already beginning to decline, then the strategic options will be designed to develop new offers or explore new markets for the business. These strategies will also be discussed in terms of the levels of competition that the business already faces and is likely to face in the near future. Competitive analysis will consider not only the number, size and type of competitors in the market, but it will also look at the maturity of the market and the ability of players to introduce barriers to participation for new entrants. The decision to move into a market may then be influenced by the possibility of a suitable acquisition or merger where there is evidence that the shakeout in the market will still maintain a viable level of demand.

This summary must also note the importance of cultural issues within the business and its environment. There are clear cultural factors to be considered if the business considers expanding into a different geographical market. Many of the studies have interpreted this as being international, where the cultural differences occur in the operations of two different nation states, but it is also possible to find these situations within countries, between north and south for instance or between different cultural groups in the same country. Boddingtons had brewed and sold beer for over a century in Manchester and the North west of England, but when they tried to expand their market in the south of the country they advertised with a beautiful woman with a stereotyped northern accent. It was not entirely successful, until it was taken up as a joke and became acceptable to talk about because 'we all knew it was so bad'. Any hospitality business thinking about entering a culturally different area has to consider how it would have to change its goods and services to meet the demands and the perceptions of the local customer and of the local cultures. We have noted at the beginning of the book that even McDonalds change their standard menu to meet the specific needs of the local population. Part of the business decision goes beyond the recognition of cultural differences, as it involves a sophisticated resource audit to understand whether the business has the capabilities – be they financial, human, technological and intellectual – to introduce the necessary adaptations and still continue the success of the core offer. One aspect of this intercultural working which is often overlooked is that it is not a simple one-way process as the new host culture can impact on the businesses' own organisational cultures in their head offices and other operations. Some of the values found necessary to create businesses in other cultures may not sit easily with the operating cultures of long established businesses and therefore the hospitality businesses should also consider the extent to which the route and direction they choose might have an impact upon their own organisational cultures.

We cannot overlook the basic consideration of resource allocation, as budgets are always limited then declaring priorities and directions is also a statement of committing resources into certain areas and not others. We have suggested that the hospitality businesses that are seeking to create sustainable business ventures would find the VIRUS (Valuable, Inimitable, Rare and UnSubstitutable) model helpful. Here we are looking for developments that meet the criteria of being Valuable, Inimitable, Rare and UnSubstitutable. Proposals should be weighed considering not only their absolute call on resources, but also the risk factors that are involved in committing those resources. New product development is particularly expensive and if combined with expansion into a new market, may also carry very high risk factors. Hospitality businesses should not be risk averse, nor should they invest in situations where they have not conducted full resource audits and undertaken thorough risk assessments.

Finally, the literature has come to recognise the role of the stakeholders within business development and the stakeholders of the hospitality businesses should be involved in the discussions about its strategic direction as they will also be impacted upon by the decisions that the business takes. The stakeholders of the business, including such diverse interests as banks, shareholders, governments, employees, customers, suppliers and community groups, will all have different needs and expectations that should be identified and responded to. Mendelow (1991) classified different stakeholder groups by their different levels of power and interest. This included suggestions on how key players, those identified as possessing high levels of either power or interest, should be managed by keeping them informed (high level of interest but low level of power) and keeping them satisfied (high level of power but low level of interest). Shamefully, the advice includes a suggestion for minimal effort, for those stakeholders with low levels of power and interest. It is not so long ago that the customers could have found themselves in this category of stakeholder and this would have prevented the move towards customer-centred business models being adopted. The choice of business model directly affects the classification of which groups constitute key stakeholders for hospitality businesses and we would argue that the trend towards customer-centred business models can be seen in the increasing recognition of the role of the consumer within the functions and decision-making processes of the businesses.

We have also considered the range of different development methods of hospitality businesses – moving from the forms of organic development to mergers and acquisitions, strategic alliances, franchising and management contracting. Our presentations attempted to critically test the various development patterns by considering the different costs and benefits experienced by those pursuing specific methods, as well as offering an appraisal of some of the risks involved in the development of these methods. Any decision on a method for development should be based on the consideration of all the alternatives available within the specific context of the development and the choice should be determined by a situationally specific calculation of how the existing resources of the businesses and those that may be mobilised externally can be brought together most effectively to satisfy the demands of the development. For example, we would see the expressed desire of a business to enter quickly into a new market as may be suggesting a development strategy based on acquisition, alliance or franchising as these allow rapid access to the market and include some experience of the market to be explored. However, we can also envisage a situation where a large and well-resourced business wants to expand into the same market but they can do so with an organic growth model, because they have the confidence in their own internal resources and capabilities to believe that they make the entry successfully. We see the feasibility study as an essential tool in the assessment and validation of the choice of entry method, especially as it can take a long-term view of the development as well as the medium- to short-term operational and cost implications that the development may have for the business.

We have also looked at new product development (NPD) system and looked into the important links between NPD and the idea of innovation within the hospitality industry. We see this as one of the clearest articulations of the model presented in this book as the exploration of the issues surrounding the definition, types, processes and importance of NPD within hospitality demonstrates our central concern for customer-centred operations and the ability of businesses to read their markets. Not all innovations are new but are innovative because they bring something which has been tried elsewhere, in other forms and other places, to a new market. We presented the assessment around six critical success factors and these are represented here in Figure 11.2.

The final contribution we made in this book was to offer an inclusive framework designed to show the different phases involved within the

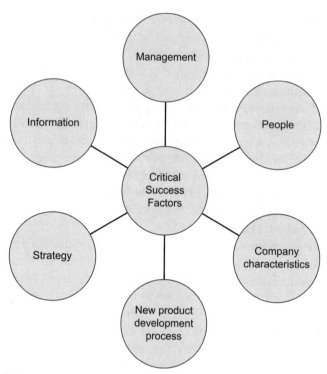

FIGURE 11.2 *Critical success factors in hospitality business development.*
Adapted from Craig and Hart (1992).

hospitality renovation process. We believe that the clarification of the relationships between renovation, innovation and new product development was an important starting point. We have reinforced the sense of the importance of the relationships between new products and innovation and property renovation in the hospitality industry by dealing with the various aspects of renovation in the hospitality industry. This included a full discussion of the definition, types, process and importance of renovation aimed at uncovering the ways the end users (current or potential customers) and users (employees, supervisors and managers) could be fully involved in every stage of the process in order for the hospitality businesses to gain the maximum benefits from renovation in terms of profitability, customer and employee satisfaction. We believe that this new model differs fundamentally from previous approaches in three important ways: (a) we move beyond a linear model by suggesting that the renovation process should be seen as a cycle since it is an ongoing process in hotels; (b) we have extended earlier models as we give weight to other forces or drivers of renovation in addition to the customer; and (c) we have recognised that particular consideration must be given to the marketing element in the process. However, our model consists of four fundamental interrelated phases, which will be found to be common to any type of renovation. We believe that the viability of the project proposals should be assessed by the project team not only throughout all of the stages but also throughout the whole process.

We want to end where we began – by pointing out the complexities in what may appear to be straightforward business developments. In order to do this we want to consider the development of the hospitality industry under the water. It appears quite simple – an underwater hotel is a hotel that is under water. This is both true and untrue. What we can see emerging is that the offer is more complex than would first appear. It is not just luxury hotels that can offer this facility. This is clearly a differentiated area within hospitality, but it is by no means straightforward and has attracted a wide range of players into the market. We will explore the developments by revisiting the key themes we have introduced throughout this book.

We must therefore ask where the market is for such developments and what drives the offer. The authors are old enough to remember a world without underwater hotels – in fact if you are reading the first edition of this book then it is quite likely that so are you! However, we also remember a world where a visit to an aquarium meant looking at small fish in small tanks. Aquaria were transformed by the introduction of new technologies in plastics and glass that allowed the creation of larger and larger tanks. The first appearance of a walk through underwater tunnel was both sensational and scary. How long would it last and could it really keep the sharks at bay? Now it is a taken for granted element in every new build all the way around the world.

We can trace a similar trajectory for hotel accommodation. It begins with accommodation by the water, then we built over the water, which we enriched by putting viewing panels into the floors of the rooms. We had hotels with aquaria in them and then we had a hotel with a restaurant with a living sea view. Now the implied demand has led the developers to explore ways of making the hotel experience itself underwater.

The questions that our models prepare us to ask are very relevant here. What are the trends in the markets that make these sorts of development thinkable? What are the market dynamics that will lead to viable market segments? What has been the customer reaction? And how did the developers identify the latent demand for these facilities?

Adventure tourism is a growing market and the Dive Centre Holiday has long been a feature of the tourism portfolio. The serious divers are a considerable niche market and the people who want to dive add to this number. Being aware of the fads and fashions that underpin market changes, it is also possible to point to a number of significant television programmes that have featured diving from David Attenborough's Blue Planet and the various shark jockeys (such as Ian 'Shark' Gordon and Rob Stewart) and increased the interest in underwater activities. The building experts have also developed the experience to offer such an opportunity to prospective developers so we can see how an emergent idea meets a technological possibility.

What is generally regarded as the first underwater hotel is in Key Largo, Florida and is a wonderful experience but not a straightforward five star luxury experience. To begin with, the market is limited as all guests have to hold a scuba diving certificate! The entrance is seven metres below the surface and the only way in is by diving. The Jules Undersea Lodge is in reality a converted research laboratory that was used in Puerto Rico. It features two bedrooms, a living room and – probably most importantly – the three 42-inch round portholes in the two bedrooms and the communal living area. (For further information, please see www.jul.com.) A similar idea can be found in Sweden, although there is fortunately no need to dive. The Utter Inn in Vasteras has a floating hut on the surface of Lake Mälaren which is your access to your room three metres below the lake (www.privateislandsonline. com/utter-inn.htm).

There are questions to be asked about the feasibility studies that were undertaken on these relatively small-scale developments. However, the pricing structure in Florida suggests that customers are willing to pay for the diving experience and the accommodation at high premium rates and this therefore justifies the running of the research laboratory and its support systems. The Utter Inn is slightly different and can almost be seen as a hobby or an art installation rather than as an accommodation project. Paying guests are a bonus – the rates of around £50 a night are not unreasonable for a very different experience, but what the business model is that underpins the offer is difficult to identify.

Catering to a different market, we can see the projected developments of underwater luxury. Hydropolis (www.hydropolis.com), a luxury Dubai underwater resort, will boast glass-bubble accommodation 20 metres down and a giant ballroom and concert hall that rises above the sea surface enabling open-air shows and views of the surrounding skyline. The proposed opening date in late 2009 has been put back but with rooms priced at US$5500 per night for one of the 220 suites that is clearly designed as a more luxurious offer. Guests will arrive at a grand entrance on Jumeirah Beach from where they will be whisked by train through a 515-metre transparent undersea tunnel to the resort.

Here we can see a different business model in operation. The Jumeirah group are very professional and thorough in all that they do and make sure that the vast resources they have at their disposal are used to generate very healthy rates of return. The use of their beach outlet associates them with the project although the funding has been secured through the Dubai Development & Investment Authority. As the developer admits, no bank would put up the 550 million Euros that the project required because it was seen as a high-risk investment and there were no pilots. Making the case to convince investors had to demonstrate both that the hotel is safe and that it will bring returns on investment. We also look forward to seeing the renovation model for these hotels as the complexities of renovation in and under water will need to be processed very carefully.

There are some who see the underwater experience as appealing to too small an audience and therefore developers have proposed mixed developments, incorporating some underwater elements and some more traditional land-based experiences. In the Maldives we can see this different way of approaching the underwater provision. Here the focus has been on taking the services underwater with the development of underwater spas and restaurants. Huvafen Fushi in the north Atoll offers the opportunity to visit the underwater spa. They claim that the underwater spa centre has been designed so that it recreates the picture and colours of the Indian Ocean. If dining underwater is your thing, you can also dine five metres below the Ocean at the Conrad Maldives, where the luxury resort features the glass bubble Ithaa undersea restaurant which guarantees the quality of the view to match the food served (www.conradmaldivesrangali.com). The five-star Poseidon Undersea Resort (www.poseidonresorts.com) planned to open in Fiji in 2009 will offer underwater rooms with panoramic views but these will be complemented by 457-square metre Beach Front Bungalows with private plunge pools and wraparound verandas to offer a complex multi-experience resort. The reaction of some people that these developments could not be safe has been addressed in the development. The underwater rooms will be pressurised and will have a safety dome with an entrance hatch for divers in the event of any emergency. As a further precaution, the design of the hotel ensures that sections of the hotel can be sealed off. A typical package here is envisaged as two nights underwater and four by the beach.

The concern for safety in all these ventures is obvious and points to at least one major point of contact with potential customers as the perception of safety and security is paramount. This will be especially true for developments like the Hydropolis where the aim is to attract those who cannot dive and even those who cannot swim. It will be necessary to be able to demonstrate convincingly that these hotels are safe and that the customers can feel relaxed and enjoy themselves there.

These examples show the richness and complexity of the offers that make up the hospitality industry. We have attempted to develop a systematic and grounded business approach to the understanding of the development of these offers through the introduction of the literature on hospitality businesses and also through the examination of case studies that have explored the actual developments in the industry. We believe that linking the academic and the practical is the only way to obtain a full understanding of the forces that shape hospitality development. The future of the hospitality industry lies in the hands of the people reading this book as you will become the key players in the industry in the not too distant future. We have not supplied you with all the answers; in fact if you read this book carefully you will find that we have not provided you with any answers. What we have attempted to do is to elaborate the principles that underpin sound business processes and tried to demonstrate why and how they can help develop successful hospitality businesses. Our models are theoretical but they are grounded in practice and the rigorous application of them within the context of specific hospitality business developments can only help to guide the direction of the business towards success.

We hope you have enjoyed this book and will find the challenge of developing the hospitality industry sufficiently interesting to become the next generation of hospitality entrepreneurs. Enjoy the journey!

Chapter 1

REFERENCES AND ADDITIONAL READING

Ansoff, I., 1988. New Corporate Strategy. John Wiley & Sons, New York.

Booz, Allen, Hamilton, 1982. New Product Management for the 1980's. Booz, Allen and Hamilton Inc., New York.

Bowie, D., Buttle, F., 2004. Hospitality Marketing: An Introduction. Butterworth-Heinemann, Oxford.

Cooper, R., 1999. Product Development for the Service Sector: Lessons from Market Leaders. Perseus Books, Cambridge, Mass.

Cooper, R.G., 1993. Winning at New Products: Accelerating the Process from Idea to Launch, second ed. Addison-Wesley Publishing Company, Reading, Massachusetts.

Cousins, J., Foskett, D., Gillespie, C., 2002. Food and Beverage Management, second ed. Prentice Hall, Harlow.

Davis, B., Lockwood, A., Pantelidis, I., Alcott, P., 2008. Food and Beverage Management, fourth ed. Elsevier, Oxford.

Hudson, S., 2008. Tourism and Hospitality Marketing. Sage, London.

Johnson, G., Scholes, K., Whittington, R., 2008. Exploring Corporate Strategy, eighth ed. Prentice Hall, London.

Kotler, P., Bowen, J., Makens, J., 2003. Marketing for Hospitality and Tourism, second ed. Prentice Hall, New Jersey.

Lashley, C., 2000. Hospitality Retail Management. Butterworth-Heinemann, Oxford.

Lashley, C., Morrison, A. (Eds.), 2000. Franchising Hospitality Services. Butterworth-Heinemann, Oxford.

Lashley, C., Morrison, A. (Eds.), 2000. Search of Hospitality. Butterworth-Heinemann, Oxford.

Lee-Ross, D., Lashley, C., 2008. Entrepreneurship and Small Business Management in the Hospitality Industry. Elsevier, Oxford.

Lockwood, A., Medlik, S., 2002. Tourism and Hospitality in the 21st Century. Butterworth-Heinemann, Oxford.

Medlik, S., 2000. The Business of Hotels, fourth ed. Butterworth-Heinmann, Oxford.

Morrison, A., 2001. Hospitality and Travel Marketing, third ed. Delmar Publishers, New York.

Morrison, A., Rimmington, M., Williams, C., 1999. Entrepreneurship in the Hospitality. Tourism and Leisure Industries. Butterworth-Heinemann, Oxford.

Palmer, A., 2001. Principles of Services Marketing, third ed. McGraw-Hill, London.

Pender, L., Sharpley, R. (Eds.), 2005. The Management of Tourism. Sage, London.

Pizam, A., Holcomb, J. (Eds.), 2008. International Dictionary of Hospitality Management. Elsevier, Oxford.

Sloan, D. (Ed.), 2004. Culinary Taste. Butterworth-Heinemann, Oxford.

Waller, K., 1996. Improving Food and Beverage Performance. Butterworth-Heinemann, Oxford.

Williams, A., 2002. Understanding the Hospitality Consumer. Butterworth-Heinemann, Oxford.

Wood, R. (Ed.), 2000. Strategic Questions in Food and Beverage Management. Butterworth-Heinemann, Oxford.

Chapter 2

REFERENCES AND ADDITIONAL READING

Brotherton, B., 1999. Towards a definitive view of the nature of hospitality and hospitality management. International Journal of Contemporary Hospitality Management 11 (4), 165–173.

Clarke, A., Chen, W., 2007. International Hotel Management. Butterworth Heinemann, Oxford.

Dittmer, P., 2002. Dimension of the Hospitality Industry, third ed. Wiley, New York.

Hoffman, D.K., Bateson, J.E.G., 2006. Services Marketing: Concepts. Strategies & Cases, third ed. Thomson/South-Western, Cincinnati, OH.

King, C.A., 1995. What is hospitality? International Journal Hospitality Management 14 (3/4) 219–234.

Kotler, P., 1994. Marketing Management, eighth ed. Prentice Hall, Englewood Cliffs, New Jersey.

Lashley, C., 2000. Hospitality Retail Management: A Unit Manager's Guide. Butterworth-Heinemann, Oxford.

Lashley, C., Lynch, P., Morrison, A. (Eds.), 2006. Hospitality: A Social Lens. Elsevier Science, Oxford.

Medlik, S., Ingram, H., 2000. The Business of Hotels, fourth ed. Butterworth-Heinemann, Oxford.

Teboul, J., 2005. Service is front stage, We are all in services...more or less Palgrave Macmillan. Available from: <http://www.notsoboringlife.com/outdoor-recreation/camping/camping-guide-types-of-camping/>; <http://www.safarinow.com/cms/accommodation-types/irie.aspx>.

Timothy, D., Teye, V., 2009. Tourism and the Lodging Sector. Elsevier, Oxford.

Chapter 3

REFERENCES AND ADDITIONAL READING

Capon, C., 2004. Understanding Organisational Context: Inside and Outside Organisations, second ed. Person Education, Harlow.

Dale, C., 2000. The UK tour operating industry: a competitive analysis. Journal of Vacation Marketing 6 (4), 357–367.

Evans, N., Campbell, D., Stonehouse, G., 2003. Strategic Management for Travel and Tourism. Butterworth-Heinemann, Oxford.

Grant, R.M., 2007. Contemporary Strategy Analysis, sixth ed. Blackwell, Oxford.

Henry, A., 2008. Understanding Strategic Management. Oxford University Press, Oxford.

Johnson, G., Scholes, K., Whittington, R., 2008. Exploring Corporate Strategy, eighth ed. Prentice Hall, London.

Porter, M.E., 1980. Competitive Strategy: Techniques for Analyzing Industries and Competitors. Free Press, New York.

Chapter 4

REFERENCES AND ADDITIONAL READING

Aaker, D., Shansby, J., 1982. Positioning your product. Business Horizon 25, 56–62.

Aaker, D., Batra, R., Myres, J., 1992. Advertising Management. Prentice Hall International, London.

Ansari, A., Economides, N., Ghosh, A., 1994. Competitive positioning in markets with non-uniform preferences. Marketing Science 13 (Summer), 248–273.

Arnott, D., 1992. Bases of financial services positioning, unpublished PhD thesis. Manchester Business School, Manchester.

Bohans, G.T., Cahill, M., 1993. Determining the feasibility of hotel marketing repositioning. Real Estate Review 22 (1), 63–74.

Boyd, H.W., Walker, O.C., Larreche, J.C., 1995. Marketing Management: A Strategic Approach with a Global Orientation, second ed. Irwin, London.

Bowie, D., Buttle, F., 2004. Hospitality Marketing: An Introduction. Butterworth-Heinemann, Oxford.

Brassington, F., Pettitt, S., 2006. Principles of Marketing, fourth ed. Pearson, Harlow, Essex.

Brooksbank, C., 1994. The anatomy of marketing positioning strategy. Marketing Intelligence & Planning 12 (4), 10–14.

Brown, P., 1985. Forget satisfying the consumer – just outfox the other guy. Business Week. October 7, 55.

Day, G., Wensley, R., 1988. Assessing advantage: a framework for diagnosing competitive superiority. Journal of Marketing 52, 1–20.

Evans, M.J., Moutinho, L., Raaij, W.F.V., 1996. Applied Consumer Behaviour. Addison-Wesley Publishing Company, Harlow.

Frabotta, David, 2001. Finding the right fit. Hotel & Motel Management 216 (2), 30–34.

Hanson, F, 1972. Backwards Segmentation Using Hierarchical Clustering and Q-Factor Analysis. ESOMAR Seminar.

Hassanien, A., Baum, T., 2002. Analysing hotel positioning through property renovation. Tourism and Hospitality Research: The Surrey Quarterly Review 4 (2).

Higley, J., 2000. Fairfield replays suites card. Hotel & Motel Management 215 (3), 2. 66.

Hill, Roger G., Fay Andrew, J., 1992. Reposition to profitability. Lodging December, 18–22.

Hooley, G.J., Möller, K., Broderick, A.J., 1998. Competitive positioning and the resource-based view of the firm. Journal of Strategic Marketing Vol 6 (No 2), 97–115.

Hooley, G., Saunders, J., 1993. Competitive Positioning: The Key to Market Success. Prentice Hall, New York.

Jain, S.C., 1997. Marketing Planning & Strategy, third ed. South-Western Publishing Co., Cincinnati, Ohio.

Kotler, P., 1997. Marketing Management, third ed. Prentice Hall, Englewood Cliffs, NJ, pp. 60.

Kotler, P., 1997. Principles of Marketing. Prentice-Hall Inc., Englewood Cliffs, New Jersey.

Kotler, P., Armstrong, G., 1989. Principles of Marketing, fourth. Prentice-Hall, Englewood Cliffs, NJ.

Kotler, P., Armstrong, G., 2007. Marketing: an introduction, eighth ed. Pearson Prentice Hall, New Jersy.

Lewis, R., 1980. The positioning statement for hotels. The Cornell Hotel and Restaurant Administration Quarterly 21 (3), 6–12.

Lewis, R., Chambers, R.E., Harsha, C.E., 1995. Marketing Leadership in Hospitality. Van-Nostrand Reinhold, New York.

Loudon, D.L., Bitta, D., 1993. Consumer Behavior: Concepts and Applications, fourth ed. International Editions, McGraw-Hill.

Lovelock, C., 1984. Positioning the service organization in the marketplace, in, C.

Lynch, R., 2000. Corporate Strategy, second ed. Pearson Education Limited, Harlow.

Nozar, R.A., 2001. Initiatives solidify brand's repositioning. Hotel & Motel Management 216 (5), 3–24.

Palmer, A., 1998. Principles of Services Marketing, second ed. McGraw-Hill, London.

Porter, M., 1985. Competitive Advantage: Creating and Sustaining Superior Performance. The Free Press, New York.

Powers, T., 1997. Marketing Hospitality, second ed. John Wiley & Sons Inc., New York.

Ries, A., Trout, J., 1986. Positioning: The Battle for Your Mind. McGraw-Hill, New York.

Sherif, H.S.A., 1986. Marketing hotel operations: an investigation into the marketing behaviour of national and international chain affiliated hotels. Unpublished PhD thesis. University of Strathclyde.

Trout, J., Rivkin, S., 1995. Strategic Planning in Industrial Marketing: an interaction approach. European Journal of Marketing 20 (3), 5–20.

Urban, G.L., Hauser, J.R., 1980. Design and Marketing for New Products. Englewood Cliffs. Prentice-Hall, New Jersey.

Walsh, J.P., 2000. Changing flags. Hotel & Motel Management 215 (17), 34–36.

Wind, Y., 1982. Product Concepts:Concepts, Methods and Strategy. Addison Wesley, Reading, M.A.

Wind, Y., 1990. Positioning Analysis and Strategy. In: Day, G., Weits, B., Wensley, R. (Eds.), The interface of Marketing and Strategy. Jaipress, Greenwich, CT, pp. 382–412.

Chapter 5

REFERENCES AND ADDITIONAL READING

Brennan, R., Henneburg, S.C., 2008. Does political marketing need the concept of customer value. Marketing Intelligence and Planning 26 (6), 559–572.

Buzzell, R.D., Gale, B.T., 1987. The PIMS Principles. Linking Strategy to Performance. The Free Press, New York.

Carlzon, J., 1989. Moments of Truth. Harper & Row, New York.

Chapman, R.L., Soosay, C., Kandampully, J., 2002. Innovation in logistic services and the new business model: a conceptual framework. Managing Service Quality 12 (6), 630–650.

Clarke, A., Chen, W., 2007. International Hotel Management. Butterworth Heinemann, Oxford.

Dick, A.S., Basu, K., 1994. Customer loyalty: toward an integrated conceptual framework. Journal of the Academy of Marketing Science 22 (2), 99–113.

Fredericks, J.O., Salter II, J., 1995. Beyond customer satisfaction. Management Review 84 (5), 29–32.

Gronroos, C., 2000. Service Management and Marketing: A Customer Relationship Management Approach, second ed. Wiley, Chichester.

Gummesson, E., 1996. Relationship marketing and imaginary organisations: a synthesis. European Journal of Marketing 30 (2), 31–44.

Gummesson, E., 2002. Relationship marketing and the new economy: it's time for de-programming. Journal of Services Marketing 16 (7), 585–589.

Heskett, J.L., 1986. Managing in the Service Economy. Harvard Business School Press, Boston, MA.

Heskett, J.L., Sasser Jr., W.E., Hart, C.W.L., 1990. Service Breakthroughs: Changing the Rules of the Game. The Free Press, New York, NY.

Jackson, B.B., 1985. Build customer relationships that last. Harvard Business Review November/December, 120–127.

Kandampully, J., 2006. The new customer-centred business model for the hospitality industry. International Journal of Contemporary Hospitality Management 18 (3), 173–187.

Kangis, P., Zhang, Y., 2000. Service quality and customer retention in financial services. Journal of Financial Services Marketing 4 (4), 306–318.

Lewis, B.R., 1996. Customer care in services. In: Glynn, W.J., Barnes, J.G. (Eds.), Understanding Services Management. Wiley, New York, NY.

Li, Y.-H., Huang, J.-W., Tsai, M.-T, 2009. Entrepreneurial orientation and firm performance: the role of knowledge creation process. Industrial Marketing Management 38 (4), 440–449.

McDougall, G., Levesque, T., 2000. Customer satisfaction with services: putting perceived value into the equation. Journal of Services Marketing 14 (5), 392–410.

Parasuraman, A., Berry, L.L., Zeithaml, V.A., 1990. Guidelines for conducting service quality research. Marketing Research. December, 34–44.

Parasuraman, A., Grewal, D., 2000. The impact of technology on the quality-value-loyalty chain: a research agenda. Journal of the Academy of Marketing Science 28 (1), 168–174.

Scott, R.C., 2001. Establishing and maintaining customer loyalty and employee identification in the new economy. Management Communication Quarterly 14 (4), 629–636.

Shah, R.T., Parasuraman, A., Staelin, R., Day, G.S., 2006. The path to customer centricity. Journal of Service Research 9 (2), 113–124.

Sheth, J., Sisodia, R.S., Sharma, A., 2000. The antecedents and consequences of customer-centric marketing. Journal of the Academy of Marketing Science 28 (Winter), 55–66.

Sivadas, E., Baker-Prewitt, J.L., 2000. An examination of the relationship between service quality, customer satisfaction, and store loyalty. International Journal of Retail & Distribution Management 28 (2), 73–82.

Slater, S.F., Narver, J.C., 1994. Market orientation, customer value, and superior performance. Business Horizons 37 (March/April), 22–28.

Slater, S.F., Narver, J.C., 1995. Market orientation and the learning organization. Journal of Marketing 59 (July), 63–74.

Vargo, S.L., Lusch, R.F., 2004. Evolving to a new dominant logic for marketing. Journal of Marketing 68, 1–17 (January).

Vargo, S.L., Lusch, R.F., 2004. The four service marketing myths: remnants of a goods-based, manufacturing model. Journal of Service Research 6 (4), 324–335.

Verhoef, P.C., Lemon, K.N., Parasuraman, A., Roggeveen, A., Tsiros, M., Schlesinger, A., 2008. Customer experience creation: determinants, dynamics and management strategies. Journal of Retailing 85 (1), 31–41.

Wang, Y., Lo, H.-P., 2003. Customer focused performance and the dynamic for competence building and leveraging: a resource based view. Journal of Management Development 22 (6), 483–526.

Zeithaml, V.A., 2000. Service quality, profitability, and the economic worth of customers: what we know and what we need to learn. Journal of the Academy of Marketing Science 28 (1), 67–85.

Zeithaml, V.A., Berry, L.L., Parasuraman, A., 1991. The nature and determinants of customer expectations of service. Report 91–113, May. Marketing Science Institute, Cambridge, MA.

Zeithaml, V.A., Berry, L.L., Parasuraman, A., 1996. The behavioural consequences of service quality. Journal of Marketing 60 (2), 31–47.

Chapter 6

REFERENCES AND ADDITIONAL READING

Baker, K., 2008. Project Evaluation and Feasibility Analysis for Hospitality Operations. Pearson Education Australia.

Barringer, B., 2010. Preparing Effective Business Plans: An Entrepreneurial Approach. International Edition. Pearson, London.

Birt, I., 2006. Writing your Plan for Small Business Success. Pearson, London.

Bowdin, G., Allen, J., O'Toole, W., Harris, R., McDonnell, I., 2006. Events Management, second ed. Elsevier, Oxford.

Buchanan, R.D., Espeseth, R.D., undated. Developing a Bed and Breakfast Business Plan. Available from: http://web.aces.uiuc.edu/vista/pdf_pubs/b&b.pdf.

Clarke, A., Chen, W., 2007. International Hotel Management. Butterworth Heinemann, Oxford.

Cooper, C., Fletcher, J., Fyall, A., Gilbert, D., Wanhill, S., 2005. Tourism Principles and Practice, third ed. Pearson, Harlow.

Drummond, S., Yeoman, I. (Eds.), 2001. Quality Issues in Heritage Visitor Attractions. Butterworth Heinemann, Oxford.

Egerton-Thomas, C., 2005. How to Open and Run a Successful Restaurant. John Wiley & Sons.

Fullen, S, 2005. Opening a Restaurant Or Other Food Business Starter Kit – How to Prepare a Restaurant Business Plan and Feasibility Study. Atlantic Publishing Co.

Godsmark, C., 2005. How to Start and Run Your Own Restaurant: An Insider Guide to Setting Up Your Own Successful Business. How to Books Ltd.

Ingram, H., Ransley, J. (Eds.), 2000. Developing Hospitality Properties and Facilities. Butterworth Heinemann, Oxford.

Jones, C., Jowett, V., 1998. Managing Facilities. Butterworth Heinemann, Oxford.

Leask, A., Yeoman, I. (Eds.), 1999. Heritage Visitor Attractions – An Operations Management Perspective. Cassell, London.

Mullins, J., 2006. The New Business Road Test: What Entrepreneurs and Executives Should Do before Writing a Business Plan. Pearson, London.

Nykiel, R.A., 2007. Handbook of Marketing Research Methodologies for Hospitality and Tourism. Haworth Press.

Ormerod, M., Newton, R., 2005. Briefing for accessibility in design. Facilities 23 (7/8), 285–294.

Pyo, S.-S., Chang, H.-S., Chon, K.-S., 1995. Considerations of management objectives by target markets in hotel feasibility studies. International Journal of Hospitality Management 14 (2), 151–156.

Ransley, J., Ingram, H. (Eds.), 2000. Developing Hospitality Properties & Facilities. Butterworth-Heinemann, Oxford.

Ransley, J., Ingram, H., 2000a. What is "good" hotel design? Facilities 19 (1/2), 79–86.

Ransley, J., Ingram, H., 2000b. Does good design improve a hotel's profits? WHATT Journal 1, 1–11.

Schmidgall, R.S., Hayes, D.K., Ninemeier, J.D, 2002. Restaurant Financial Basics. John Wiley & Sons.

Stutely, R., 2006. The Definitive Business Plan. Pearson, London.

Swarbrooke, J., 2002. The Development and Management of Visitor Attractions, second ed. Butterworth Heinemann, Oxford.

Yeoman, I., Robertson, M., Ali-Knight, J., McMahon-Beattie, U., 2004. Festival and Events Management – An International Arts and Culture Perspective. Elsevier, Oxford.

Chapter 7

REFERENCES AND ADDITIONAL READING

Ansoff, I., 1968. Corporate Strategy. McGraw-Hill, Maidenhead.

Capon, C., 2008. Understanding Strategic Management. FT/Prentice Hall, Harlow.

Evans, N., Campbell, D., Stonehouse, G., 2003. Strategic Management for Travel and Tourism. Butterworth-Heinemann, Oxford.

Faulkner, D., Bowman, C., 1995. Essence of Competitive Strategy. Prentice Hall, London.

Grant, R.M., 2007. Contemporary Strategy Analysis, sixth ed. Blackwell, Oxford.

Haberberg, A., Rieple, A., 2008. Strategic Management: Theory and Application. Oxford University Press, Oxford.

Johnson, G., Scholes, K., Whittington, R., 2008. Exploring Corporate Strategy, eighth ed. Prentice Hall, London.

Lynch, R., 2009. Corporate Strategy, fifth ed. Pitman, London.

Mendelow, A., 1991. Proceedings of the Second International Conference on Information Systems. Cambridge.

Porter, M.E., 1980. Competitive Stratergy: Techniques for Analyzing Industries and Competitors. Free Press, New York.

Porter, M.E., 1985. Competitive Advantage. Free Press, New York.

Prahalad, C.K., Hamel, G., 1990. The core competence of the organisation. Harvard Business Review 68 (3), 79–91.

Thompson, J.L., 2001. Strategic Management, fourth ed. Thomson Learning, London.

Chapter 8

REFERENCES AND ADDITIONAL READING

Bader, E., Lababedi, A., 2007. Hotel Management Contracts in Europe. Available from: <http://www.4hoteliers.com/4hots_fshw.php?mwi=2196>.

Brandenburger, A., Nalebuff, B., 1997. Co-opetition. HarperCollins, London.

Capon, C., 2008. Understanding Strategic Management. FT/Prentice Hall, Harlow.

Evans, N., Campbell, D., Stonehouse, G., 2003. Strategic Management for Travel and Tourism. Butterworth-Heinemann, Oxford.

Faulkner, D., Bowman, C., 1995. Essence of Competitive Strategy. Prentice Hall, Hemel, Hempstead.

Grant, R.M., 2007. Contemporary Strategy Analysis, sixth ed. Blackwell, Oxford.

Haberberg, A., Rieple, A., 2001. Strategic Management: Theory and Application. Oxford University Press, Oxford.

Johnson, G., Scholes, K., Whittington, R., 2008. Exploring Corporate Strategy, eighth ed. Prentice Hall, London.

Lynch, R., 2009. Corporate Strategy, fifth ed. Pitman, London.

Medcof, J.W., 1997. Why too many alliances end in divorce. Long Range Planning 30 (5).

Mendelow, A., 1991. Proceedings of the Second International Conference on Information Systems. Cambridge.

Porter, M.E., 1980. Competitive Strategy: Techniques for Analyzing Industries and Competitors. Free Press, New York.

Porter, M.E., 1985. Competitive Advantage. Free Press, New York.

Prahald, C.K., Hamel, G., 1990. The Core Competence of the Organisation. Harvard Business Review 68 (3), 79–91.

Thompson, J.L., 2001. Strategic Management, fourth ed. Thomon Learning, London.

Chapter 9

REFERENCES AND ADDITIONAL READING

Alam, I., 2002. An exploratory investigation of user involvement in new service development. Journal of the Academy of Marketing Science 30 (3), 250–261.

Alam, I., Perry, C., 2002. A customer-oriented new service development process. Journal of Services Marketing 16 (6), 515–534.

Ansoff, I., 1988. New Corporate Strategy. John Wiley & Sons, New York.

Baker, M., 2000. The Marketing Book, third ed. Butterworth-Heinemann, London.

Baldwin, J.R., Johnson, J., 1996. Business strategies in more- and less-innovative firms in Canada. Research Policy 22 (3), 225–263.

Barczak, G., 1995. New product strategy, structure, process and performance in the telecommunication industry. Journal of Product Innovation Management 12, 224–234.

Booz, Allen, Hamilton, 1968. Management of New Products. Booz, Allen and Hamilton Inc., Chicago.

Booz, Allen, Hamilton, 1982. New Product Management for the 1980's. Booz, Allen and Hamilton Inc., New York.

Bowie, R., Buttle, F., 2004. Hospitality Marketing: An Introduction. Elsevier Butterworth-Heinemann, Burlington, MA.

Bradford, Hudson T., 1994. "Innovation through Acquisition". The Cornell Hotel and Restaurant Administration Quarterly 35 (3), 82–88.

Buttle, F., 1996. Hotel and Food Service Marketing: A Managerial Approach, second ed. Reinhart and Winston, London.

Churchill, G., 1979. A paradigm for developing better measures of marketing constructs. Journal of Marketing Research XVI, 64–73.

Churchill, G.A.J., 1995. Marketing Research: Methodological Foundations, sixth ed. The Dryden Press, Orland.

Ciappei, C., Simoni, C., 2005. Drivers of new product success in the Italian sport shoe cluster of Montebelluna. Journal of Fashion Marketing and Management 9 (1), 20–42.

Cooper, R., 1999. Product Development for the Service Sector: Lessons from Market Leaders. Perseus Books, Cambridge, Mass.

Cooper, R.G., 1983. A process model for industrial new product development. IEEE Transactions on Engineering Development 30 (1), 2–12.

Cooper, R.G., 1993. Winning at New Products: Accelerating the Process from Idea to Launch, second ed. Addison-Wesley Publishing Company, Reading, Massachusetts.

Cooper, R.G., Kleinschmidt, E., 1987. New products: what separates winners from losers. Journal of Product Innovation Management 4 (3), 169–184.

Cooper, R.G., Kleinschmidt, E.J., 1993. Uncovering the keys to new product success. IEEE Engineering Management Review Winter, 5–18.

Cooper, R.G., Kleinschmidt, E.J., 1995. New product performance: keys to success, profitability and cycle time reduction. Journal of Marketing Management 11, 315–337.

Craig, A., Hart, S., 1992. Where to now in new product development research? European Journal of Marketing 26 (11), 3–46.

Crawford, C.M., 1994. New Product Management, fourth ed. Irwin, Illinois.

Crawford, M.C., Di-Benedetto, A., 2000. New Product Management, sixth ed. McGraw-Hill, Boston.

Curry, S.J., Clayton, R.H., 1992. Business innovation strategies. Business Quarterly 56 (3), 121–126.

Dillman, D., 1978. Mail and Telephone Surveys: The Total Design Method. John Wiley & Sons, New York, NY.

Easingwood, C.J., 1986. New product development for service companies. Journal of Product Innovation Management 3, 264–275.

Ennew, C.T., Binks, M.R., 1996. Good and bad customers: the benefits of participating in banking relationship. International Journal of Bank Marketing 14 (2), 5–13.

Griffin, A., Page, A.L., 1993. An interim report on measuring product development success and failure. Journal of Product Innovation Management 10 (4), 281–308.

Griffin, A., Page, A.L., 1996. PDMA success measurement project: recommended measures for product development success and failure. Journal of Product Innovation Management 13 (2), 478–496.

Hair Jr., J.F., Anderson, R.E., Tatham, R.L., Black, W.C., 1998. Multivariate Data Analysis, fifth ed. Prentice Hall, Upper Saddle River, NJ.

Hart, S., 2000. New product development. In: Baker, M. (Ed.), The Marketing Book, fourth ed. Butterworth Heinemann, Oxford, pp. 314–334.

Hart, S.J., Baker, M.J., 1994. The multiple convergent processing model of new product development. International Marketing Review 11 (1), 77–92.

Hassanien, A., Losekoot, E., 2002. The application of facilities management expertise to the hotel renovation process. Facilities 20 (7/8), 230–238.

Heany, D., 1983. Degrees of product innovation. In: Lovelock, Christopher (1996). Services Marketing, third ed. Prentice Hall International, London.

Huang, X., Soutar, G.N., Brown, A., 2003. New product development processes in small and medium-sized enterprises. Journal of Small Business Management 40 (1), 27–43.

Hunt, S.D., Sparkman, R.M., Wilcox, G.B., 1982. The pretest in survey research: issues and preliminary findings. Journal of Marketing Research 19 (4), 269–273.

Hüsig, S., Kohn, S., 2003. Factors influencing the front end of the innovation process: a comprehensive review of selected empirical NPD and explorative FFE studies. Proceedings of the 10th International Product Development Management Conference. Belgium, Brussels. June 10–11.

Jensen, B., Harmsen, H., 2001. Implementation of success factors in new product development – the missing links? European Journal of Innovation Management 4 (1), 37–52.

Jiménez-Zarco, A.I., Martinez-Ruiz, M.P., Gonzalez-Benito, O., 2006. Success factors in new service performance: a research Agenda. Marketing Review 6 (3), 265–283.

John, A., Snelson, P., 1990. "Success factors in product innovation: a selective review of the literature". Journal of Product Innovation Management 5 (2), 114–128.

Johne, A., 1996. Avoiding product development failure is not enough. European Management Journal 14 (2), 176–180.

Johne, A., Storey, C., 1998. New service development: a review of the literature and annotated bibliography. European Journal of Marketing 32 (3/4), 184–251.

Jones, P., 1995. Developing new products and services in flight catering. International Journal of Contemporary Hospitality Management 7 (2/3), 24–28.

Jones, P., 1996. Managing hospitality innovation. Cornell Hotel and Restaurant Administration Quarterly 37 (5) 86–69.

Keegan, W.J., Moritary, S., Duncan, R.T., Paliwoda, S., 1995. Marketing. Canadian edition. Prentice-Hall Canada Inc., Ontario.

Kelly, D., Storey, C., 2000. New service development: initiation strategies. Library Consortium Management 2 (5/6), 104–122.

Kotler, P., Armstrong, G., Saunders, J., Wong, V., 2002. Principles of Marketing, third EUROPEAN edition. Prentice-Hall Inc, Essex.

Kotler, P., Armstrong, G., 2004. Principles of Marketing. Englewood Cliffs, tenth ed. Prentice-Hall Inc., New Jersey.

Kotler, P., Bowen, J., Makens, J., 2003. Marketing for Hospitality and Tourism, second ed. Prentice Hall, New Jersey.

Laage-Hellman, J., 1987. Process innovation through technical co-operation. In: Hakanasson, H. (Ed.), Industrial Technological Development. A Network Approach. Croom Helm, London.

Lancaster, G., Massingham, L., 1999. Essentials of Marketing, third ed. McGraw Hill, London.

Laugen, B.T., Acur, N., Boer, H., Frick, J., 2005. Best manufacturing practices: what do the best-performing companies do? International Journal of Operations & Production. Management 25 (2), 131–150.

Leonard-Barton, D.A., 1992. Core capabilities and core rigidities: a paradox in managing new product development. Strategic Management Journal 13, 111–125 (Summer 1992).

Lewis, R., Chambers, R.E., 2000. Marketing Leadership in Hospitality, third ed. Van-Nostrand Reinhold, New York.

Lovelock, C., 1996. Services Marketing, third ed. Prentice Hall International, London.

Mahajan, V., Wind, J., 1992. New product models: practice, shortcomings and desired improvements. Journal of Product Innovation Management 9, 128–139.

Martin, C.R., Horne, D.A., 1995. Level of success inputs for service innovations in the same firm. International Journal of Services Industry Management 6 (4), 40–56.

Miner, T., 1996. Customer-focused menu marketing. The Cornell Hotel and Restaurant Administration Quarterly 37 (3), 37–49.

Morrison, A., 2001. Hospitality and Travel Marketing, third ed. Delmar Publishers, New York.

Moenaert, R.K., Souder, W.E., 1990. An information transfer model for integrating marketing and R&D personnel in new product development projects. Journal of Product Innovation Management 7, 91–107.

Mohammed-Salleh, A., Easingwood, C., 1993. Why European financial institutions do not test-market new consumer products. International Journal of Bank Marketing 11 (3), 23–28.

Palmer, A., 2001. Principles of Services Marketing, third ed. McGraw-Hill, London.

Rothberg, R., 1967. Corporate Strategy and Product Innovation. The Free Press, New York.

Rothwell, R., 1994. Towards the fifth generation innovation process. International Marketing Review 11 (1), 7–31.

Saleh, S.D., Wang, C.K., 1993. The management of innovation: strategy, structure, and organizational climate. IEEE Transactions on Engineering Development 40 (1), 14–21.

Saren, M., 1994. Reframing the process of new product development: from 'stages' models to a 'blocks' framework. Journal of Marketing Management 10, 633–643.

Scheuing, E.E., Johnson, E.M., 1989. A proposed model for new service development. Journal of Services Marketing 3 (2), 25–35.

Shani, A.B.R., Shani, J., Sena, T.O., 2003. Knowledge management and new product development: a study of two companies. European Journal of Innovation Management 6 (3), 137–149.

Shepherd, C., Ahmed, P.K., 2000. NPD frameworks: a holistic examination European Journal of Innovation Management 3 (3), 160–173.

Shoemaker, S., 1996. Scripts: precursor of consumer expectations. The Cornel Hotel and Restaurant Administration Quarterly 37 (1), 42–53.

Tracey, M., 2004. A holistic approach to new product development: new insights Journal of Supply Chain Management: A Global Review of Purchasing & Supply 40 (4), 37–55.

Wind, J., Mahajan, V., 1997. Issues and opportunities in new product development: an introduction to the special issue. Journal of Marketing Research 34 1–13.

Chapter 10

REFERENCES AND ADDITIONAL READING

Aeberhard, W., 1995. Hotel renovations: a designer's view. European Hotelie 19 (2), 59–65.

Alexander, 1996. Facilities Management and Practice. E&FN Spon, London.

Anonymous, 1994. The renovation continuum. Lodging Hospitality 50 (12), 14

Austen, A., Neale, R., 1984. Managing Construction Projects. ILO, Geneva.

Baltin, B., Cole, J., 1995. Renovating to a target market. Lodging Hospitality 51 (8), 36–39.

Baum, C., 1993. The 6 basic features any business hotel must have. Hotel 27 (11), 52–56.

Baum, C., Wolchuck, S., 1992. Problem: losing market share? Solution: renovate Hotels 26 (11), 94–104.

Berg, P., Skinner, M., 1995. CapEx: do you spend enough? Lodging Hospitalit 51 (11), 103–105.

Booz, Allen, Hamilton, 1982. New Product Management for the 1980's. Booz, Allen and Hamilton Inc., New York.

Boykin, P.J., 1991. "Rejuvenat Properties with Four Design Options". Hotel & Motel Management Vol. 206 (Iss.6), 27–28.

Bruns, R., 1996. Coming back: better than ever. Lodging 54 (3), 23–25.

Chipkin, H., 1997. Renovation rush. Hotel and Motel Management 212 (2), 25–28.

CIRIA (Construction Industry Research and Information Association), 1994. A guide to the management of building refurbishment. Report 133, London.

Cooper, R.G., 1993. Winning at New Products: Accelerating the Process from Idea to Launch, second ed. Addison-Wesley Publishing Company, Reading, Massachusetts.

Doswell, R., 1970. Towards an integrated approach to hotel planning. In: West, Amanda, Hughes, Janet (1991) (Eds.), An Evaluation of Hotel Design Practice. The Service Industries Journal 11 (3), 326–380.

Dube, L., Cathy, A.E., Renaghan, L.M., Judy, A., Singuaw, 2000. Managing for excellence. The Cornell Hotel and Restaurant Administration Quarterly 41 (5), 30–39.

Fairhead, J., 1988. Design for Corporate Culture. NEDO, London.

Fox, C.A., 1991. Be choosy when choosing designer, contractor. Hotel & Motel Management 206 (9), 38–78.

Fox, C.A., 1993. Work scheduling avoids revenue loss during renovations. Hotel & Motel Management 208 (19), 85.

Griffin, A., Page, A.L., 1993. An interim report on measuring product development success and failure. Journal of Product Innovation Management 10 (4), 281–308.

Hassanien, A., 2005. Hotel renovation within the context of new product development. International Journal of Hospitality & Tourism Administration (IJHTA) 6 (2).

Hassanien, A., 2006. An analysis of hotel property renovation in large hotels: a multiple case-study. Journal of Structural Survey 24 (1), 41–64.

Hassanien, A., 2006b. Renovation practices of three star hotels in Egypt. International Journal of Hospitality & Tourism Administration (IJHTA) 7 (1).

Hassanien, A., 2007. Exploring the relationship between hotel renovation and hotel inspection. International Journal of Hospitality & Tourism Administration (IJHTA) 8 (4).

Hassanien, A., Baum, T., 2001. Hotel product renovation as a product modification-marketing tool. In: Gatchalian, C., Vincent, C.S., Reil, C. (Eds.), Shaping the Future of Tourism: Mix, Match and Move (277–282). Proceedings of the Seventh Annual Conference of the Asia Pacific Tourism Association. Makati, Philippines.

Hassanien, A., Baum, T., 2002a. Analysing hotel positioning through property renovation. Tourism and Hospitality Research: The Surrey Quarterly Review 4 (2).

Hassanien, A., Baum, T., 2002. Hotel innovation through property renovation. International Journal of Hospitality & Tourism Administration 3 (4), 5–24.

Hassanien, A., Losekoot, E, 2002. Applying the expertise of Facilities Management to the hotel renovation Process. Facilities 20 (7/8).

Knapp, F., 1991. The Sheraton palace: preserving the past, positioning for the future. The Cornell Hotel and Restaurant Administration Quarterly 32 (4), 13–21.

Jones, P., 1995. Developing new products and services in flight catering. International Journal of Contemporary Hospitality Management 7 (2/3), 24–28.

Jones, P., 1996. Managing hospitality innovation. Cornell Hotel and Restaurant Administration Quarterly 37 (5), 86–95.

Koss-Feder, L., 1994. Renovations increase as lenders return. Hotel & Motel Management 209 (15), 12.

Koss-Feder, L., 1994. Renovation takes guest-sensitive approach. Hotel & Motel Management 209 (15), 16.

Lawson, F.R., 1995. Hotels & Resorts: Planning, Design and Refurbishment, second ed. Butterworth Architecture, Oxford.

Lerner, M.S., 1996. Maximizing return on renovation. Hotels 30 (11), 18–22.

Lewis, E.L., Brush, S., 1998. "Renovation, Refurbishment and Redevelopment: Is the Difference more than Semantics?". Loading Hospitality Vol 54 (Iss. 4), 48–54.

Losekoot, E., van Wezel, R., Wood, R.C., 2001. 'Conceptualising and operationalising the research interface between facilities management and hospitality management'. Facilites 19 (7/8), 296–303.

Lovelock, C., 1996. Services Marketing, third ed. Prentice Hall International, London.

Lynn, W., Seldon, J., 1993. Like new but how? Lodging 48 (6), 54–57.

MacDonald, J., 1995. A new look – a new tomorrow. Hotel & Motel Management 210 (6), 30–32.

Moss, M.A., 1996. Applying TQM to product design and development. M. Dekker, New York.

Nehmer, J.C., 1991. The art of hotel renovation. Lodging Hospitality 47 (8), 22–24.

Paneri, M.R., Wolff, H.J., 1994. Why should I renovate? Lodging Hospitality 50 (12), 14–19.

Powers, T., 1998. Marketing Hospitality, second ed. John Wiley & Sons Inc., New York.

Ransley, J., Ingram, H., 2001. What is good hotel design? Facilities 19 (1/2), 79–86.

Rowe, M., 1995. Renovation has its risks. Lodging Hospitality 51 (3), 40–42.

Rowe, M., 1996. The trials of teamwork. Lodging Hospitality 52 (2), 20–23.

Ruttes, W., Penner, R.H., Adams, L., 2001. Hotel Design: Planning and Development. Architectural Press, Butterworth-Heinemann, Oxford.

Seacord, S., 1997. Stay open or close? Lodging Hospitality 53 (4), 47–52.

Stipanuk, David M., Roffmann, Harold, 1996. Hospitality Facilities Management and Design. American Hotel & Motel Association, Michigan.

Sullivan, D., 1994. On renovation and the bottom line. Lodging Hospitality 50 (12), 29–30.

Tull, D.S., Hawkins, D.I., 1993. Marketing Research: Measurement and Method, sixth ed. Macmillan Publishing Company, New York.

Turner, B.T., 1968. Management of design. In: West, Amanda, Hughes, Janet (1991). An Evaluation of Hotel Design Practice. The Service Industries Journal 11(3), 326–380.

Verginis, Wood, 1999. Accommodation Management - Perspectives for the international Hotel Industry. Thomson Business Press.

Watkins, E., 1995. Don't just sit there...renovate! Lodging Hospitality 51 (4), 18–27.

West, A., Hughes, J., 1991. An evaluation of hotel design practice. The Service Industries Journal 11 (3), 326–380.

West, A., Purvis, E., 1992. Hotel design: the need to develop a strategic approach. International Journal of Contemporary Hospitality Management 4 (1), 15–22.

Index